Murav'yov's journey to Khiva through the Turkoman Country

Journey to Khiva
through the Turkoman Country

by Nikolay Murav'yov

Oguz Press London
1977

First published in Russian, by Avgust Semyon Printing House, Moscow 1822

Translated into French by M.G. Lecointe de Laveau and published by Louis Tenré, Paris 1825.

Translated into German by Philipp Strahl and published by G. Reimer, Berlin 1824.

First English edition, translated from the German edition by Capt. W.S.A. Lockhart F.R.G.S., under the title 'Muraviev's Journey to Khiva through the Turkoman Country 1819—20', published by the Foreign Department Press, Calcutta 1871.

The lithographs were taken from 'Atlas of the Journey to Turkmenia and Khiva of Nikolay Murav'yov, Captain of the Guards and General Staff'', published as a companion volume to the Russian edition by Avgust Semyon Printing House, Moscow 1822.

Oguz Press Limited
P.O. Box 127 London NW8
Introduction © Oguz Press, 1977.

Printed by J & P Weldon Limited, London.
The cover and prelims designed by Richard Foenander.

Contents

Table of Illustrations

Foreword

'Journey to Khiva through Turkoman Country' was first published in Moscow in 1822, two years after its author's return to Russia and was an instant success. Possessing all the perennial ingredients of the best-seller, it could hardly have failed; its hero, an intrepid young soldier, disguised as a Yomud Turkoman tribesman, had travelled through some of the most romantic and dangerous territory in the world. He had survived confinement in the Khan's fortress and, his mission successfully concluded, he had returned to the capital to present himself to his Tsar and to Society.

Yet *Journey to Khiva* was not only an adventure story. It also contained a picturesque and entirely authentic account of an ancient and mysterious country and its famous nomad inhabitants who had succeeded in thwarting Russia's efforts to subdue or civilise them since Peter the Great's first expedition a century earlier. To the European reader, the Turkoman represented the true Noble Savage, an almost exact equivalent to America's Red Indians of the same period.

Arrangements for translation rights were being negotiated even before the book's publication in Russia; the French edition was issued in Paris in 1823 and the German version in Berlin in 1824.

It is an interesting question why no London publishing house thought it worth while to issue an English translation. The English reader had only a resume, contained in a pamphlet entitled 'Russian Missions into the Interior of Asia' published by Sir Richard Phillips in 1823.

Whatever the reason, no London publisher saw sufficient in this foreign adventure story to entertain his English readers. Ten years later it would certainly have been different. By then, England had become highly interested in Turkestan and its inhabitants through the books of Alexander Burnes and James Baillie Fraser and the many and varied accounts which began to appear in the *Journal* of the newly founded Royal Geographical Society.* In the decade after that, the British reading public knew of the incarceration of

---

*'Travels into Bokhara', by Alexander Burnes, John Murray, London 1834, 1835 and 1839 reprinted in 1973 in three volumes.
'Narrative of a Journey into Khorasan, in the years 1821-1822', by James Baillie Fraser, Longman, London, 1825.
'The Country of the Turkoman', Oguz Press, London 1977; an anthology of travellers' tales and other items from the archives of the Royal Geographical Society from 1835 to 1885.

Colonel Stoddard and Captain Connolly by the villanous Emir of Bokhara and of the journey undertaken by the eccentric priest, Dr. Joseph Wolff to save them.

Murav'yov's vivid account of the country of the Turkoman was not translated into English until, almost half a century later, the Indian government was belatedly compiling its information files on the area. This edition, translated from the German by Capt. W.S.A. Lockhart, was published without illustrations by the Foreign Department Press in Calcutta. Its purpose was to serve as one of the principal sources for a political and military reference work to be written on the Khanate of Khiva, a task assigned to a Captain Collett, deputy assistant Quartermaster-general. In 1873, the year in which the Foreign Department completed its Political and Military Treatise on Khiva, the Russian army succeeded in its capture.

Today Nikolay Murav'yov's diaries stand as the earliest authentic description of the Turkoman in their country. They also form one of the most entertaining travellers' tales from an area which, during much of the world's history, stirred the imagination of its peoples.

For this new edition, the original lithographs have been taken from Murav'yov's 'Atlas' published as a separate volume in 1822 in Russia. We have also included the *Notes* (p.175) contributed by the famous German philologist Julius von Kalproth to the Paris edition of 1823 which contains a mass of information on the population groups of 19th century Central Asia. It also contains an intriguingly horrible recipe for Kalmuck tea which alone would justify its inclusion. The translation of local names which have been included in the text, were made by Dr. Freytag, Professor of Oriental Languages at the Rhein University, Bonn for the Berlin edition of 1824.

Turkoman names

The early 19th century travellers to Central Asia had great difficulty in deciding how to spell the local names. On the one hand, most Turkoman were illiterate, on the other, few European travellers, even if they could read Arabic, had any command of Turkish dialects. They therefore had no alternative to simply giving their own phonetic rendering of what they heard. Further complications were introduced when translators grappled with the problem of transliterating the strange sounds from Russian Cyrillic into German or English. Somewhat surprisingly the English translation of Murav'yov con- tains few names which can not be understood by the European who is familiar with the modern versions of Turkoman tribal or place names. The reader will have little difficulty in recognizing Burnes's *Tuka*, Fraser's *Tuckeh*, Strahl's (Murav'yov's German translator)

Teke and Lockhart's *Takka* as the Tekke tribe. Burnes's *Choudor* was transliterated as *Tschabdur* by Strahl and *Chobdur* in the English edition. The Ersari gave more trouble. Burnes called them *Ersaree* but Strahl wrote *Err Sare* and Lockhart *Ar Sare*. A professional translator set the task of transliterating the original Russian version, produced *Yer Saryo*.

To provide a modern glossary would have served little purpose since it would only have replaced an old approximation by a new; no European spelling can capture the sound of words spoken by Turkoman and the standard phonetic forms used by Turkish scholars would, in any case, be unintelligible to the layman.

In the title and introductory section the phonetically more accurate transliteration *Murav'yov* has been employed.

Robert Pinner, London 1976

Introduction

Captain Nikolay Nikolayevich Murav'yov's mission to Khiva in 1819—20 was by no means the first expedition of its kind, however it was the first to meet with any success. Murav'yov succeeded in crossing the barren steppes between the Caspian and the Amu-Darya, in being granted an audience by the ruler of the Khivan khanate, Mahomed Ragim Khan, and in returning to the Caspian accompanied by envoys from Khiva, with gifts and messages of goodwill to the Russian governor-general in Georgia.

As Murav'yov himself notes, in the preface to his diary, there had been several earlier attempts to establish, or rather re-establish, friendly relations with the rulers of Khiva. In 1700, when the khanate was under the rule of Bukhara, the Khivan Khan Shakh-Niaz sent an ambassador to Peter the Great requesting him to place Khiva under Russian protection. Permission was granted by the Tsar in June of that year and from then until 1714 there was a Khivan embassy in St. Petersburg.

At that time extravagant rumours were circulating about the fabulous wealth of Khiva. The banks of the Amu-Darya were said to be covered with golden sand and a legend told that the gold-bearing river had once flowed into the Caspian and could return to its old course at will. Peter, curious to find out more about this territory, dispatched an exploratory expedition, with the eastern shore of the Caspian and the Irtysh heights as its twin starting points. This expedition succeeded in finding the old course of the Amu-Darya, thus verifying at least part of the legend. It also collected some of the first reliable information about the topography of the area.

Soon after, in 1716, Prince Bekovich set out with a detachment of infantry and cavalry, three and a half thousand strong. His aim was to take possession of the old course of the river, follow it to the Khivan khanate and force the Khan to accept Russian rule. While in Khiva he was to examine the golden sands, but his most important task was to discover the shortest and easiest routes to North India.

India was the goal, the driving force behind Russia's constant attempts to expand eastwards. Russian merchants traded with India and the lands east of Khiva, but always through Khivan merchants. The latter brought their silk and woollen cloth, Chinese dishes, tea, tobacco and black lambskins from Bukhara to the Caspian, and there exchanged them for Russian linen, metal goods, spun gold and silver, glass, paper and sugar. This trade was complicated and sporadic and the Russians, having heard tales of the wealth of India that far outshone stories of Khivan riches, were anxious to establish direct relations. At the very least their object was to strengthen existing trade links by establishing a base on the eastern shore of the Caspian.

Prince Bekovich's first task was to win the friendship of the nomadic Kalmyk and Turkoman tribes on the eastern shores of the Caspian and to fortify his base. This achieved, he sent his envoys to Khiva with presents and cordial messages of good will. At last, in July 1717, he set off towards Khiva himself. Whatever his real intentions, it is reported that his convoy was so large that it caused much agitation among the tribes. Not surprisingly, the Khivan Shirgazi, hearing of this martial advance, found it difficult to believe that Bekovich meant anything but war and dispatched his Turkoman and Uzbek troops to meet them. The tribes were no match for Bekovich's well equipped army and after a short battle, the Russians entered Khiva. The Russian Prince might have been the better soldier but he badly underestimated Shirgazi. When Bekovich entered the city, the Khan welcomed him like a brother. There had been a battle? He had known nothing of this. The wild Turkoman and Uzbek had acted without his knowledge or authority. Bekovich was invited into the capital. The Russian troops were quartered most hospitably throughout the city. This achieved, the Khan promptly arrested and executed the entire mission. Bekovich himself was flayed alive and his body sent as a gift to the neighbouring Khan of Bukhara.

Not until fifty years later did the Russians try again. In 1771 Catherine the Great ordered Count Voynovich, at that time Commander of the Russian Navy at Astrakhan, to build a fortress and a harbour on the Caspian coast near Astrabad. When Voynovich arrived with his fleet, he was at once made to feel at ease. His charming host, the local Persian ruler Aga Mukhamed Khan, could not have been more hospitable. Of course Voynovich could build his harbour. It would be a wonderful thing to have and, naturally, the installation would need a fortress to protect it. When the Russians had completed the construction work the Khan came to admire and to dine on board Voynovich's frigate. In return Aga Mukhamed invited his host and all his officers to a feast at a residence nearby. When they had all arrived, the Khan had them put in irons and announced an ultimatum. Either Voynovich would immediately order the destruction of the fortress and the harbour, or he would face execution. The Russian had no alternative. When the installation had been demolished, Aga Mukhamed's slaves helped the Count and his officers into the sea to swim to the ships.

The slow but determined pressure exerted by the Russians could not be held back for ever. Gradually, they expanded eastwards, taking the Kizyl-Kaysak steppe and establishing a new line of fortifications to the south-west of the Aral Sea. The reaction in Khiva was to capture and enslave as many Russians and as many other foreigners as possible.

By the beginning of the 19th century relations between Khiva and the Russians were at their worst. Subkhankulov, the last envoy to be sent to Khiva before Murav'yov's mission, returned with a message from the Khan to the Governor of Orenburg. Any new Russian envoy who crossed the borders of the Khivan Khanate, would either be executed or treated as a slave.

In a new effort to open the trade route to the east through Khiva, and on the suggestion of Admiral N.S. Mordvinov, yet another attempt was made to fortify a trading base on the eastern shores of the Caspian. Mordvinov's scheme was to approach the Turkoman Tribesmen in the area and offer them Russian citizenship. The project was put into the hands of General Yermolov, the Russian army commander in Georgia who realised that two pre-conditions were essential for success: friendly relations with the Khan of Khiva and detailed intelligence about the Khanate, its people and its terrain. Yermolov saw the fortifications on the Caspian as the first step to the conquest of the Central Asian states and ultimately of the invasion of India to the south while also providing an effective defence against the possibility of attack by Persia.

The envoy chosen by Yermolov was Murav'yov. His task was to establish relations with the Khan and to survey Khiva and the surrounding desert. He was to gather all the information he could about the Khanate, its ruler and its people. Murav'yov was to travel in his own name rather than in that of the Russian Government since, if he failed in his mission, he might lose his life but Russia would not lose face. It was also to be a small expedition. For one thing Murav'yov did not have the resources for a large detachment, for another the Khan would be less likely to see a small group of men as a threat to him or his territory.

Nikolay Murav'yov was born in 1794, the second of five sons of a distinguished father who had abandoned an academic career to serve in both the Navy and the Army and who had reached the rank of Lieutenant-Colonel as Senior Adjutant to his relative Admiral Mordvinov. By the time Nikolay embarked on his mission he had left the service to set up the first military training establishment in Russia which he financed out of his own pocket.

It was natural that all five sons should enter the army and in 1811 Nikolay joined his elder brother Aleksandr as an officer in the Quarter Masters section in St. Petersburg. It was equally natural, that in the wake of the French Revolution, Nikolay and his brother's officers should react to the winds of liberal thought that were sweeping Europe.

The immediate purpose was to abolish serfdom; the ideals were those of Rousseau's *The Social Contract*. At the same time, the young officers believed firmly in the integrity and even the sanctity of the Tsar and far from wishing to depose him, it was their aim to free him from what they saw as the corrupting influence of the Court.

The autumn of 1811 saw the first clandestine meetings of a circle whose aim was to establish a republic on a northern island, unspoilt by civilization, commerce or law. Among its members were Nikolay's two cousins, Artamon Zakharovich Murav'yov and Matvey Ivanovich Murav'yov-Apostol. Another member was Lvovich Pushkin, the uncle of Aleksandr Pushkin. Nikolay himself was elected President. However less than a year after its formation the circle broke up when most of its members departed with the Russian army for action against the French. In the battle of Borodino, Nikolay Murav'yov distinguished himself by receiving five official orders.

Political intrigue resumed after the French retreat. Nikolay, his brothers and friends, formed an artel, a community whose members lived together, shared their domestic expenses and discussed political and social reform. The members of the original 1811 circle were joined by two young liberal poets Del'vig and Kyukhel'beker and by a number of former members of the Lycèe which had been established by Tsar Aleksandr for the sons of noblemen. The expanded group called itself the Holy Indivisible Artel.

It would be wrong to suggest that Nikolay's life was filled with politics. On the contrary, much of his time was occupied with two much greater problems. His financial affairs were never stable, since he had no private means and they deteriorated further when he was promoted to Staff Captain after Borodino. He also wished to marry Admiral Mordvinov's daughter Natasha. While Mordvinov approved of Nikolay as an officer and a gentleman, he strongly disapproved of the prospect of supporting an impoverished son-in-law. Nikolay was permitted to visit the house but forbidden any thought of marriage until his prospects improved. No improvement was forthcoming. Nikolay's father, now a Major-General, still had his military school to support. All Mordvinov could advise the young couple was patience. By 1816, Mordvinov's own patience had failed him. Seeing no prospect that Nikolay's situation would improve, he ordered him out of St. Petersburg.

Nikolay applied to General Yermolov who was preparing for his new post in the south. The General agreed immediately, offering to take Nikolay on a diplomatic mission to Persia provided that he promised to remain with him in Georgia when he took up his command of the Caucasian detachment.

Politics were not entirely forgotten in the south; Nikolay kept up his correspondence with members of the artel. He even tried, not very successfully, to set up a branch in Tblisi, but the new politics had little appeal for the provincial army officers.

In St. Petersburg in the meantime, the mood was changing. The Tsar who, before the French campaign, had promised to set up committees to examine Government structure, to introduce liberal institutions and to discuss the emancipation of the serfs now made it clear that he had no such intentions. As a result the Murav'yov artel became considerably larger and although, as distinct from the more extreme revolutionary groups, the young officers still held the Tsar's life sacred, they had become increasingly disillusioned with him. That year the artel reformed itself into the *Soyuz blagodensteva*, a group which flourished until 1821, the year which saw the emergence of the northern and southern societies which planned the Decembrist uprising in 1825. Nikolay Murav'yov received news of these changes from a colleague who had visited St. Petersburg. He also learnt of the arrest of his brother Aleksandr, ostensibly for neglect of duty. Aleksandr was released but had to resign from service.

Yermolov's mission to Persia was delayed. While waiting for permission to depart, Murav'yov suggested that he and a small group of officers and men should survey the territory between Tblisi and Mozdok, 190 miles to the north. The expedition was a success and resulted in similar surveys in Gumry Kars and beyond the Arpachy river. On one expedition Murav'yov penetrated behind the Persian border to Echniadzan, the centre of the Armenian church. Using false papers and posing as a pilgrim he obtained information from the patriarch about the Persian forces. On another occasion he crossed the Arpachay to a Turkish settlement and it was on these excursions that he decided to learn both Persian and Turkish.

Early in 1817 Yermolov began his mission to Teheran. In Tabriz the group were received by Abas-Mirza, the Shah's son and Murav'yov took the opportunity to survey the terrain and to report on the military strength of their host. The Persian troops, he noted, were led by English officers but he was less than impressed by their appearance and their equipment. In Teheran, Yermolov and the Shah exchanged gifts and expressions of goodwill. Murav'yov was disillusioned with Persia, a country incomparably rich and beautiful in his imagination turned out to be drab, arid and hardly able to support its population.

Nikolay Murav'yov was the obvious choice for Yermolov's mission to cross the Caspian Sea. He was an experienced surveyor, accustomed to difficult and dangerous journeys. He had also been able to observe the General's technique in dealing with difficult potentates and he now had a command of oriental languages. Murav'yov himself was less enthusiastic about the idea, aware that there was no certainty of returning alive.

Three years later, in 1820, after the events described in this book, Nikolay Murav'yov had returned from his adventures, had been promoted to Colonel and allowed to take his report personally to St. Petersburg.

Yermolov's intentions were not altogether altruistic. Murav'yov's task was to persuade a less than eager Tsar to authorise the General to continue his expansion programme by building a fortress in Krasnovosk Bay before sending trade missions to Khiva and Bukhara.

In St. Petersburg Murav'yov was welcomed with enthusiasm by society and with caution by the authorities. General Yermolov had realised perfectly well that he was out of favour. The Tsar who had originally pronounced the whole scheme as unsound, could not be expected to acknowledge its success with much enthusiasm. When, during his audience, Murav'yov attempted to support his General's proposals, the Tsar was polite, praised Nikolay's successful mission, and promised nothing. Shortly afterwards, Nikolay was warned that he would be wise not to linger in the capital. Murav'yov stayed only to arrange for the publication of his diaries and returned to Georgia.

During the 1820's Nikolay served in the Caucasus and thus missed The Decembrist uprising in 1825 in which his brothers Aleksandr and Mikhail were arrested. His elder brother was exiled to Verkhneudinsk in Siberia where he became active in local government and eventually became Chairman of the Tobol'sk administration and Governor of Arkhangel'sk. Mikhail, who had resigned his commission before the uprising, was able to prove his innocence. Later he rejoined the service and became Vice-Governor of Vitebsk.

Nikolay Murav'yov remained in the army for most of his life. In 1826–27 he fought against the Persians; in 1828–29 against the Persians; in 1828–29 against the Asian Turks. He took part in the Polish war in 1831 and two years later he commanded the Russian detachment which was sent to the Bosphorus to help the Sultan against the Egyptian Pasha Megmet-Ali and assisted in the conclusion of the Unkyar-Iskelesiysky Treaty of 1833.

At no time after the Decembrist affair, did Nikolay participate actively in illegal politics although he continued to support the emancipation of the serfs. In 1836 he was dismissed from the service for helping to protect exiled Decembrists and for criticising the army administration. A few years later, having served his penance, he was allowed to rejoin the Grenadiers, in time to play a leading role in the campaign against Hungary. In 1854, fully rehabilitated, he was appointed Governor General in the Caucasus and Commander in Chief of the Caucasian army. This was the time of his most famous exploit. During the Crimean war he commanded the troops which took the fortress of Kars after a long siege, an achievement which earned him the name Murav'yov-Karsky throughout Russia. This was to be his last campaign. He retired not long after his 60th birthday. The last years of his life, until his death in 1860, were spent in the traditional occupation of retired Generals, writing his memoirs.

Jessica Routley, London 1976

I dedicate this book to my companions, steadfast in helping the weak, devoted to their mother country and trusting in fate.

Also to my parents. The book would be nothing without their inspiration and the patient co-operation of my respected father

Your obedient son
Nikolay Murav'yov

Author's Preface

ALEXIS PETROVITSH JERMALOF, Military Governor of Georgia, General of Infantry in the Russian Imperial Service, &c., &c., conceived the project of sending an expedition to the Eastern Coast of the Caspian Sea, in order to establish friendly relations with the nomadic Turcomans inhabiting that district.

His desire was also to found a harbour on the same coast, where Russian merchantmen could find a safe anchorage, and land their cargoes in security : the harbour to be protected by a small fortified work.

Peter the Great had originally entertained this scheme as part of his grand project of establishing a direct and permanent trade with India through the great Steppe commonly called Tartary, a project defeated by the treachery of the Khivans, who put Prince Bekovitsh and all the troops he had led into their territory to the sword. This people, contrary to treaty and to their most solemn guarantees, took him prisoner, and, on the pretence that sufficient provisions were not procurable for his large army, compelled him to distribute his force among the different villages, which enabled them to butcher the Prince and destroy his troops in detail.

The three remaining Russian detachments at Mangushlak, Alexander Bay, and Krasnavoda were now forced to take to their ships and return to Astraccan, abandoning the fortifications they had already commenced. The unhappy fate of Prince Bekovitsh taught us a lesson of Khivan faithlessness and blood-thirstiness, and since then all intercourse between Russia and Khiva had ceased.

The first step now to be taken for the furtherance of our scheme was to secure the alliance of the Turcomans. The latter lead a wandering life, with their flocks and herds, on the eastern shore of the Caspian, ignoring all industrial pursuits and living by theft and robbery. They wage continual war with the Persians, a war which, fed by sect animosity, never slumbers but to burst forth again with fresh fury.

It is true that in the year 1813 General Nicholas Feodorvitsh Ratishtsheff, then Military Governor of Georgia, sent a certain Derbent merchant, Ivan Muratoff, by birth an Armenian, to the Turcomans. This person, from former commercial connections with Astrabad, had made many acquaintances there. He communicated the Governor-General's proposals to Sultan Khan, who at that period exercised a kind of sovereignty over several Turcoman tribes, whom he had equipped for war and led several times to victory over the Persians. Sultan Khan was rejoiced at the promise of support made him by the Russian Governor-General (probably hoping thereby to raise himself in time to supreme rule over the unruly Turcomans), and immediately sent General Ratishtsheff a deputation composed of Chiefs from the several tribes and the most eminent men of the nation, soliciting only a few privileges and the protection of the Russian Government. Unfortunately the Envoys (among them Kiat Aga, of whom frequent mention will be found in the following pages) reached the Russian General's camp at Karabag in Giyulistan at the moment when that officer was concluding a treaty of peace with Abul Hossein Khan, the Shah of Persia's Plenipotentiary. The latter, aware how dangerous to Persia the Turcomans might become, once under Russian protection, demanded that Russia should enter into no negotiations with them. The Governor yielded, and dismissed the Envoys with valuable presents. This disappointment threw the Turcomans into great distress, and finding themselves unable to offer further resistance to Persia, they submitted and gave hostages. Those, however, who remained recusant retired either to Balkan Bay, whither the Persians could not pursue them, or fled to Khiva, and were welcomed by the present Ruler, Mahomed Ragim Khan (a sworn enemy to the Kajar dynasty). Sultan Khan was among the latter, and lives under the Khan's protection to the present day. To Major Ponomarev, Commandant of Elisabetopol, was entrusted the management of the Turcoman negotiations, I, as Staff Officer, making, in concert with him, a survey of the eastern coast of the Caspian. The additional duty allotted to me was to proceed alone to Khiva, negotiate an alliance with the Khan, and furnish a description of the country and its inhabitants. The entries in my diary were written secretly and in as succinct a style as possible. They were originally only intended as memoranda for my own perusal and that of a few intimate friends, but on my return home, finding so many desirous to hear about the country I had visited, and my adventures there, I determined to publish these rough notes.

I only relate what happened to myself or came under my own observation, and would remind the reader that it is no easy task for a foreigner to make his notes and record his thoughts in writing amongst a people in the highest degree suspicious. It was never my intention to write a book, or much now given briefly would have been elaborated, and much other matter condensed or omitted. If, in the course of this narrative, names frequently occur which appear of trivial importance, I think I shall be forgiven when I explain that my object has been to assist any future Envoy who may be sent to the same country by giving him at the outset some insight into the circumstances and characters of the persons he may have to deal with.

MURAVIEV.

FIRST PART

Chapter I

Visit to the Turkoman inhabitants
of the Eastern Coast of the Caspian Sea

On the 17th of June 1819 Alexis Petrovitsh Jermalof,
the Commander-in-Chief in Georgia, made over to Major
Ponomarev and myself all the necessary documents, and
repaired to the Caucasian frontier, where the war with the
Tchetshes demanded his presence.

The Armenian Muratoff, who had already been among
the Turcomans in the time of Nicholas Ratishtsheff, was
to accompany us as interpreter.

On the same day I made my preparations for the
journey, and offered up fervent prayers for divine aid in
the Tiflis * Cathedral. Major Ponomarev had a separate
special commission. The gifts he took over were designed
only for the Turcomans. Among the instructions which
I received from the Governor, and to which I was strictly
to adhere in my negotiations with the Turcomans and in
Khiva, were the following :—

"Your capacity for making yourself liked, as well as
your acquaintance with the Tartar language, can be turned
to good account. Do not regard the arts of flattery from
an European point of view ; they are constantly used by
Asiatics, and you need never fear of being too lavish in
this respect. You will be able to make other useful
researches, which a residence among those tribes will suggest to you better than I can do, especially as the race
you are going to is one regarding which we have but
scanty information. Your qualifications and your zeal give
me good grounds to expect that this attempt to establish
friendly relations with the Turcomans will not be a fruitless one, and that the account you will give them of our
Government will open the way to future proceedings."

On the 18th of June I left Tiflis, and reached the
post of Sagala, where just then lay a detachment of 250
Cossacks, who were proceeding on active service to Dag-i-stan
against the Leksis.

---

* Sir Robert Ker Porter (in his *Travels in Georgia, Persia, &c.: London,*
1821) states Tiflis to possess 3,684 houses and 18,000 inhabitants.

The night of the 19th I passed at Tausk. It rained terribly the whole day.

On the 20th the heat was intolerable. Reached Elisabetopol (called by the natives Hansha), a very beautiful town, surrounded by gardens, and stayed there until the 1st of July, as Ponomarev's military business with the Commandant of the place could not be concluded before then.

In front of the city, on the Tiflis road, stands an old fortress, which in the time of Prince Zizianow was occupied by the Khan Javot, whose guns are still to be seen on the towers. This fortress is now in ruins; in its interior are the remains of some splendid stone buildings. It has secret subterranean passages, which, however, have all either fallen in, or threaten to do so. These are said by the inhabitants to contain treasure brought in during the time of the siege. The most precious treasures of the former Khan are also said to have been buried here in a garden outside the fortress, and to have been disinterred by the son of the murdered Khan Javot. This, however, is only report. Within the walls of the fortress my attention was attracted by an enormous tree, measuring 27 feet in circumference.

On the evening of the 1st we left Elisabetopol in a light cart, which broke down on the road. This accident forced me to pass the night in the open, half way to Kurge, which I had hoped to reach. When the moon rose I started again, and reached Turgan on the night of the 2nd, the heat having been unbearable during the whole day. At Mingitshauer I crossed the Kur by a ferry.

My way had hitherto lain through a barren steppe, relieved here and there by patches of salt marsh, but now the country quite changed its character. The banks of the Kur are very beautiful, offering on either side a pleasing prospect of wood and garden, from which peep the Armenian homesteads.

To my front, as I left the river, lay a range of sterile hills, the radiation from which greatly added to the heat; but to the right stretched a vast plain, richly cultivated and populous, in the midst of which were the ruins of the town of Arevsh.* Very early on the morning of the 3rd I left Turgan, and by night reached New Shamakha, † formerly the residence of Mustapha, Khan of Shirwan. The Khan's

---

* Arevsh. In *Soimalov's Description of the Caspian*, A.D. 1726, this town is called Arrash.

† New Shamakha—Lat. 40° 34' N.

predecessors had always made Old Shamakha their capital, but from the earliest days the majority of the people had settled in the fertile country around the site of the new town. Mustapha abandoned the capital of his ancestors, and built New Shamakha in order the better to overawe his subjects by his presence in their midst; but the plain was at once deserted, the inhabitants betaking themselves to the mountains and settling at Fith, to which place the Khan was obliged to shift his residence. New Shamakha is now only a Cossack station.

The road ran for about four and a half miles through the flat country, and then over the precipitous hills separating New from Old Shamakha. This mountain road, although nothing to speak of in the way of length, was still so steep, that the horses were quite exhausted, and it was with great difficulty that I reached the station by evening. What a glorious spectacle now rewarded my toils! The rich champaign beneath me stretching away to the horizon; the picturesque hills amongst which I stood; the numerous Armenian villages, some on the slopes, some in the hollows, surrounded on every side by sheaves of corn; the husbandmen all busy at the harvest,—all these combined to make up a gorgeous and magnificent scene. Apart from the picturesque, however, that fruitful plain is remarkable for the culture of silk-worms, which is carried on to a great extent, especially in the neighbourhood of Shamakha, and which brings wealth and prosperity to the country.

Old Shamakha,* or Kognashahar (i.e., "old town"), presents an imposing appearance with its ruins, its baths, mosques, and palaces.

Even the fortifications excite our admiration for the builders of this ancient capital. The Khan's castle stands on rising ground, which affords a fine view of the town. The Post Office is established in a caravanserai of noble proportions. At some distance from the fortress stands the citadel built by Lutra, a virgin Czarina, whose remains rest here. Some deep excavations within the walls are said to mark the site of her tomb. The common people believe that these cavities were ransacked by Mustapha in the hope of treasure, but that the spirit of Lutra frustrated his endeavours.

On the 5th I started from Old Shamakha, and, passing two staging places on the road, finally reached Glubokaya-balka, where I passed the night. This is only a Cossack post in the

---

* Old Shamakha was sacked by the famous Nadir Shah in 1726.

middle of a barren and waterless steppe. The aspect of the country changes here, and the eye encounters a steppe studded with the ruins of towns and hamlets, only relieved by some hills, and at wide intervals by occasional patches of pasture land. On the following day I reached the Cossack post of Arbat, a well-built and regular fortress, where I overtook the cart with the presents which had left Elisabetopol before me. On the 7th I reached Baku.* From the heights before the city I got a good view of the whole place, and of the sea and shipping. The town is girt by a double wall, turreted and embrasured and furnished with guns. The interior is handsome and extensive, but the bald hills without the walls have an unpleasing appearance. The scarcity of wood and water in the neighbourhood is a great drawback to its value as a fortress, and the situation of the place generally is bad. The streets of Baku are narrow ; the buildings high and not bad-looking : the town possesses a numerous population, a fair market, and excellent caravanserais, and it has an important trade with Astraccan. Ship-building goes on in the port, but the craft ply only along the coast, and do not go further than Ghilan. A lofty tower stands on the shore, known as the "Maiden Tower," a name which it owes to the following tragical story :—In ancient times a Governor of Baku fell in love with his own daughter, and desired to place her in the position of his wife. For long the girl resisted his importunities, but at last consented, making it a condition of her compliance that her father should build a high tower for her on the sea beach, wherein she might hide her shame. The tower was quickly built, and the daughter, enticing her father to the topmost pinnacle on the pretence of showing him the height, seized her opportunity as he bent to gaze beneath, and pushed him over the parapet, flinging herself after him into the sea.

We found the two (2) ships which had been equipped for us lying in port all ready, so we laid in necessaries and went on board, taking with us one officer and thirty men from the Baku garrison. The vessels were the Corvette *Kasan*, 18 Guns, under Lieutenant Bassargin, which had arrived from Astraccan the year before (1818), and the Merchant sloop *St. Polikarp*, under Lieutenant Ostrolopov. This last was not armed, being only intended as a transport for the troops and spare baggage. The naval officials on board the

---

* Baku, compounded from the Persian words بـاد wind, and كو a street.

corvette were as follows :—Lieutenant Bassargin, two sub-officers, Juriev and Ivanov, the Chaplain, the Surgeon, For-mizin, Lieutenant Linitzki of the Artillery, and the Pilot and Master. The force, all told, amounted to 160 men. On the evening of the 8th we accepted the invitation of the ship's officers, and went on shore to a small house called the " Sea Bath ;" on our way we passed the ruins of the great caravanserai lying at a distance of seven miles from the shore and completely submerged, with the exception of a few turrets rising above the surface. It is unknown how or when this building sank into the sea, but it is most likely the result of an earthquake. At this point there is a depth of about 18 feet, and it is noticed that every 13 years important changes take place on this part of the coast, the sea some-times receding from, and sometimes encroaching on, the land.

The whole neighbourhood is well worthy of attention both on account of the naphtha which it produces and the mighty ruins which lie scattered on every side and invite historical research.

On the 17th of July we went on board the corvette again, and at 6 o'clock on the following evening (18th) weighed anchor, and stood for the Island of Sara, whither the trans-port had preceded us on the 15th. At first we had a good breeze, but it fell in the night, and we spent the whole of the next day in tacking without making any perceptible progress. On the night of the 20th there fell a dead calm, and we lay motionless for two hours and a half, but at day-break we sighted Sara, and by noon we moored close by the island. This island is six miles in length, in form a crescent, its beach shelly, and its whole surface covered with sedge and rushes, except here and there where Russian squatters have planted a few osiers. In former days all the water was brack-ish in the wells here, but the Russians introduced wooden linings for the latter, and, by continually emptying and clearing them, managed to obtain a supply of fresh water.

The transport now made sail for the fortress of Lenko-ran to take in wood.

The distance from Sara is about 12 miles. We lay at anchor until the 24th, and all this time it rained without ceasing.

On the 24th, at 7 A.M., we weighed, with a good breeze from N.E., which lasted till midnight, and we were sanguine of sighting the Turcoman coast on the following day, when suddenly the wind died away, and we hardly made 1½ knots an hour. This state of things lasted for two whole days— no breeze and torrents of rain; and it was not until the evening of the third day that the sky cleared.

We wished to steer on the so-called "Silver Hill" of which we had heard, but none of the crew were acquainted with the coast.

At last the Turcoman land came in view, and we recognised the Ak-Tapa (white hill), which runs from the coast in a north-easterly direction. It is of a considerable length, and diminishes in height as it approaches the sea. We anchored in 4½ fathoms at a distance of 5½ miles from the shore, and, on searching the beach with our telescopes, made out some "Kibitks" (Turcoman carts). It was accordingly resolved that I should land next morning and reconnoitre the country, while Petrovitsh, the Interpreter, endeavoured to establish intercourse between us and the inhabitants. The 12-oared long-boat was therefore lowered from the corvette and armed with a 12-pounder and two falconets. The party altogether numbered 24 men, six of whom carried muskets, and as we counted on returning the same evening, we only took provisions and water for the day. After a pull of an hour and a half we came within 120 yards of the beach, and were obliged to anchor, as there was not sufficient water to admit of our getting closer in; so we got on land with only our arms and clothes. Forty yards from the water line were a lot of mounds, evidently thrown up by the action of the wind on the sand, and covered with bushes. I ascended one of these, and discovered, by means of my telescope, that the Ak-Tapa, instead of being an isolated hill, was a great mountain, which must be connected with some other chain. It was about eight miles distant, and seemed to be so entirely cut off by water from the place where I stood, that I imagined myself to be on a detached island.*

At first I wished to explore towards the north, in order to discover the bay where the Turcomans conceal their "Kirshimas"† (boats), but Dobritsch, the artillery officer, Petrovitsh, and a sailor, called Agejeve, who had been here

---

* I found out afterwards that the apparent sea was only a salt steppe or a dry lake, covered with crystallized salt, which, shining through the moving vapours formed by the heat, had quite the appearance of water from a distance.

† Kirshima. This word is derived from the Turkish Kiriji, i.e., a flat-bottomed boat.

Captain Muraviev's first night on the eastern bank of the Caspian Sea

before, advised me to try to southward instead, more in the direction of Astrabad; and I acted on their advice, having further a hope of coming on a river by so doing. I accordingly went along the beach with four sailors and Petrovitsh, whilst the rest of the party in the long-boat kept up with us. Before starting we bored for water, but found it quite salt and undrinkable. We went steadily along the shore for 11 miles, found the traces of camels, horses, and bare-footed men, and at last a post with a mark on it, among the bushes, which made me think that the Turcoman carts might be concealed there. I crawled to the place through the undergrowth, but found only a sand hill with a lot of dry brushwood on it, in the midst of which the post had been stuck up. Wearied and disappointed, I determined at 3 P.M. to go back to the corvette, leaving Petrovitsh on shore to try and find out some of the inhabitants.

We were carrying out this plan, when suddenly a strong gale got up from seaward, and when only 1,500 paces away from land, we found we could make no head against it; the waves broke over us, and Juriev advised that we should put back.

This storm caused me great anxiety, for we were without provisions and water, and it seemed quite possible that it might continue to blow for a week; and the chance of a sudden attack from the Turcomans gave me another ground for uneasiness. Resolved to make the best of it, I landed the two falconets and occupied a couple of hillocks, throwing round the bivouac a chain of sentries, whom Juriev and I visited alternately from time to time during the night. We also lit a huge fire to indicate our whereabouts to the corvette. The fine, blinding dust which was blown about caused great annoyance to us all. I dug for fresh water here, but unsuccessfully, the water we got at being brackish and unfit for drinking purposes.

In the evening Petrovitsh came in with the news that he had not found a living creature in the neighbourhood, so, exhausted with fatigue and thirst, we passed a most wretched night in the sand. Next day (30th) our situation became more critical every hour; the storm raged with increasing fury, the provisions came to an end, and our thirst became more and more insufferable, so much so, that some of the men dipped their last biscuits in the sea-water, hoping thereby to allay their dreadful pangs,—we were, indeed, at the last extremity, and immediate action became imperative; so I resolved on penetrating further into the steppe, to the hills visible in the distance, in the hope of discovering some Turcoman habitations ("Yurts" as they are called), or, at any rate, striking fresh water. I therefore directed Juriev to shift our position to a point nearer the sea and to make it more compact, posting only one look-out party during the day. I was on the point of starting, when of a sudden the long-boat began to sink; we all rushed into the sea, threw everything overboard, and with great difficulty managed to haul the boat up on to the beach, when we found she had sprung a leak, but not of a very serious nature. We now armed and set out for the opposite edge of the steppe, the party consisting of the artillery officer, Petrovitsh, myself, four sailors, and two pioneers.

For upwards of an hour we waded through heavy sand, and were quite worn out, when suddenly we sank to the knee in a black bog, which formed the centre of a great dried-up salt lake. Here I had bitter experience of the deceitfulness of the famous "mirage," for this dry salt lake had from afar the appearance of a piece of water, with people on the banks; but when we reached it, lo! the water was nowhere, and the men had turned into bushes, and instead of plunging into a cold stream, we found ourselves stuck in a morass! We had to retrace our steps, and on the way back I dug for water in three different places, but found it all brackish.

I may mention that in this search I employed a means which I had heard of in Persia by which time is saved: this is simply to fire down the hole one has dug, which brings the water into it immediately. The plan was perfectly successful, in so far as obtaining water went, but it unfortunately could not alter the quality of the same. Worn out and disappointed, I now returned to my party, and determined not to make any further attempts, but to trust to the storm's going down. At last the weather improved, and we resolved to despatch the sub-officer and 12 sailors to the corvette in the long-boat. When the moon rose the long-boat put off. I sent a note by it to Ponomarev describing in a few words our situation, begging him for help, and telling him that, in the event of any mishap, we should make for Astrabad on foot. By noon (31st) the long-boat returned with but a small supply of provisions and a letter from Ponomarev entreating us to return. Meanwhile the sea had gone down, so we embarked, and in two or three hours reached the corvette in safety. I took the latitude, and found that we were in 37°24'37"N.

According to Count Voinovitsh's map * this would place us directly opposite the "White Hill," but the ordinary ship's chart placed us far to the north of this point, so I came to the conclusion that the hill before us was the "Green Hill." Strengthened in this opinion by the circumstance that the Astrabad mountain chain was not in sight, we made up our minds to try for the "White Hill" further south. In the evening we weighed anchor, but the wind was unfavourable, and we made little progress.

On Sunday morning (August 1st) we were told that three Turcoman craft were in view near the shore. We went on deck and made out 10 boats ; they had sails set, and were steering northwards. We were very anxious to pick up at any rate one of the number, and accordingly fired a gun as a signal, but they did not understand it, and made all sail away from us. We now fired two rounds at them, but they were out of range, so we sent a boat in pursuit with an armed party, and Petrovitsh among them. An attempt was made to cut off the last " Kirshime," but when the crew saw their situation, they promptly ran her ashore and fled into the bush, their number being 5 men and 3 women. Our party likewise landed and gave chase. Petrovitsh managed to stop one of the men and assure him that we had no hostile intentions, but had come only with friendly designs. On this they all came out of their hiding-place and begged for mercy. We again assured them they had nothing to fear from us, and then let them all go, except the owner of the boat, who was an old man of sixty, and held in great respect by his countrymen. His name was Dowlat Ali.

In spite of all our caresses and friendly assurances he would not believe us, but looked on himself as a captive, and seemed by his downcast bearing to expect a terrible fate.

From his replies to our interrogations it appeared that we really had been opposite the "White Hill," and that the "Silver Hill "† lay somewhat to the south. The "Yurts" of these Turcomans are situated between the two above-mentioned hills, on the sea-coast. The place is called Hassan Kuli, and

---

* Journal of Count Voinovitsh's Expedition to the Caspian in 1781-82: Moscow, 1810.

† The Silver Hill received its name from the Turcomans (by whom it is called Gumish Tapa) on account of the silver coins they frequently used to find in earthen vessels among the ruins. The coins were about the size of a shilling, and as the natives could not decipher the superscription, they put them down to Alexander the Great's era. The bricks $1\frac{1}{2}' \times 2''$ of these ruins have for long been an article of trade between the Turcomans and Persia.—STRAHL.

here dwells the elder Kiat Aga,* who had gone as Envoy to General Ratishtsheff as far back as 1813. The Turcomans graze their herds on the "Silver Hill," and although it is at a pretty good distance off, it is still their favourite resort, being convenient for their boats, on which their entire trade depends.

Their water-supply they obtain from the river "Giurgen-Jai,"† which falls into the sea by the Silver Hill, and flows about half a day's ride from their village. It is a whole day's ride from the Giurgen-Jai to Astrabad. On the road there is another little river called Khwaja Nafas ‡.

Dowlat Ali spoke of the ruins of many great cities as existing in the country of the Turcomans, among others, one on the Silver Hill, ascribed by the natives to Alexander the Great.§ The Sultan Khan or Jadukar of whom Petrovitsh had so often spoken was now at Khiva, where he had taken refuge from the Persians at the close of the war of 1813. From what I could gather from Dowlat Ali, I think I may safely assert that the Turcomans have no common Ruler, but that they are split up into tribes, each tribe acknowledging its own particular elder or Chief. Dowlat Ali could only mention five such Chieftains, but assured me that there were many more. He further said that the people of Khiva live in great amity and constant intercourse with the Turcomans; and that from here to Khiva was a 15 days' ride.

We could get no more out of him. He showed much discomposure at being alone among foreigners, and desired to be speedily landed, promising to send Kiat Aga to us. This determined us on casting anchor opposite the place where he said we should find some "Yurts," but the vast shallows compelled us to stand so far off from the coast that we actually lost sight of it. In the evening, at a general consultation, we decided, on Ponomarev's suggestion, to put Dowlat Ali and Petrovitsh ashore, and to await their return and Kiat's opposite to the Silver Hill. We hoped also to get nearer the shore opposite this hill and to obtain a fresh supply of water, as well as to have greater facilities for opening negotiations

---

* Kiat Aga's portrait will be found in the Appendix. It presents a characteristic type of the Turcoman features.—STRAHL.

† Jai in Russian means tea, in Turkish a river.—STRAHL.

‡ Khwaja is the epithet applied to a Mussulman pilgrim to Mecca. Khwaja Nafas signifies literally pilgrim's breath.

§ The Persians generally ascribe the ruins which they cannot account for otherwise to Alexander the Great, in the same way that the Swiss make Cæsar the founder of all their old towers, &c.—STRAHL.

Portrait of Petrovitsh

with the Turcomans and searching for the best spot for the con-templated harbour. Until close on evening we lay at anchor, waiting for the wind to fall and enable us to land Petrovitsh and Dowlat Ali, but before night-fall it was settled that we should go on at once to the Silver Hill, whence I should start on my journey to Khiva. In the night we saw the reflection of fire in two parts of the heavens. This was put down by Dowlat Ali to the dry grass having caught fire.

We then cast anchor and awaited daybreak. At 7 A.M. we came to the Silver Hill, and found our sloop which had preceded us from Sara, and had been lying here for three days.

Lieutenant Ostolopov, the Commander of the Sloop, pre-sented Nazar Margan to us, the Chief of the Nomadic Tur-comans who wander in the district lying round the hill. His appearance was pleasing, but was apparently not borne out by his real character. From him we learnt that there were 200 Turcoman families * in this " Ahl " (village), who had set-tled here for good. They are agriculturists, and seem pros-perous. We entertained Nazar Margan hospitably, and he undertook to conduct Petrovitsh to Kiat Aga, who was just then attending some fair, or engaged in some commercial transactions with the Persians. The dignity of a Kiat is very considerable among the Turcomans. He is generally acknowledged as their head by the elders of several tribes, yet in a very optional manner, " for," say they, " God is our only Governor." These people cherish an unconquerable hatred of the Persians. We were presently visited by eight Turcomans, whom we feasted with " pilau," and did all we could to ingratiate ourselves with them. The matter in hand being Petrovitsh's conveyance to the Kiat, Nazar Margan, who had previously agreed to conduct him for three ducats, rose now in his demands to five, and eventually to 10, ducats. Then Ponomarev lost all patience, and sent them all out of the corvette, retaining only Nazar Margan, but that gentle-man now refused to undertake the commission, and referred us to Dowlat Ali. The latter willingly agreed, but when we made him a small present, Nazar became so excited by envy, that we had to pacify him with some flints and a pound of gunpowder. Petrovitsh started the same evening. We may predicate of the Turcomans that their simple mode of living stands in remarkable contrast to their insatiable lust for gold.

---

* A Kibitke can be estimated at six souls. The word signifies in Rus-sian a half-covered, badly built, four-wheeled cart, among the nomadic hordes it means a family.—STRAHL.

The Silver Hill does not appear very lofty. The Turcomans say that the ruins of a town, called Gushi Tappa, are to be seen on its slopes. I found the latitude here to be 37° 5′ 22.″

This morning (4th August) I went on board the sloop, and from that proceeded in a skiff with Ostolopov to get a nearer look at the Giurgen River, which falls into the sea a mile and a half to the south of the Silver Hill.

The sloop's boat, carrying 10 soldiers, 2 falconets, and 1 cannon, followed us, but at about a mile from shore the shallows stopped its further progress. The sailors now dragged the skiff ashore, and I got into a "Kulass" (i.e., a hollowed-out log in use with the Turcomans as a canoe) and proceeded about a mile up the river mouth.

The river Giurgen flows through a swamp, has a muddy bottom, is from 12 to 24 yards in breadth, and has low banks, from which stretches on either side the morass, covered with a 3-foot high grass. The water tastes brackish and smells marshy. From its gentle fall, the river has a sluggish flow. It frequently dries up in summer, yet is never entirely without some water. A mile from the mouth I noticed "Baktsha" (cultivation), proving that the Turcomans of this part are agriculturists. At this point the river is over 6 feet deep, the banks higher and dry, but these sound banks only extend to a distance of 400 or 800 yards, and, further up, the river crawls again through bog and fen. At this point also there is a ford, where the Turcomans cross their herds, and through which the high road to Astrabad runs. I got a good view of the Silver Hill from here. It lies 3 miles or so 33° north-west from the ford. Here dwell some Turcomans, with whom I conversed for about two hours; they invited me into their village, but I promised them a visit on the following day. They said it was the universal wish of their countrymen that the Russians should restore the razed fortress on the Silver Hill, "for," said they, "we should then be able to revenge ourselves on the Persians for their ravages. We Turcomans are stupid people, or we should have rebuilt the place ourselves before now, but that is a job we cannot manage. If we were all called out, we should muster over 10,000 men, and could then chastise the Persians, as, indeed, we did five years ago at this place, when we defeated the Sirdars and captured many head of cattle."

I asked them if they would not like some arms. They looked at one another with beaming countenances, clucked their tongues, and were evidently overjoyed at the thought.

They have constant intercourse with Khiva, and assured me that with an escort of 5 or 6 men one might safely make the journey thither.

According to them Khiva is a large town, and the ruling Khan immensely rich. The Turcomans of this district are agriculturists; the soil is fruitful, and they are cattle-breeders to a large extent. They are also powder manufacturers, and it seems that their only deficiency is in mechanical works. A wood lies at a distance of 11 miles from the river, and extends to Astrabad. It is reported to be of vast dimensions and to furnish good timber. I learned that the day before my arrival Petrovitsh had been at this " Ahl." He had started in a Kirshime on his way to the Kiat, accompanied by Dowlat Ali and two villagers.

6th August.—This morning the sloop's boat was sent to bring off Nazar Margan and the notables of the " Ahl." They arrived at the corvette towards mid-day. One of the Chiefs appeared as the representative of Khan Dowlat Ali. Nazar Margan exerted himself to the utmost to persuade us that it was quite unnecessary to send Dowlat Ali a special invitation ; but it is probable that his motive was the hope of himself receiving the present intended for the Khan. When Khan Dowlat Ali did arrive, he explained that he did not come earlier, as he did not wish to infringe the custom which forbids Khans to pay visits without invitation.

The true cause was, however, that he did not want to connect himself with us, as he had an awe of the Persians, to whom he owed his Khanship. Dowlat Ali Khan showed more intelligence than the other Turcomans ; he had served in Aga Mahomed Khan's army, and been present at the sack of Tiflis. He had now fallen away from the reigning Shah, Fatteh Ali, and been forthwith elected Chief at his own birth-place. We gained no further intelligence from him beyond what we had already heard from the others ; he acknowledges no one as having a claim to sovereignty over the Turcomans, and seems to be more Persian than Russian in his tendencies. He named to us also several of the most notable among the elders or Chiefs, such as Kiat Aga of the " Ahl" Hassan Kuli, Tagan Kulij Khan of the village of Gerai, Tepe Mirza Khan of the same place, and Kodsham Kulibai and Tagan-Cazi of Atrek. The River Atrek runs 11 miles north of the Giurgen. " Ahls " lie on the banks of both rivers, but along the whole course of the Giurgen are to be seen the ruins of fortifications and cities.

Ponomarev wrote to all the above-named Chiefs, inviting them to visit him. He presented the Khan with a piece of gold brocade, and entrusted the letters to him for delivery; but we kept Nazar Margan on the corvette as a hostage.

This person now told us that he had it from Dowlat Ali that the Turcomans imagined that next autumn would see the arrival of many Russian ships with troops and guns, and that they were all in great dread of this. At length Petrovitsh arrived to-day with Kiat Aga. The latter is superior to all his countrymen in shrewdness, and acknowledges no superior. For some time Sultan Khan ruled over the Turcomans, but soon abandoned the Government, and fled to Khiva, probably from fear of the Persians. He had really no particular right to the Government, and held the reins solely from his superior abilities. He would appear to have come originally from the confines of Khiva or India, and devoted himself to the study of magic, whence his soubriquet of "Jadugar." At first Kiat Aga was suspicious and distrustful, and when Ponomarev unfolded to him the plan of our Government he demurred for a long time. At last, said he—" If your motives are upright, I am ready to serve you, but you will gain your end much better in 'Cheleken.' There I have relations, and the coast, too, is far more adapted to the construction of the work you contemplate, and it is only a 15 days' ride from there to Khiva.

" I am ready to accompany you to Cheleken myself, and as there are some of Sultan Khan's people there, I shall send your Agents with them to Khiva." I now landed at the Silver Hill, and thence went to pay a visit to Dowlat Ali Khan in his " Ahl," and discovered that the hill I had seen was only the walls of a large building which had been covered with sand from the east side of the steppe, and thus from a distance resembled a natural rise. The inhabitants have cultivated this sandy soil to a certain extent. On the other side of the building, towards the sea, there are many ruins visible. The distance to the " Ahl " is a little over 1,500 paces. I halted my escort of 12 men in front of the village, and went alone to the Khan, who received me most cordially. A number of people assembled at his house (Kibitke), and his wife did not withdraw. He entertained me with sour camel's milk and bread, and begged that I should let my party enter the village, which I gladly agreed to. Mirza Khan, to whom Ponomarev had written, was already in the " Ahl." He visited me at Dowlat Ali Khan's house, and expressed his desire to accompany me back to the corvette, but afterwards

Portrait of Kiat Aga

changed his mind, and said he would await the arrival of the three other invited Chiefs. The Khan was very anxious to see our soldiers "play with their muskets" as he expressed it, "for," said he, "we have heard from all sides that the Russians are so highly instructed, that when one man strikes the ground with his foot, 300, or even more, will do the same thing simultaneously, and this I should much like to see." I made the soldiers go through some manoeuvres and fire, which filled all the spectators with astonishment.

The dwelling-places of the Turcomans are constructed like those of the Tartars in Georgia, that is to say, they consist of rush mats stretched on long poles, the whole being covered with felt.

Their women are not kept in privacy, and the features of the latter are agreeable and pretty regular, their dress consisting of coloured "Shirovari," a long red chemise and a head-dress which has much in common with the Russian "Kokoshniks," only it is two or three times as high. This head-dress among the wealthy is edged with gold or silver. The hair is shown on the forehead, but combed modestly off on either side and plaited into a long tail behind.

7th August.—This morning I visited the Silver Hill, taking with me workmen and implements in the hopes of procuring some coins among the ruins, so as to establish the age of the ancient city. It was, however, necessary first to divert the attention of the Turcomans from my intentions, so I landed an officer with some soldiers and a drummer, and while these entered the "Ahl" and went through military exercises, I proceeded undisturbed with my researches. I cannot give any satisfactory explanation with regard to these ruins. The Silver Hill is, as above mentioned, only the shell of some huge building or fortress, which has been covered with sand from the eastern side; nevertheless within those walls I found tombs, and, indeed, got at some human remains, buried after the Mahomedan fashion, *i.e.*, resting on one side with the head towards the north-east. I think these must be Turcoman tombs and very ancient. The great wall is about 600 feet long and over 12 feet in height. It consists of beautiful burnt bricks, and it is noteworthy that after every three layers of Georgian bricks there is one layer of Russian. Beneath the wall I discovered a small vault, which I rummaged, but found in it nothing but broken glass and ashes.

From this wall there runs a tongue of land, apparently the handiwork of man, into the sea, to the distance of about 280 yards.   In several places I found the remains of buildings, round towers, stair-cases, and such like, faced in the most regular manner with great bricks over a foot thick.   Here also there are great heaps of loose bricks, stretching into the sea to the distance of one or two hundred yards.   It struck me that those ruins were not the work of ordinary decay, but rather that the structures had succumbed to an earthquake (like the caravanserai on the road from Baku), as the walls were all of a fair height, and seemed to have been cut sharply off, so to say, at a certain point.

The people about have found many gold and silver coins here, and the tradition is that the fortress was built by the Russians, * who once possessed this sea-board.   I dug down into one of the round towers, but came upon nothing, except some *débris* of glass and earthenware jars, possessing none of the characteristics of Russian work.   I would have pursued my researches further and have worked down to the very foundation, but the tremendous heat quite overpowered the labourers I had employed.

The description of the Silver Hill given in the History of the Russian Naval Expedition to the Caspian Sea in the year 1782 under Count Voinovitsh does not in the least agree with my own personal observations.   In that account the Silver Hill is described as an island, which it most certainly is not. It is therefore reasonable to suppose that the discrepancy is due to the frequent alterations on the shores of the Caspian, caused by alternate encroaching and retiring of the sea.   The Kiat and other Turcomans declared that the Silver Hill really had been an island, and had only become one with the dry land five or six years ago.   I landed early with Kiat, and made a survey of the country between the Silver Hill and the River Giurgen, then went up stream, and came across another little river running into the Giurgen from the north, its banks covered with sedge.   Kiat declared that formerly an arm of the sea separated the Silver Hill from the main land at this point, and further told me to warn my people who had gone out for water not to scatter, but to be on the look-out, as the

---

* They probably believe the pirate Stenka Rasin to have been the founder, but erroneously so, for Rasin never visited the Eastern Coast of the Caspian. The Silver Hill is the last fortress in the wall now called Kisim Alai (gold giving). Along this wall were scattered smaller forts, such as Kuru-Segri, Jorshan, and many others, the traces of which and of the wall are to be found at the present day all along the right bank of the Giurgen.   Native traditions do not throw any light on the age of this wall, but some information is given in the *Bibliothique Orientale d' Herbelot,* who holds it to be the boundary between Turan and Iran.

A Turcoman woman

Persians had bribed the Turcomans of other " Ahls " to shoot us from the cover of the reeds.

11th August.—The heat was insupportable, and when, at 2 P.M., I had completed my survey, I took refuge in the " Ahl," and was received in a very friendly manner by Dowlat Ali Khan and Nazar Margan. Kiat told me that the " White Hill," called in Turkish Ak-Tapa, had originally gone by the name of " Ak Bartlain," derived from a swamp grass known in Russian also as Bartlain.

There is a spring in a cleft on this hill, from which spouts a jet of salt water with great noise.

17th August.—Kiat, Dowlat Ali Khan, and Kojam Kuli Bey (another of the Chiefs) now assembled on board the corvette, but Mirza Khan and Tagan Kolij Khan did not put in an appearance. They sent us a message telling us to wait for them, but I believe they only wanted an opportunity when their coming would not excite the suspicion of the Persians,—a consideration which was always present in their minds. But Ponomarev would not wait for them. He proposed to the three Chiefs that they should send Kiat as Envoy to the Russian Governor in Georgia, giving him letters of credit and the powers of a plenipotentiary. They received this proposal with great satisfaction, and desired to gain the acquiescence of all the elders, and indeed the Cazi, himself, their spiritual Ruler, who, according to what they said, would appear to be the head of the tribe of Yomud. Kiat undertook to bring the consent of the other Turcoman Chiefs of the Yomud tribe within four days, so we determined to put him ashore, and then to proceed to Hassan Kuli and await his return at that place. Then we were to go to the Bay of Krasnavoda, lying by the Balkan, and get the Chiefs of that district to subscribe to the above-mentioned letters, and after that we were to make arrangements for my journey to Khiva.

The dignity of the Khans is not hereditary; they are appointed by the Persians, and the people obey them from a regard for their superior wisdom or virtues. All are free, and no Turcoman is the slave of another. The fields are tilled by slaves, whom they either purchase or capture.

The power of the Ak Sakhkali (lit., white beards), or head Chiefs elected by the people, appears to be greater than that of the Khans, and the position is hereditary so long as the successor's qualifications inspire confidence.

24th August.—I went ashore, and took leave of Dowlat Ali Khan, who for the fourth time offered me the present of a stallion, which, however, I had to reject, because I could not take him with me. Then I returned with Kolij Beg and a relation of Kiat's to the corvette, which had already weighed anchor. We distributed presents among them, and learned from Kiat's relation that the Turcomans on the Persian frontier acknowledge the sway of the Persians, whilst those on the Atrek River, and further north, do not recognize their authority. On the whole, it is impossible to say of this people who is their real Ruler. We landed Kiat's cousin, and directed him to go at once to Hassan Kuli, and let the Kiat know of our shortly-to-be-expected arrival.

The Turcomans have no decided or earnest character, and none of that love of justice which characterizes the Caucasian type.

This miserable race is devoid of all ideas of hospitality. Their only thought is money, and for a trifle they are prepared for any baseness. They have no idea of obedience or discipline, but if a clever and enterprising individual starts up, they acknowledge him as their head without questioning his right to the post. Sultan Khan's case is one in point. They are equally devoid of public spirit and of modesty. A man calls himself a Chief or an elder only to make something by it, and his neighbour forthwith adopts a higher title to spite him, such as Ak Sakkal, &c. The language of the Turcomans is Turkish, and their dialect resembles that spoken in Kasan. None of them, except the priests (Mullas), can read or write. They are Mahomedans and followers of Omar.

Although strict in observing religious ceremonies and in praying at the prescribed hours, they are totally ignorant of the first principles of their faith. Physically they are a fine race, tall and broad-shouldered. They wear a short beard, and greatly resemble the Calmucks in their features. They dress after the Persian fashion. The women dress their hair with great care, and attach a number of jingling silver gew-gaws to the plaits behind. If I happened to stray unexpected into an Ahl, I would find them in the simplest attire, but before I left they would all be sitting in front of their houses, dressed in their very best. These remarks apply only to the Turcomans of the "Silver Hill," who have acquired Persian manners and customs to a certain extent. The Northern Turcomans differ from these tribes considerably. We arrived in the corvette before Hassan

Kuli, but on account of shoals had to keep out to sea, so far that the land was invisible to the naked eye. With the telescope we descried a number of Turcoman craft. The latitude was here ascertained to be 37° 27′ 51″.

27th August.—Ponomarev and I now went ashore with a quantity of presents. It took us two hours to reach land, and we had hardly done so, when such a breeze sprang up from the seaward that we could not regain the corvette until the 31st.

On account of the shallow water we could not bring our boat nearer than 600 yards from land. Kiat came to meet us, with all the inhabitants of the Ahl, and we found a Kibitk prepared for our especial residence and provided with handsome carpets. There are 150 Kibitks in Hassan Kuli. Boatbuilding is carried on here to a certain extent, timber being brought for the purpose from the Silver Hill district. I found the remains of an old redoubt, built years before by Kiat as a safeguard against the attacks of the Kaklas, who, it appears, are much dreaded by the Yomuds.

The name of Hassan Kuli is derived from that of the founder of this tribe, who settled here in ancient times. This strip of land was then an island, but in these days it is connected with the main land on the north side, and forms a peninsula, separated from the land on its east side by an arm of the sea 11 miles long by five and a half broad. Both this estuary and the peninsula run due north and south. The peninsula is only 1,600 feet across and four miles long. Opposite the Ahl, E. S. E., on the other side of the estuary, the little river Atrek falls into the sea. On its banks there are many Yurts of Turcomans belonging to this same Yomud tribe, and the inhabitants of Hassan Kuli depend on it for their supply of fresh water. Kiat took great pains to amuse us with Turcoman sports. These consisted in shooting at a mark both with guns and bows and arrows, wrestling, and running races, and the competitors were incited to do their utmost by the money which Ponomarev dealt out with no sparing hand. Their fire-arms are most inferior, and their powder has no strength. They seldom hit the mark. Some of the competitors were wonderfully well-dressed. The tribe leads a pretty lazy life, and it may therefore be assumed that they derive a large profit from the one trade they engage in, *viz.*, carrying naphtha and salt to the Persian market. They annually dispose of about 2,000 " Puds " (Russian) of these articles. This trade belongs more particularly to the Turcomans dwelling round the Bay of Balkan, who procure both.

the salt and naphtha from the Naphtha Island, but the inhabitants of Hassan Kuli purchase their stock from them, and take it at a good profit to Persia; hence the circumstance of the latter possessing so large a number of boats (Kirshimes). Very fair carpets are manufactured at Hassan Kuli; the people are, in fact, clever workmen on the whole. Their silver-smiths strike all sorts of medallions and coins, which serve for the adornment of the women. Their musical instrument is a two-stringed guitar.

They till their land and graze their flocks and herds on the Rivers Atrek and Giurgen. From the insufficiency of their own corn-crops, they are obliged to draw to a consider-able extent on Persia for grain. On the peninsula itself water-melons are the only vegetables that thrive. The yearly take of fish has for some time back been reduced to a half of what it used to be. In winter they catch many swans, uti-lizing only the down. On the coast snipe or wood-cock always abound (called by the people " Jiluk " and Kunkaitak). On the steppes and the reedy banks of the Atrek wolves are to be met with, also foxes, wild goats (" Jairan "), wild pig, jackals, &c. The wind almost invariably blows on to the land here, which renders communication difficult. It is very desirable that the Hassan Kuli estuary should be carefully surveyed and sounded. At present one cannot assume that large vessels could find an anchorage in it, although light craft probably could. The following are some of the princi-pal Chiefs of Hassan Kuli :—Il-Mahomed, Khan Haldi, Dowlat Ali, and we may add the name of Kiat. There are others who are on bad terms with Kiat, so the Ahl is divided into two factions, of which Kiat's is at present the stronger.

28th August.—Towards evening Petrovitsh arrived from the Atrek River, whither he had proceeded the day before, and brought with him the Cazi and Kojam Kuli Bey, who are much respected by the Turcomans. Although the Cazi was very young, they paid the greatest deference to him, because he had inherited the dignity from his father, who had commanded universal confidence. We soon won him over by presents. The necessary documents had now been subscribed to by the principal Chiefs, but Ponomarev still desired that Kiat should proceed as Envoy to our Govern-ment by the votes of all the Turcomans. He accordingly assembled all the Chiefs before the Cazi and Kiat, and the latter was elected *nem. con.* for the post of Ambassador.

But Kiat took offence because we had made out the list of notable Turcomans without consulting him, and because we had given presents to Meer Said, Haji Mahomed, and Tamari Kuli (who had been made " Sirdars " for their valour), and he was the more irritated because, as it seemed, he had previously promised presents to several individuals on his own account (who were now disappointed). He accordingly wanted to make us feel his displeasure and ex- perience the influence he held over the others, and therefore persuaded his adherents, Il-Mahomed and Khan Haldi, to accept nothing from us, and to avoid coming near us even. We soon, however, pacified him by intimating that we would not give any more rewards without his consent. Meanwhile one of the Chiefs rejected his present, as being of too little value. Ponomarev gave him a fresh one, but when the others saw this, they also all demanded more costly gifts, and even a ragged Mulla had the presumption to return his portion to us with signs of displeasure. Ponomarev now lost patience, and abused them roundly. That turned out to be the true way of restoring order, for tranquillity re-appeared in the Ahl directly.

30th August.—When the wind fell a little we started back to the corvette, and got on board after a four hours' sail. Kiat alone came with us, for he would permit no one to accompany him and share his pretended labours, probably from dread lest he should lose for himself some portion of the rewards and distinctions which he looked forward to from our Government.

31st August.—We weighed anchor, but had to spend the day in tacking backwards and forwards. Kiat informs me that the Turcomans dwelling to the south of the Bay of Balkan, both along the coast and in the interior of the steppe, are divided into three tribes, *viz.*, Yomuds, Takkas, and Kiok- lans. The last named tribe (Kioklan) is distinguished for its predatory habits, and will often fall upon the Yomuds themselves and carry off their property. These two tribes have, consequently, been at war for a long time, having enjoyed peace only during Sultan Khan's days. The predatory Takkas were quelled by the Khan of Khiva in 1813, when he marched through their territory against the Persians with an army of 30,000 men. The name Yomud is derived from a patriarch of that name, who had three wives. The first bore him two sons, *viz.*, Juni and Sharab, the second bore him Kujuk, and the third Bairam Shah. From those four sons sprang the four chief clans of the Yomud tribe, each clan distinguishing itself by the name of its founder. These four clans live together in the closest bonds of union, and afford each other mutual protection. The first and second (Juni and Sharab) are particularly remarkable for the closeness of their relations. These two tribes number about 15,000 families, the third (Kujuk) 8,000, and the fourth (Bairam Shah) 14,000. As just mentioned, these clans are closely allied with one another, but the Bairam Shah clan has an extraneous alliance with Khiva. Each clan has its particular Chieftain. Hojam Kuli Bey is the Chief of the Sharab tribe, but the Cazi is Mahomed Tagan.

This individual stands high in the eyes of the Yomuds, partly by reason of his ancient family, and partly because his forefathers have always filled the office. The Yomuds graze their herds in summer on the banks of the Atrek and Giurgen; in winter they inhabit the country about the Ak-Tapa and further in the interior. The Chief of the Junis is Nadir Khan; he lives in Atta Bai, where also dwells the Cazi by name Dowlat Murad. The Kujuk Chieftain is Ana Wardi Khan, but he has fled to Khiva. The Cazi of this clan is dead, and no successor has been appointed to his office. The Bairam Shah Chief is Mang Ali Sirdar; he also, with many of his clan, has fled to Khiva.

In time of need the tribe of Yomud can place 30,000 men in the field, but hardly a thousand of these are properly armed. I asked Kiat about the Gulf of Karabogass, which is said to absorb the waters of the Caspian, and he assured me that that was the belief of the Turcomans.

1st September.—To-day we were becalmed, and had to anchor opposite the Green Hill. The latter is conical in form, and has three times the diameter at the base that it has at the summit. There is a chasm on this hill similar to that on the Ak-Tapa (White Hill), from which salt water is thrown up having a very pungent smell. The Turcomans call the Green Hill "Bartlauk" or "Hios Bartlauk," *i.e.* sky-blue. A little to the south of this hill, and quite by the sea-side, there stands an old mosque called "Mama Kuss," or Maiden's breast. From the Silver Hill to Hassan Kuli the distance is 33 miles; from Hassan Kuli to Ak-Tapa (White Hill) 20 miles; and from the latter to the Green Hill 25 and a half miles.

2nd September.—Towards noon we sighted Naphtha Island: the Island of Agurchin was on our larboard, but we could not distinguish it by reason of its low beach and the distance which intervened. I found the latitude to be 39° 10′ 20″ N. at the entrance to the bay south-east of Naphtha Island. The latter island as well as the before-mentioned hills to the eastward have the appearance at a distance of great yellow heigths. In Count Voinovitsh's work, quoted before, these islands are very well and exhaustively described and their position correctly given in the appended map. In those days Dervish was still a separate island, lying southward of Naphtha Island Point, but for 15 years it has formed one with the latter, probably owing to volcanic agency. In the afternoon we anchored about five miles from the Ahl on the south side of Naphtha Island. Ponomarev and I visited the Ahl, which, however, consists of only 15 Kibitks (families), who have been settlers here for long. The people support themselves by traffic in naphtha and salt, which they sell to the Turcomans of Hassan Kuli and the Silver Hill district. The naphtha springs lie on the other side of the island, which is also inhabited. The islanders say that, all told, they may aggregate 100 families. They all belong to the Sharab tribe. The island possesses only four wells, the water of which is pretty good, but slightly brackish.

In the middle of Naphtha Island there are several patches of pasture land, which support camels and sheep, but the people have no horned cattle. An insignificant wood supplies sufficient fuel for the winter, which, according to them, is very rigorous here. The landing-place by the Ahl affords good shelter to the Turcomans' small craft, as it is protected by a tongue of land running parallel to the east shore. In the roads large ships can lie in perfect security, as there are good anchorages everywhere. Some of the islanders remembered Count Voinovitsh (as far back as 1782), whom they styled "Count Khan."

3rd September.—At daybreak we weighed anchor and steered S. S. W. for the strait between the islands of Dervish and Agurchin or Aidak.

The depth of water was very varying. As we had an adverse wind night overtook us before we had made much way, so we anchored opposite Agurchin. We observed a pillar on the north side of the island, which, according to Kiat, consisted of four trees, each 18 feet high, tied together, and had been erected 10 years before to the memory of a Dervish who once dwelt here and had made the pilgrimage to Mecca. This is now the Turcoman burial-place, and the monument serves as a guide for people coming from a distance. In summer Agurchin is left uninhabited, save by flocks of sheep, which graze about without shepherds. In winter a few families occupy the island, which contains no fresh water whatever, so the people are constrained to make use of the frozen sea-water, which, on becoming ice, loses all its acrid and salt taste. The wood supply is sufficient for all requirements in the way of fuel. The Turcomans assert that, in summer time here, the wild goats (Jairani) go from two to three months without water. It is difficult to give credence to this, although one thing is certain, that there is neither a drop of salt or fresh water in the interior. Is it not, then, probable that these animals allay their thirst by means of the morning dew, which is frequently very heavy in this place? Our original intention was to have passed through the strait dividing Dervish and Agurchin, but this was frustrated by the insufficient depth of water, so we resolved to round Agurchin to the southward.

6th September.—We now steered for the Gulf of Krasnavoda, and anchored in 11 fathoms at a distance of eight and a half miles from Naphtha Island.

7th September.—When day broke the Krasnavoda Mountains were in sight. We weighed anchor, but were immediately assailed by a violent gale from the east, which drove us far out to sea.

8th September.—We ran into the sound between the Cape of Krasnavoda and Naphtha Island, and made out the Balkan range, so called from its highest peak, which starts up abruptly from the eastern side of the bay. This mountain chain extends all round the bay. The wind did not permit us at first to go along the western shore, so as to let me land at the "Oog" rock, from which point Kiat recommended I should start for Khiva, and we only arrived off it by evening. Count Voinovitsh's narrative, in general very correct, makes out that there is a sand-bank here covered in some places by only two feet of water, but this is not now the case, for we found a depth of over 3 fathoms right up to the beach. This discrepancy is probably due to the same earthquake which converted Cheleken (Naphtha Island) and Dervish into one island. The mountains on the northern shore of the Bay of Balkan present a yellowish appearance, and conspicuous among them are two rocky heights of a perfectly black colour.

10th September.—In the forenoon we entered the Bay of Krasnavoda, and anchored 1,500 yards from land in three fathoms. All along the coast there are pasture lands and springs of fresh water, just like on Krasnavoda Point, which has an abundance of excellent drinking water. This promontory afforded us protection from the violence of the sea, like a breakwater. The northern shore of the Balkan Bay is lofty, and consists partly of high rocks. On the tongue of land there are several Yurts, and a population of about 50 Turcoman families; it is nine miles in length by three across. As ships find a secure harbour in this bay, it seemed better adapted for the site of our projected fort than any of the places we had hitherto examined. The necessary wood is obtainable from Cheleken and Darji, and, indeed, the inhabitants assert that timber is to be found on the heights of the Balkan range also. On arrival we immediately sent Kiat ashore to get hold of somebody who would accompany me on my journey to Khiva; we then landed in a body, and refreshed ourselves at a well hewn out of the rock.

12th September.—At daybreak I landed, and, going with my gun into the hills, succeeded in making a fair bag of snipe. The hills which here form the coast line are very steep, and consist of masses of a friable rock, which crumbles under the feet, rendering one's ascent by no means easy. From the heights one has a glorious and extensive view of the whole country round. Our ship lay at anchor opposite a cape; the latter is intersected by two rocky ridges, not very lofty, between which runs a level valley south-eastwards to the sea and south-westwards to the Krasnavoda promontory. On the other side of this valley there is a rocky declivity, forming the boundary to the mighty steppe stretching away towards Khiva.

14th September.—The most eminent Chiefs of the Turcomans inhabiting the shores of the Bay of Balkan now assembled on board the corvette. These were Mulla Kaib, Hakim Ali Bey, Meer Said (from Hassan Kuli), Niyaz Bulad Bey, Mahomed Mizaz Margan, Tagan Niyaz, and Kyal Yarshik, the owner of the well opposite to where we anchored. They stayed on board all day, and only left us late in the evening. Ponomarev and I went ashore and gave the Chiefs an entertainment, which they repaid by showing us some wrestling, shooting, and the like. No business was done with the Chiefs on this day; only Kiat exerted himself in endeavours to bring them into the humour to accept our proposals. He named a trustworthy man, my "Jarvidar"*

---

* Sarwadar (سَروَه دار) is the Turkish for a guide.

to Khiva, but the individual himself would not agree, so Kiat sent for another man, by name Said, who arrived on the following day.

15th September.—To-day Kiat re-appeared on board the corvette with all the Chiefs, who, by way of signing the agreement, smudged their fingers with ink and smeared them on the paper.   Mulla Kaib at the same time confirmed and ratified their joint consent, whereupon the allotted presents were distributed among them.

Meanwhile I was making terms with Said, who was willing to start for Khiva on the 21st September (according to their reckoning the 12th of the month "Sulhaji").   He agreed to take me to my destination and to bring me back for 40 ducats, whereupon I advanced him half of that sum as a "handsel."

17th September.—I went on shore to purchase a horse for the Khiva trip.   They brought me, however, such a wretched animal, old and small, that I would hardly have given two ducats for it; still they had the effrontery to ask me 20.   I therefore determined to do without a horse altogether, and to make the long journey on a camel instead.

Chapter II

Journey to Khiva and stay in that Khanate

17th September.—I was now ready for the journey to Khiva, and set out on it, furnished with two letters to the Khan—one from the Governor-General, Alexis Petrovitsh Jermalof, the other from Major Ponomarev. The contents of the former were as follows :—" The Governor of Astraccan and Georgia, provinces of the world-renowned, most powerful, and most prosperous Russian nation, and of all the inhabitants of the country from the shores of the Black Sea to the borders of the Caspian, tenders friendliest greetings to His Highness the illustrious Ruler of the province of Khiva, and wishes him long life and much happiness. He has the honor to intimate that by means of the trade which brings the people of Khiva to Astraccan he has for long been acquainted with His Highness' subjects, members of a race brilliantly famous not only for valour, but also for magnanimity and a noble intellect. Much rejoicing, moreover, at the wide-spreading fame of His Highness' great worth, deep wisdom, and distinguished virtues, the undersigned yearns earnestly for a more intimate acquaintance with His Highness, and longs to establish friendly relations with that august personage, wherefore, as a consequence of this address, indited in an hour favoured by Heaven, in that it opens the gate of friendship and harmony between us, he cherishes the pleasing hope that in future, by virtue of these sentiments and their reciprocity on the part of His Highness and His Highness' subjects, the happy path shall be opened up by which the great advantages of Russian trade may be enjoyed and eternal peace and unity be founded on genuine faith and loyalty between the two nations.

" The bearer of this, who has also been charged with verbal messages by the undersigned, will have the honor personally to assure His Highness how desirous the undersigned is to make up a fair bouquet of mutual alliance from the garden of friendship with His Highness, which bouquet shall be firmly bound together by an uninterrupted peace. It will further be the bearer's duty to report, on his return, the reception that shall have been accorded him, and the sentiments entertained by His Highness, so that the undersigned may know if he is to have the pleasure, next year also, of sending an envoy with friendly tokens, and charged with the assurance of deepest regard.

" In conclusion, he prays that God may lengthen His serene Highness' days, and bless him with glory and prosperity. He has the honor to be His Highness' obedient well-wisher.

" JERMALOF,

" *General of Infantry.* "

Copy of Major Ponomarev's letter.

" LONG life to the serene, illustrious, and renowned Governor of the province of Khiva.

" Alexis Petrovitsh Jermalof, Governor of Astraccan and Georgia, dependencies of the mighty and prosperous Russian Empire, and Ruler over all the races dwelling between the Black Sea and the Caspian, being desirous of establishing commercial relations with the Turcoman inhabitants of the Caspian shores, has sent me to that people. These relations will be all the more firmly established if your Excellency entertain ideas on the subject similar to those of our Governor-General. Then the people, who are most deserving of protection from both sides, shall indeed be blest, and this end will be the easier attained if your Highness' subjects receive your permission to carry their merchandize through the Turcoman territory down to the Bay of Balkan, whither also the Russian traders will repair. By this course the caravans will reach Astraccan in a shorter time, and will enjoy immunity from the robberies and extortions of the Kirgis Kazaks, which they have now so often to submit to on their journey through the country of that tribe.

" The Russian nation having for long been acquainted with Khiva, and friendship having always existed between the two powers, it seemed expedient to the Governor-General to send Nicholas Muraviev as ambassador to your serene Highness, in order to declare the deep respect which he entertains for you, the illustrious Ruler of the Khiva Khanate. At the same time the envoy is commissioned to discuss by word of mouth sundry matters with your Highness. With much gladness I hasten to despatch the envoy, and whilst I express through him my profound respect for your Highness, I am at the same time animated by the sincere desire that during the auspicious days of your illustrious reign our mutual friendly relations may be more firmly bound together by a garland of roses which shall never fade, and may be celebrated in the thrilling song of melodious nightingales from the kingdom of consolation and heavenly joy.

" I have the honor to be,

" Your Highness' most obedient servant.

" PONOMAREV, *Major.* "

_____

18*th September.*—I passed this night in one of two Kibitks on the shore with the elder Kyal Yarshik Sufi : our chaplain, Lieutenant Linitzki, and Midshipman Juriev, accompanied me.

19*th September.*—On this day I commenced my journey, and left the sea-coast behind me. My guide Said, who lived by the spring of Suji Kabil, had sent me 4 camels by one of his relatives, named Abul Hossein, and with these and two horses in addition I struck into the steppe. I had only my servant and Petrovitsh, the interpreter, with me, but I made up for the deficiency in men by a good gun, a pair of pistols, and a large dagger, all of which I never had off my person once during the entire journey. Petrovitsh was always ready and willing, faithful to me and of good heart. His outward man was certainly not prepossessing, but he often cheered me, even in the most gloomy moments, by his comical humour. Kiat and Takan Niyaz accompanied me to Said's dwelling-place. When I reached the summit of the mountain range forming the coast line of the Bay of Balkan, the great steppe through which ran my path lay at my feet, a vast sandy flat with scanty patches of bush here and there. There are some salt water springs not far from the coast, round which the Turcomans have set up their Yurts.

Nowhere does vegetation or grass meet the eye, and nevertheless herds of camels and sheep wander all about, feeding on the dry bushes with which the steppe is thinly studded. The careless and inert Turcomans buy their necessary grain in Astrabad or Khiva, living for the rest entirely on camel's milk. Plundering is their only trade. They waylay Persian travellers at Astrabad and sell them as slaves

in Khiva, often for very high sums.   Here I rode up to see
my acquaintance Mulla Kaib, and was entertained with camel's
milk.   Further along the road I came to pasture land border-
ed by some insignificant hills, belonging probably to the
Balkan range.   Before evening I reached Said's abode.   This
village (" Oba ") is inhabited by Turcomans of the Kulta
family, who are descended from Jafir Bey, a scion of the
Sharab clan (Yomuds and one of the two principal Turcoman
tribes).   These Turcoman races are scattered over the whole
of the steppe from the Caspian Sea to well nigh the Chinese
frontier.   They are split into numerous small septs, each
having a Chief of its own selection, whose orders are obeyed,
or, rather, who commands deference by reason of his age,
his past plundering exploits, or his wealth.   The " Oba " Suji
Kabil contains about 50 dwelling-places and three springs of
good fresh water.   It is 17 miles eastwards from the sea.   I
put up with Said, who treated me most cordially.

20th September. —This whole day I had to pass in Suji
Kabil, for the Mullas declared that we must not start until
the 21st, which they considered to be an auspicious day, and
all endeavours to get my guides away were, consequently,
futile.   Afterwards I discovered that the elder of the Kalta
tribes had been anxious to persuade Said into not accompanying me.   The cause of this was his friendship for Hakim
Ali Bey, the elder of the Kirind Shik tribe, whose brother
had at first offered to accompany me for 100 ducats, instead
of which I had closed with Said for 40.   In spite of all the
means of persuasion employed, Said remained true to his word,
and, contrary to the expectation of all his friends, he received
me into his house.   This unusual behaviour, so antagonistic
to the mean principles on which the Turcomans frame their
actions, as a rule, was due to the offices of Kiat, who
availed himself of his personal influence to help me, in
the hope that he might forward his own ends with our
Government on my safe return.   He had therefore talked
over Said into accompanying me, and directly after my
arrival at Suji Kabil, he twice visited the before-mentioned
elder in his Yurt.   In considering his character, Said is
one of the best Turcomans I ever knew.   His manners
were, indeed, rough and uncouth, and he was rather dull,
but he was also firm, determined, and intrepid, a good
horseman, and renowned for his plundering raids into Persia.
His actions were often so contradictory, that one could
hardly conceive them to emanate from one and the same

person. When he was 16 years old he rode with his aged father into the field. On the third day's journey from their Yurt they suddenly came on a band of horsemen belonging to the hostile tribe of Takka.

The father was well mounted, but the son had a sorry nag. As there appeared no means of escape the old man dismounted, and, handing over his horse to the son, said— " Said, I am old, and have lived long enough ; thou art young, and canst maintain the family, save thyself, and farewell. As for me I die here." Said replied as he drew his sword—" If thou wilt not save thyself, come on ; we shall die together, and the children shall be orphans, for I am resolved to fight like a man." With these words he also sprang from his horse. Time and the nearness of the enemy forbade further dispute, so they sought safety in flight, and urged their horses until night fell and enabled them to elude their pursuers. When they reached home the father declared in presence of the whole tribe that his son far surpassed him in valour. I found the character of these Turcomans of the desert much superior to that of the dwellers by the sea, and think this is due to the former not having experience of the knavery practised by the traders who annually bring their wares to the coast. Kiat seized the opportunity now of asking me for gifts for Hakim Ali Bey and Ana Durda, two Chiefs who were travelling with me to Khiva, but entirely on their own business. Before starting I made some small presents to Said's wife and the wives of the other men whom he had hired to accompany us.

I wrote a letter to Ponomarev from Suji Kabil.

21st September.—At daybreak I left Suji Kabil, riding on a large and powerful camel, which I had great difficulty in sticking to when it rose to its feet from the kneeling posture. The caravan consisted of 17 camels, belonging to four different individuals bound for Khiva to buy grain. The principal personage among them was Said, the next his cousin, Abul Hossein, the third Kulji, and the last Ak Nafas. The whole team followed the leader in a long string,* each camel being tied to the one in front of him. After going on for

* On the leading camel sat Fatima, by birth a Kurd, and formerly Said's father's concubine. She had been 12 years his slave, and now, wishing to improve her lot, begged her master to sell her in Khiva. On his refusal to part with her, she threatened to commit suicide; so he gave in. It is incredible what this woman endured on the road. Clothed only in rags, she led the caravan day and night, hardly slept or ate, and, when we halted, attended to the camels, cooked her master's food, &c.

17 miles we halted towards noon, and united ourselves to the caravan led by Hakim Ali Bey. The further inland we proceeded, the more our caravan increased in numbers owing to our being joined every now and then by single Turcomans who lived by the side of the road, so that by the third day, when we found ourselves in the perfectly barren portion of the steppe, our numbers had swollen to something like 200 camels and 40 men. The quarrel between Hakim Ali Bey and Said did not affect me. We rode apart, and took up our night quarters in separate places. My caravan was well armed, and if, as I suspect, Hakim Ali Bey started with the intention of robbing us, he was certainly only deterred by fear of our superior weapons. He never greeted me, but would sit apart with his companions before his fire, talking contemptuously of us ; nevertheless on one occasion I managed to alienate some of his people through the medium of tea, for which all Turcomans have a passion. Perhaps an additional motive for Hakim Ali Bey's avoiding me lay in his dread of an unfavourable reception from the Khan of Khiva on my account. Whatever the cause may have been, I never was off my guard, and never laid aside my arms once during the 16 days and nights we were in the steppe.

In the afternoon we reached a small eminence called Kasil Aiyag, which is probably an offshoot from the Balkan chain. We pursued our way 17 miles further, then halted for the night, having to our left rear the Yurts clustered round the Siulman well. During the whole journey I suffered less from the unpleasant jolting and the unaccustomed ride on camel-back than from the terrible *ennui*, for I found myself alone without a soul to talk to. The heat was great, but not intolerable. The steppe presented a most dreary aspect, a very picture of death, or depopulation caused by some mighty convulsion of nature. Not an object betrayed signs of life ; no grass nor verdure refreshed the eye : only here and there a stunted patch of bush struggled for existence in the sand. Then to add to my depression came thoughts of the distance between me and my home, and of the risk I ran of falling into captivity and perpetual slavery. Dreadful pictures which haunted me throughout the whole journey ! I was dressed like a Turcoman, and went by the Turkish name of Murad Beg, which saved me from much inquisitive questioning, for, although all the caravan people knew who I really was, I was always taken for a Turcoman of the Jafir Bey tribe by the strangers we met *en route*. Our course lay due

Portrait of Hakim Ali Bey

east. To-day's eclipse of the moon lasted over an hour, and discomposed the Turcomans not a little.

They asked me the cause of the eclipse, declared that the moon was only darkened in this manner at the death of one of their Chiefs or elders, and suggested that the omen augured ill for our reception at Khiva. I now perceived that I must enlighten them as to their mistaken notions, and the case of the wise man of old occurred to my memory, who on a similar occasion replied by throwing his cloak over the head of the enquirer. I did this to Said, and asked him if he saw the fire beaming before him; on his saying no, I sought to explain the movements of the heavenly bodies and how one comes at times to obscure the other. The Turcomans did not understand me at first, as they thought I included all the stars, but at last it came home to their comprehension, and they said— "Yes; you are truly an Ambassador, a chosen man, for you are not only acquainted with the affairs of earth, but also know what is going on in the heavens." Their astonishment increased when I indicated to them which edge of the moon would first emerge from the shadow.

22nd September.—We started at 1 A.M.; night cold, dew heavy. After going 20 miles we arrived at dawn at the Siuli well, where there are 20 Yurts. This well is 15 fathoms deep; water nauseous, but drinkable. There is a large burial-ground here. The grave-stones appear to me to be made of limestone : they are fairly large, well cut, and ornamented to a certain extent. I am inclined to attribute their origin to the Turcomans. The inhabitants say that this cemetery is very old, and that the same kind of stone is to be found on the sea-coast. I wrote a second time to Ponomarev from this place, and entrusted the letter to Ashar Mahomed, a man who had accompanied me thus far. We continued our march for 11 miles further, always going due east, and then halted. To our right appeared the Balkan range, on whose slopes there is said to be good pasturage and water supply. We certainly saw many horses grazing there.

23rd September.—At midnight we resumed our course, and, after getting over 17 miles, arrived at the well of Damur-jam a little after sunrise. The well lies a little off the road to the right, and about 40 families graze their herds here. On the road opposite this pasturage there is another well, called Yassak Jam, which caravans, however, do not stop at, as its water is brackish. The well of Damurjam is situated in a depression of the ground, quite level and surrounded by banks.

which looks as if this were the dried-up bed of a lake formerly existing here. As I had hardly closed my eyes for two whole days and nights I dismounted from my camel, and, while the beasts were being fed, sank into a profound sleep. On awaking I found myself surrounded by women and children, all taking careful stock of me. In order to divert my mind a little I tried to read, and this certainly did me good, and cheered me up in this desolate waste, where only the rising and setting sun and the moon claimed my attention, and served as signals to the caravan for rest or toil. There was no growth of any kind on the extinct lake bed. At the distance of five and $\frac{3}{4}$ miles from Damurjam we called a halt, but no grass was to be found here. This deprivation did not entail any suffering on our camels, and as we were told that we should not meet with water for several days, we had filled our leather bags at the Damurjam well. Here our caravan received a fresh increase. After two hours' rest we went on 23 miles further in the direction E. N. E. $\frac{1}{4}$ E. From Damurjam I wrote to Ponomarev, enjoining him to keep a sharp eye on the family of Hakim Ali Bey, who excited my suspicion. Our road lay continuously over the bed of a dried-up lake. Eight miles from Damurjam, to the right, we saw the Yurts by the well of Haroidan, the water of which is exceptionally good. It is curious that the water all over this steppe should not be of the same quality, but so it is, and close to salt water a perfectly fresh spring will often be struck. Several of the wells about here are 40 fathoms deep, and have their sides strengthened with beams, but the people cannot say who sank them. Before midnight we took the road again, and, having covered 23 miles in the direction E. by N., halted before sunrise. After going about five miles we saw a great lake, called by the Turcomans " Kuli Dariya," or Aji Kuyusi. It extends 57 miles from north to south, and is connected with the Gulf of Karabogass.

It appears that this great water is as little known to geographers as the Gulf of Karabogass, which has not yet been explored by any navigator from the evil reputation it bears for whirlpools. The Turcomans take their craft, indeed, with perfect safety all along the shores of this gulf for the seal fishery, but they have never yet dared to enter the mouth of the Kuli Dariya, and mention its name with mysterious awe. They say—" Why should we venture up it? The animals all fear to drink from it, for its waters are bitter and deadly ; why, not even a fish lives in it." According to them the Kuli Dariya absorbs the waters of the Caspian, for the current from the latter into the Karabogass Gulf is extraordinarily strong. The Kuli Dariya decreases in a very marked manner, and traces of its former limits are visible far in the interior of the steppe. Its northern shore is rocky. A belief obtains among the people that all birds flying across this lake are struck blind. Not far from the spot where we halted a road runs on the left hand along the side of the Kuli Dariya to Mangushlak, and where the two roads meet, we saw a great burial-place, with stones similar to those at Siuli. According to the inhabitants these are the tombs of some Yomuds who were slain here in one of the Kirgis Kazaks' raids.

24th September.—At sunrise we started, and halted after a stretch of 23 miles on nearly the highest point of the Sare Baba range, running from north to south. We had to cross a number of deep fissures and chasms, formed probably by the torrents which fall into the Kuli Dariya. This neighbourhood is called Bahljaringri. The road was of limestone, and in the most execrable state. For the first 11 miles it was a steady and gentle ascent, but the Sare Baba range was visible from much further off. We suffered much at this night's halting-place, for a high wind drove the sand over us; the cold was very considerable, and we had difficulty in finding enough sticks to make a small fire with. Before midnight we were on the move again, and soon got down from the heights. The road is, indeed, very steep, but so regular as to resemble the handiwork of man instead of a natural track. On the highest point of this range there is a mound called " Kur," where a strong wind always blows. Here stands a monument in honor of one of the Turcoman patriarchs by name Ar Sare Baba. His numerous descendants, a tribe formerly established on the shores of the Bay of Balkan, have now settled in Bokhara. Ar Sare Baba is said to have lived long ago, and to have been distinguished for his many virtues and great learning. As he wished to be buried on the summit near the high road, so that passers-by might pray for him, he gave this mountain his own name. His monument consists of a pole, to which are attached some coloured rags, and round it is a cairn of stones, stags' antlers, and potsherds. The latter offering is contributed by all passing Turcomans, even those who belong to other tribes. No one dares to desecrate this grave. Quite close to the latter there is an old burial-ground. We had scarcely got down from this height when it seemed as if we had arrived in quite a different climate. The air was soft and mild, and the road ran through deep sand, which, however, was not quite destitute of vegetation.

25th September.—At length, on the 25th, at 3 A.M., after a 20 miles' ride, we arrived at the well of Tuar. Our course had been east by north. Not far from the well, to the right of the road, we saw some Yurts of the Atta tribe, which formerly stood actually by the well. As this tribe is a small one, and is often harassed by its neighbours, it seeks protection from the Khan of Khiva. Its members seldom venture on plundering expeditions, as they are so widely scattered, but for all that, they are not the less predatory in their tendencies or actions when a favourable opportunity arises. They differ from the other Turcomans very widely in costume, and more particularly in feature; indeed, their customs and mode of living generally have little in common with the other tribes. They cannot number more than 1,000 Kibitks. In my opinion, this tribe must be an offshoot from those races which populate the country known to us as Tartary. At Tuar there are six wells of good water, but the neighbourhood is barren, and, except just by the foot of the mountain, we had not seen a blade of grass, or a shrivelled bush, the whole way. Not far from here there is a neat stone monument in honor of Jaffir Bey, one of the former Yomud Chieftains, whose clan is the most warlike and numerous of all; it boasts nearly 2,000 families, and maintains a certain pre-eminence among the other sections of the great tribes. My guide Said belonged to this section, and seemed, like the other members of it, proud of his descent. There are two roads from Tuar to Khiva; the natural one goes straight on, but it has two drawbacks, *viz.*, it is not well off for water, and it runs nearer than could be desired to the Yurts of the Takka tribe, who are a most violent and unscrupulous set, always at war with their neighbours. Raids from the one side or the other are almost incessant, and the Yomud caravans are frequently plundered by the Takkas, although the latter are also Turcomans. The scarcity of water is in winter made up for by snow. In the summer time caravans of horses only take this route. The other road goes off to the left, and bends round to the north-east. It is a longer route by two days than the first mentioned one, but has a better water supply, and is less dangerous. Notwithstanding the latter consideration, Said loaded his firearms at Tuar, and advised me to do the same to mine.

We rode nearly 34 miles north by east. The steppe is here a little undulating. Hakim Ali Bey continued to treat me most discourteously, and although we were all in imminent danger of being attacked by robbers, he would never wait for me, so that we might be all together. I did not, however, solicit him on this point, as I knew I had little support to look for from him in the hour of need; in fact, I remained further and further apart from him. At night, however, I took all necessary precautionary measures. Once some of the people of his caravan came to me and urged me for safety's sake to join them. I replied—"If you are afraid, you had better join me." They said nothing more, and went away. Nevertheless one of his associates attached himself to my caravan with a servant and 16 camels, perhaps attracted by my tea, but more probably (as he remained with me the whole day) in the hope of receiving a considerable reward from me, which, however, I did not bestow. I succeeded in seducing him as well as his comrades from Hakim Ali Bey, but my only motive was thereby to secure good informants when we should reach Khiva, who would keep me *au fait* with regard to Hakim Ali Bey's intentions, and his reports about me to the Khan, in case he should endeavour to revenge himself on Said through that agency. As he had noticed that I kept a diary and entered my remarks on the road, he was the first to inform the Khan of this circumstance. Before midnight we again started. The country was a little hilly. After a 17 miles' march we arrived before daybreak of the 26th at the well "Dirin."

26th September.—This well is situated in a low valley, and is faced with stone, but still the water is foul and brackish. We had, however, to fill our water bags with it, such as it was, for the steppe in front of us was entirely destitute of any water whatsoever. Dirin may be considered as the limit of the country, occupied by the sea-coast Turcomans, for at a distance of 2,000 paces from this well, on the left hand, is the last grazing ground of the Baga Yomuds, consisting of 50 Yurts. From this place to the Besh Dishik well, which formerly marked the Khiva frontier, the road runs uninterruptedly for five or six days' journey through a barren desert. This is the most trying portion of the whole journey from Balkan to Khiva. The Dirin valley has steep banks, and is the bed of a river that in former times flowed from north to south, probably that branch of the Amu Dariya called the Oxus by the ancients. Water and vegetation are wanted to enliven this fine tract of country. Nature is dead, and seems unwilling ever to permit verdure to appear in this home of brute-like men. Hakim Ali Bey now rejoined me with his caravan, and greeted me again for the first time. He said— " I do not carry my faith on the tongue, like your companions, but in the heart;" whereupon I turned my back on him and vouchsafed no reply. Many Turcomans now began to offer their services to intimate my approach to the Khan of Khiva, but knowing their untrustworthiness I rejected them all. At 10 A.M. we again set out, and halted after going 17 miles over a flat steppe. Starting the same night, we had gone 29 miles by sunrise the following day : our course lay at first to the N. E., then due E., then E. by N. On the way we came upon a small caravan travelling from Khiva. I availed myself of the opportunity to send Ponomarev a letter by Mahomed Niyaz, giving him news of my well-being and begging him to secure Hakim Ali Bey's son in case of anything untoward happening to me.

27th September.—Marching at 8 A.M. to-day, we did 25 miles. After three hours we passed the well Kasagli on our right, the water of which is salt and undrinkable.

28th September.—From the 27th to the evening of the 28th we left 51 miles behind us, but nothing on the road attracted my attention. I was only oppressed by the most deadly *ennui*. After two hours' rest we went on 23 miles further, in the direction E. by N., and halted at daybreak.

29th September.—On the 29th we had pretty cold weather. After doing another 28 miles we encamped by the well " Besh Dishik," or five openings. Our course had been E. by N. Here the water was excellent. It was a comforting reflection to me that two-thirds of the journey were now over, and that I was actually in the Khan's territory. Still more I rejoiced when it turned out there was to be a halt to-day. I had now been 10 days on the tramp, had suffered much from the bumping on the camel, had often been obliged to go on foot, and had hardly had any sleep during all this time. To the Turcomans this kind of travelling is less fatiguing, for they are able to stretch themselves at length on their camels and sleep—a feat which I could not accomplish. Here, too, for the first time I tasted some cooked food, having had nothing since we started, save black biscuit and brackish water. Our road had been through loose sand, and we had in front of us at first a wall of lofty and precipitous rocks seamed with great fissures. My companions said that this wall had formerly been sea-coast. We had only a distance of eight and a half miles between us and the well, when we were brought up by a great dry river bed, say 400 yards across and 60 yards deep. The banks were very steep, and these as well as the bed itself were covered with bushes. The course of the river bed was from N. E. to S. W. Our route would naturally have been straight across, but the precipitous nature of the banks forbade of this. We had therefore to turn to the left and go along the top of the bank, picking our way through sand hummocks 12 feet high. When we had got abreast of the Sare Kamush well, which is sunk in the river bed, we met a caravan, and I took the opportunity of again letting Ponomarev hear from me.

We had to go five and a half miles along the bank before we could descend it and make good our way to the well "Besh Dishik" for night quarters. The rocky wall, or so-called ancient 'coast' before mentioned, runs parallel with this extinct river at a distance from it of 3,000 paces. The features of this ravine, winding in all the usual curves and bends of a river through a level steppe, led me to conclude that this must be the old course of the Amu Dariya, which Peter the Great had been at such pains to have explored. My companions confirmed this, saying that, though the ravine was now called Uss Bey, a river called "Amu Dariya" used formerly to run through it down to the Bay of Balkan. This river, they said, had long since altered its course, and now ran northwards out of the Khanate of Khiva on the "Demar Kazak" side. On my return from Khiva, Kiat informed me that the mouth of this old river bed, although choked with sand, is still distinguishable on the Caspian, and that by it there stands a hut (isba) constructed on the Russian plan. No one knows who the builder of this was, but the neighbouring Turcomans are restrained from demolishing it by superstitious dread. Its existence probably dates back to the time of Prince Bekovitsh, whom Peter the Great sent hither to search for gold dust. It is quite possible that the hut may have stood for so long a time without tumbling to pieces, as very little rain falls here, and the ignorance of the present people of the Balkan as to its origin is probably to be accounted for by the former nomadic inhabitants having belonged to a different tribe. The nature of the dry bed of Amu Dariya, where it is not covered by sand drift, differs widely from that of the steppe, for it is clothed with grass and trees, and contains wells of good

spring water. The overflow of the Sare Kamush well, before referred to, runs on, forming a tiny rivulet in place of the quondam river. Beside this well stands another, the water of which is brackish, where, as in our night station, I counted six wells of good drinking water. From this place onwards the route runs pretty uninterruptedly through vegetation, from the dearth of which we had suffered some six or seven times. I was much astonished here to find myself cordially met my Hakim Ali Bey and his brother, Tagan Ali, and to see them attending to my camels. The former, moreover, actually asked my forgiveness for having kept away from me hitherto, assured me that he would make up for past faults and do his best to serve me, and protested that I might rely on him more surely than on my most trusty servant. I accepted his advances in a friendly manner and entertained him with tea, but trusted him less than ever, and took extraordinary measures of precaution on this night. I account for this sudden change as follows :—
He found he was not in a position to carry out his evil designs, whatever they were, and reflecting that I had now nearly accomplished the journey to Khiva in safety, he determined that it would be better to make up matters, so as to benefit himself through my agency with the Khan, supposing that personage to receive me favourably. Besides this, he heard from the caravans we met that the speedy arrival of a Russian Envoy was talked of in Khiva, and that the Ruler himself was in a great state of impatience for me, and the four camel-loads of gold being sent him by the Ak Padshah (White King), by which he meant the Czar. The rumour of my intended visit had been spread by the Turcomans who had gone to Khiva from the Atrek and Giurgen Rivers, and who had drawn their conclusion from the enquiries about the Khiva route which I had been making in their district.

For the matter of that, I had never made any secret of my project. From Besh Dishik we had several marches without water before us.

30th September.—At daybreak we broke up camp, marched 17 miles, and halted after sunset. There was much to attract attention and court speculation on this portion of the road. We were now on the further side of the former Amu Dariya, at no great distance from the river bed, whilst on our left hand a precipitous wall of rock (the supposed ancient coast alluded to before) stretched away into the far distance, presenting throughout a most strange appearance. The elevated plateau beyond this line of cliffs was perfectly analogous to the lower steppe which we were travelling over. For about an hour our road ran parallel to the precipice, and we diverted ourselves with the echo from it, which repeated each word distinctly several times over. In the rock, opposite the point where the road turns off to the right, there are five apertures, hewn out with great regularity, looking like the entrances to a house. My fellow-travellers told me that these five openings were called " Besh Dishik," and that the well by which we had encamped on the previous night derived its name from them. The nomadic Turcomans of the surrounding country are all assured that these apertures are the approaches to vast caverns in which from time immemorial there has dwelt a King with a numerous family, countless treasure, and beauteous daughters, but that once when some inquisitive persons tried to intrude into the caverns, they were immediately seized by an unseen hand and strangled.

When they told me of this I did not like to ask how they could possibly know the fate of the unlucky trespassers, seeing that none of them had ever come back to tell the tale, as the narrative had elicited already many different opinions ; when one individual said he did not believe the story at all, another asked him quite seriously—" Whence, then, came that voice that repeated all we said as we rode by the steep rock ?" After such an unanswerable argument the doubter did not venture further to gainsay the truth of the story, but lapsed into silence. Meanwhile I became very desirous of exploring the caverns in question, which may, perhaps, have once been the retreat of a band of robbers, so commenced the climb upwards with one of my Turcomans. The caves are more than half way up the rock. A projection juts out from beneath the entrances, and forms a sort of gallery about 400 yards long. The loose soil gave way under my feet and much impeded my ascent, and as I mounted up stones began to fall from overhead. At last I came to a huge rock, threatening to detach itself at any moment, and under this I had to crawl in order to get to the projection whence it seemed easy to gain access to the caves. My Turcoman preceded me and got safely through, but when he reached the gallery he found the bit he stood on isolated from the rest by a gap two fathoms across.

As the caravan had now got far ahead I abandoned my plan, and had to make all haste to overtake the rest. I don't know what to make of this line of rock. It does not seem improbable that it may have been the boundary either of the sea or of some vast lake. At some distance from Besh Dishik, on this side of the Amu Dariya, there were a number of canals, destitute of water, but bearing distinct traces of its having been there once.

Our course lay E. by N.

1st October.—On the night of the 30th we again started, and by the morning of the 1st October had gone 29 miles to the S. E. On our way we saw a corresponding shore of the supposed sea. Here also we saw the ruins of the fort "Utin Kila." These canals and ruins furnish incontrovertible evidence to this having once been a populous district, and to the now dried-up Uss Bai having once contained the waters of that great commercial thoroughfare, the Amu Dariya. To-day we marched another 28 miles, passing by many a dry canal and patch of copse.

2nd October.—From the night of the 1st to the morning of the 2nd October we did 25 miles, and halted at sunrise. There are some poisonous plants about here, which my fellow-travellers were very cautious to keep their camels away from. Before daybreak we came on a great Turcoman caravan of the Igdur section of the Chobdur tribe. It consisted of 1,000 camels and 200 men, who went along with a great uproar, singing, laughing, and shouting for joy at leaving Khiva and having purchased their grain at a cheap rate. They were bound for Mangushlak. Hakim Ali Bey had gone on ahead with his caravan, and I had only six Turcomans with me, so, as we met the Igdurs in a narrow part of the road, with jungle on either side, we had to wait until the whole train had passed us before we could proceed. The Igdurs asked my Turcomans what tribe they belonged to, and, crowding round us, discovered by Petrovitsh's cap that he was no Turcoman. They regarded me and my servant with great curiosity and asked what manner of people we were. "These are Russian captives," replied my men; "they came to our coasts with their ships, and we caught three of them, whom we are now going to sell." "Well done," cried the Igdurs with wild, mocking laughter; "off with them, the accursed infidels. We sold three Russians in Khiva this very trip, and got a good sum for them." Starting again we accomplished nearly 29 miles in a S. E. direction, and met a number of other caravans coming back laden with corn from Khiva. We learnt from them that the Khan had laid a fresh impost of ½ Tilla on every Turcoman camel entering the city. As, however, the Turcomans were very averse to paying this tax, and as they had petitioned for its abolition, the Khan had directed all the camels which had then arrived to be detained, but had promised at the same time to meet the Turcoman leaders at the fortress of Ak Serai in order to listen to their requests and to receive their offerings in person. In spite of this, many caravans had fled, and as it was pretty certain that the Khan must have left Khiva by then we were informed that we should most likely find him at the Ak Serai. This news was most agreeable to me, and gave me the hope of being soon able to accomplish my mission. I therefore composed my address to the Khan, and gave it to Petrovitsh to translate, ordering him at the same time to learn it by heart. But alas! how I deceived myself, how much too sanguine I was! From our yesterday's halting-place roads branched off in every direction to the various pasture lands and villages in the Khiva Khanate. Hakim Ali Bey's large caravan dispersed entirely in quest of grain, but we all remained together : many fires blazed near us, kindled by that class of people who travel into the steppe in their Arabas (carts) to fetch wood or burn charcoal, and who have an evil reputation as robbers. They did not, however, molest us. The sight of the cart ruts rejoiced and comforted me with the thought of being once more in an inhabited country and among my kind. Little did I foresee how soon misery was to overtake me and what my fate was to be.

3rd October.—Starting on the night of the 2nd, we marched 23 miles E. S. E., often through jungle, indeed, not without occasionally missing the road. Towards morning we halted, and afterwards advanced an additional eight and a half miles E. S. E., when we reached a canal to our no small joy, seeing that we had been four days without water. This canal is fed by the modern Amu Dariya, which rises in the mountain range to the north of Hindustan, flows through Bokhara, passes to the east of the city of Khiva, and falls into the Sea of Aral. In the Khanate of Khiva, which has a diameter of over 115 miles, there are numerous canals. By the first canal there is a settlement of Turcomans from different tribes. These people, although living near towns and practising husbandry, are really robbers by trade. No sooner is their harvest over than off they go a plundering to Persia, and dispose of their captives in the Khiva slave market. The villages in Khiva are all situated on canals, between which are intervals of salt steppe. The land is tilled partly by the people themselves, and partly by their slaves. One can hardly conceive the wonderful fertility of the soil here. Wheat, rice, sesame flourish, and also jogan, a small round grain the size of a little pea and white in colour, growing in thick ears like Indian corn. It is used as forage for the horses, but also as human food. All kinds of fruit thrive in this country, notably melons and water-melons. The melons are often a foot and a half long, and wonderfully sweet. Cattle-breeding is carried on to a great extent. Their domestic cattle comprise camels, cows, and sheep (some of the latter attaining to an extraordinary size). The breed of horses is excellent, but they prize those brought by the Turcomans from the Giurgen and Atrek above their own indigenous animals.

The Turcomans and Khivans who live by raids into Persia spare their horses very little. They generally ride eight days on end, doing 80 miles a day, and watering their beasts for the first time on the fourth day's journey through the parched desert. The "jogan" before mentioned is the sole article of forage, and of this each horseman carries with him enough for the whole trip. We started soon again, and marched steadily on without a halt. In the distance there appeared to be a thick fog enveloping the whole horizon. This turned out, however, to be a mass of dust, borne upwards by the wind just in the very direction we had to go : eyes, nose, mouth, and hair got the full benefit of this. The clouds of dust were so dense that nothing could be distinguished at any distance. We halted two hours before nightfall, whereupon Said went off to the Yurts on one side of the road to look for a night's lodgings for us. The people were Yomud Turcomans of the Kujuk Tatar branch and Quiruk family, under their elder Attan Niyaz Margan. Of all the Turcomans I have ever come across this person pleased me most. He had settled in Khiva and taken service with the Khan ; was regarded, however, more in the light of a partizan by the latter. Once a week he rode over to pay his respects to the Khan, and had, indeed, just returned from Khiva when I arrived. His Yurt stood on the Dash Haos canal. He received me with the hospitality that became an honor-loving and generous man, but which one seldom meets with among the Turcomans. He put himself to the greatest trouble to make me comfortable, slaughtered his best sheep, set water before me to wash with, cooked the dinner, and finally drove away the inquisitive idlers who had assembled in numbers to stare at me. He told me that my early arrival was spoken of in Khiva, wherefore counselled me not to have myself particularly announced in the city, but to ride straight through to the Shah's Court, according to the established custom, and announce myself as guest and envoy, which would ensure my being well received.

I doubted whether such a sudden and unexpected arrival on my part would please the Khan, but thanked my host for his well-meant advice, given sincerely from the benevolence of his heart, determining at the same time to pursue a different course. He now presented his four sons to me, each one handsomer than his brother. They swaggered bravely with their long pistols and fine stallions, gifts from the Khan. His second son was absent, having been despatched by his father with 30 men on a marauding expedition to Astrabad.

4th October.—Refreshed and recruited, we started in the forenoon, my brave host accompanying me for 11 miles. There was no high road or beaten track now. We rode through the steppe (covered with sand hills) lying between the Canals Dash Haos and Ak Serai. The gale still continued, and covered us with sand, overpowering us so that even our host lost the way. Here for the first time I remarked how the wind throws up a sand hill here and levels another there, and how the sand, beginning to collect round some insignificant little bush, grows up and up and becomes a hill in no time. When the wind fell I descried ruins, on both sides, of fortresses and houses, and the whole strip traversed by us was strewn with broken brick and earthenware. At length, towards evening, after a ride of 20 miles in a S. E. direction, we sighted the Ak Serai canal. The land about was well tilled, and had some trees, and a number of Yurts studded the canal bank. Our intention was to have followed the canal the same day up to a village where a cousin of Said's lived, but it turned out to be impossible, so we had to spend the night in a miserable little Turcoman hamlet.

From this point we began to see occasional buildings. The Turcomans dwell in Yurts, but keep their cattle in regular stables or sheds, which they surround either with wooden palings or mud walls for security. The inhabitants of this part come from the Bokhara border, and are unacquainted with the Turcoman tribes of the Caspian. They all got round me, and so plagued me with questions that I despaired of getting free from them. At length I threatened them with the name of Khan Mahomed Ragim, as whose guest I announced myself, but that only made matters worse; they said they neither knew nor cared about the said Khan Mahomed Ragim, and clean refused to admit me for the night now at all. Losing all patience, I shouted abuse at them, on which they immediately retired, and appeared to be consulting together at a little distance. As I was already making preparations to pass the night among their Yurts, one of them presently stepped forward from their midst and offered me his Yurt, saying that it was all ready for me, as he had had it cleared. I accepted his invitation, and entered a most miserable hovel, from which I was immediately obliged to eject a number of curious intruders who had the impertinence to squat down beside me and pelt me with their questions. My old host seemed to be of Mongolian descent from his Chinese features. He did not know who the people were who had intruded, but was very grateful to me for not turning out himself and his daughter with the rest. I gladdened his heart with some tea. On account of the great number of people about us I ordered my Turcomans to keep watch throughout the night.

5th October.—We marched at daybreak, and, after skirting the canal for three hours in the direction E. S. E., arrived at two high trees, visible from a great distance, near which Said's cousin lived. The further we went on, the more cultivation disclosed itself. The fields, covered with the richest crops, presented a very different aspect to the sandy wastes of yesterday. In the whole of Germany I have never seen such well-cultivated land as here in Khiva. Every Yurt is here surrounded by an artificial water-course unbridged. Our course lay through lonely meadows covered with fruit trees, in which the birds sang sweetly. The Yurts and mud cottages scattered over this glorious landscape have a most cheerful appearance. So charmed was I with all I saw, that I reproachfully asked my companions why they too did not bring their country under similar cultivation, or, if their soil would not admit of this, why they did not emigrate to Khiva. They replied—"Ambassador, we are gentlemen : these people are but our servants. They fear their Khan ; we fear God alone." In the country about the canals in the State of Khiva the villagers are for the most part Turcomans. These districts are very populous. The inhabitants dress well, and are a much quicker people than their brethren of the Caspian. On the road to Said's cousin's abode we met a bridal party. The bride, much bedecked with all sorts of finery, sat on a tall camel in a saddle covered with richly-embroidered silk. I was most kindly received at the village, and a small chamber was placed at my disposal; unfortunately it was very dirty and dark. When I had changed my clothes a number of Chiefs came to congratulate me on my arrival. I admitted the most notable into the room, said a few words to them, and then went out to the rest, each of whom greeted me after his own fashion.

The Khan, it appeared, had not yet left Khiva, so I immediately despatched two Turcomans, one to Khiva to give notice of my arrival, and the other to the nearest fortress, Ak Serai, to let the Khan's Agent there (an Usbeg) know about me. Here my heart rather misgave me when I overheard the conversation of my Turcomans. They were, indeed, speaking in my praise, but said that I must be a most eminent personage because I could write, and had always noted at every well how deep it was and how far distant from the next. All this reached the ear of the Khan eventually, and was afterwards the cause of my recommendation for death as a spy. Vardi Khan, a Turcoman elder, visited me to-day from Khiva. He had served with the Persians in the war of 1812, been wounded and taken prisoner by the Russians. He had then taken service with the Russian General Lissanovitsh, had left him to go back to his home, and from thence had at last fled to Khiva. He gave me some intelligence about the Khan, which made me desirous of at once starting and accomplishing the remaining 34 miles between us and Khiva, but Said utterly refused to agree to this. I stormed and swore, until he at length sent for horses, most probably giving the messenger secret instructions not to bring them. Perhaps he wanted to detain me in order to screw a present out of me for his cousin, or he may have wished to serve the leaders of the caravans which had just arrived, and who hoped to get off the new camel toll through my mediation with the Khan. At any rate, the leaders themselves had already expressed this hope to me, only I had pretended not to understand them. No horses being forthcoming, I had to spend the whole day at this place. Wherever I went I was surrounded by people. A well-dressed Turcoman, belonging to the Khan's army, interested me for a time, his conversation being very sensible. At last he looked at the buttons on my great coat, and asked with great *naïveté* if they were made of silver. He kept turning the buttons round and round, until I could stand it no longer; so I asked him in a mocking tone if in Khiva the silver had the same appearance as in Russia. The by-standers raised a loud shout of laughter, but the young man immediately left me, and said, as he struck his hand on the hilt of his sword—"Mr. Envoy, we Turcomans are a simple people, but this is overlooked and respect accorded to us for our bravery and our sharp blades, which are always ready for the service of our Khan." I pacified him by hoping that his sword would also be at the service of my Czar should my mission succeed in uniting the two Sovereigns in the bonds of peace and amity. I went to bed late, and was just dropping off to sleep, when I was suddenly roused by the information that an officer from Khan Mahomed Ragim had arrived. A handsome young man entered the room, accompanied by another much older person. They sat down on my bed, and the young man immediately began to interrogate me, in the name of the Khan, as to the cause of my visit and the intentions of my Government. I replied that I could offer no explanations except to the Khan himself, or some person specially appointed by him to confer with me, and added that I had two letters to deliver, with the contents of which I was unacquainted. I showed Abdulla (the young man) the sealed letters, and begged him to intimate this to the Khan. He rejoined that it was strange that the Russian Czar should send embassies to Khiva from two quarters at the same time, seeing that there were already four Envoys in Khiva, and he then asked me if I was in the Russian Army.

I tried to convince him that the people he referred to could not really be Envoys, but only refugees passing themselves off as such, and told him that they ought to be seized, and if they really were impostors, I promised to have them sent to Russia in chains. Abdulla nevertheless stuck to his assertion that they were *bonâ fide* Russian Envoys, and afterwards they turned out to be four Noga Cossacks, who had brought over a letter to the Khan.

"Do you drink tea?" asked Abdulla. "If so, let me make it." I said—"We people drink tea by day, and not at midnight; besides, I am ill and weary after my journey; so do me a favour, and let me rest. Farewell." They left me, and in the sequel I found that this Abdulla was the son of an eminent official in Khiva, who had formerly been in the Khan's service. The Khan had never sent him to me, and his questions had been prompted by sheer curiosity. To-day I learned that two Russians, on hearing of the arrival of a corvette on the

Turcoman coast, had fled in that direction, leaving wife and children behind, the day before I arrived at Ak Serai, but had been caught. The people of Khiva have many Russian slaves, whom they purchase from the Kirgis, who kidnap them on the Orenburg frontier. They have also numerous Persian and Kurd slaves, whom the Turcomans supply them with. A slave has, indeed, a bitter lot in Khiva. On the slightest suspicion of intended desertion he is punished with the most cold-blooded cruelty, and should it be the second offence, the poor wretch is nailed by an ear to the door, and left to endure every privation for three days. If he survive this punishment his fate is not amended, for he is a slave as before.

6th October.—This morning the hired horses arrived, but I was delayed in starting for two hours by an invitation to breakfast from an elder. I mention this circumstance, because but for it things might have gone very differently with me, that is, I should have arrived in Khiva the same day, and the Khan, surprised by my sudden appearance, would perhaps have received me well and dismissed me early. Perhaps, also, had the rumour reached him that Russians were on their way to Khiva to avenge the death of Bekovitsh, the people, by his orders, might have torn me to pieces before I ever reached the city. Such a report would spread very easily and rapidly in Khiva, and the Khan, who has never been out of his own territory and its surrounding steppes, would readily have given credence to it. I had not gone above six miles when a horseman met me at full gallop, and requested me, in the name of the Khan, to halt until the arrival of two officers sent to meet me the night before by the Khan.

I halted, and the deputies soon appeared, escorted by four horsemen. The elder of the two was a small man, about 60 years of age, with a white beard and the face of a monkey. He occasionally stammered, and then jabbered at a tremendous pace to make up for it, betraying at every word a vile character and an insatiable avarice for money. This was "Att Chapar Alla Vardi." The prefix "Att Chapar" signifies in Turkish "galloping horse," and had been bestowed on him because the Khan always employed him to proclaim his orders throughout the country. The other was a tall man, stoutish, with a slight beard, whose noble and modest bearing and superior manners quite accorded with the first words he spoke. His name was Ash Nazar, his age over 30, and he filled the post of a "Yuz Bashi," *i.e.*, Centurion, or Captain of a hundred. There is no such rank literally in Khiva, but the title is bestowed by the Khan in war time on the officers commanding divisions of his forces. Att Chapar, I subsequently heard, was a native of Astrabad, who had been brought to Khiva in his youth as a slave, where he recanted his faith, embraced the Siul doctrine, and married. His son, Khwaja Margam, rendered such important services in a battle, that he became a Court favourite, and was entrusted with the chief control of taxes and customs. Then, enjoying as he did the full confidence of the Khan, it was no difficult matter for him to advance his father and brothers to high positions. The Khan had bestowed much land and many canals on Att Chapar, and he had added greatly to his estate by his own purchase, so that he was now regarded as the third personage of the State in wealth and position. As he had a commercial connection with Astraccan he begged the Khan to be allowed to entertain me as his guest until my business should be settled, hoping probably to receive a handsome acknowledgment from me in the event of a favourable issue, or to put the Khan under an obligation by killing me, should my death be thought advisable. He now informed me that it was the Khan's order that I should accompany him to his stronghold of "Yal Kaldi," where all was in readiness for my reception. We rode 14 miles N. by E. through a splendid and populous tract, during the whole distance seeing only one piece of steppe, lying between two canals : the weather was clear and agreeable, and from a long way off the fort rose to view, with a small garden to one side of it. It is in the form of a square, with a tower at each angle. The walls, built of stone set in mud, are 21 feet high by 150 long (per face). There is only one entrance, and that by a large gate, secured with a powerful padlock. Khwaja Margam is really the owner of this stronghold. Nearly all the great landholders possess similar ones. They are not loopholed, and the interiors contain a small reservoir for water, several courts and apartments, store-houses, mills, and cow-houses. They probably owe their origin to the disturbances which invariably occur on the death of a Khan, the empty throne appearing to be the signal for a civil war. But in times of peace they are also useful in affording safe retreats during an invasion of Turcoman marauders, for such a fort provided with all necessaries can hold its own for some days against a not too numerous band of those robbers. I found from 50 to

Portrait of Att Chapar Alla Vardi

60 souls in Yal Kaldi, some living in the chambers of the building, others, with their wives and children, occupying Yurts which they had erected in the Courts. Just opposite the gateway stands a tower, and close to it a small postern leads from the interior into the garden, which contains a small muddy tank, some trees, and a fine vineyard. The garden is surrounded by a nine-foot wall, on to the outer face of which a Mulla's house and a mosque have been built. As I entered the place, Khwaja Margam's brother (one of Att Chapar's sons) came forward to meet me. He was an assistant in his brother's department, had a good figure and intelligent countenance, and altogether looked less savage and evil-disposed than his father. Att Chapar's family is distinguished by two peculiarities, *viz.*, their long beards (seldom to be seen in Khiva) and their inordinate avarice. The first day I received every possible attention. Said Nazar communicated to me a greeting from the Khan and from his elder brother, and brought me a tea equipage and tea and sugar. A pilau was prepared and all kinds of fruit given me, and a particular apartment placed at my disposal. The latter was but a dark, cold, unplastered place, but it was acceptable owing to the great heat outside. Occasionally I wandered about the Court or into the garden, but was always accompanied by a guard, which at first I conceived to be there as a mark of distinction, but discovered at last that I was really being treated as a prisoner. Four of my Turcomans were meanwhile permitted to go wherever they pleased and visit their relatives. I was assured that the Khan would give me an audience the day after my arrival, but I waited in vain for the invitation.

Then Yakoob (Att Chapar's third son), who had come from Khiva, declared as a positive certainty that I should be summoned on the day following.

8th October.—I received a visit from a certain Yakoob Bey, who spoke a little Russian. He had traded in Astraccan, lost his money there, returned to Khiva a beggar, obtained employment as a tax-gatherer, and had amassed a considerable amount of wealth again. He came from the Khan to ask me who I was, why I had come, what business I was charged with, and demanded that I should give him my letters to deliver to the Khan. Irritated at this request, I rejected it roughly, and told him that I had been sent to the Khan only, and if that personage would not receive me, he might let me go back. For the rest he might tell the Khan that I had two letters and some presents for him, which I wished to deliver

to him in person.   Hereupon he left me in a huff.   With this
Yakoob Bey came another Yakoob, by birth a Jew, but who had
long since embraced the Mahomedan faith.   As this Jew traded
with Astraccan and Orenburg, he understood Russian to a certain extent.   He often visited me, and gave me much information about the state of trade between Khiva and Russia and
Cashmeer, which latter country his brother had several times
visited.   One day a Turcoman in my service had heard at
the bazar, that of Kazavat, that the Khan had left Khiva,
and was going to receive me in a particular castle not far
from Yal Kaldi.   I communicated this news to Att Chapar
and Yuz Bashi, who, however, would not believe it, and
assured me that it was quite untrue which it was, for I heard
that same evening that the Khan had left Khiva on a 12 days'
hunting expedition into the steppe the very day that Yakoob
Bey had visited me.   Meanwhile I began to be treated more
discourteously every day.   My allowance of food became
scantier.   I was no longer allowed tea or firewood for the
kitchen ; indeed, at first I was forbidden to buy food on my own
account : this prohibition was afterwards cancelled in order to
increase the perquisites accruing to Att Chapar, who managed
my purchases for me.   The surveillance over me became
every day stricter.   I was not allowed to leave my room for a
single minute without a guard of two men, and at last they
placed a sentry over my door with orders not to admit
any one, whilst at night a man slept at the threshold, so
as to be roused any time the door opened.   My Turcomans who had been to the bazar further informed me
that, on my arrival, the Khan had at once assembled a
Council, to which all the eminent persons of the State, the Governor and Commandant of the town of Urganj (his brother Kutli Murad Inakh), and the Chief Priest (Cazi) had
been summoned ; that they had had a lengthy conference,
but that no one knew the result.   Several days after this,
however, I learned from some of the Turcoman relatives of
my companions, one among whom was in the domestic service
of the Khan, that when Mahomed Ragim heard that I had
taken notes on the road, he pronounced me to be a spy, and
said in Council that the Turcomans who escorted me were to
blame for not having murdered me en route and possessed
themselves of my gifts, for, now that I was actually there, it
was too late to think of it ; whereupon he had asked the
Cazi's advice, and the Cazi had replied that I was an un-
believer, who should be buried alive in the steppe.   The
Khan then said that he had taken the Cazi for a sharper man

than he really was, " for," said he, " supposing I have him killed, his Czar can easily come here next year and carry away the wives from my harem. It will be much better to receive him and let him take his departure; meanwhile he must just wait. I want first to know his object in coming." There was great difference of opinion as to the latter point. Some opined I had come to obtain the release of the Russian captives; others that it was to demand satisfaction for two Russian ships which had been burnt ten years before in the Bay of Balkan by the Atta Turcomans (who, since their expulsion from the shores of the Caspian by the Yomuds, had become Mahomed Ragim's subjects); others, again, thought that my mission must be with the view to demanding vengeance for the death of Bekovitsh, &c.

They spoke of a Russian fleet said to have arrived off the Turcoman Coast, and to have been engaged in erecting a large fortress there, which was half finished, and suggested that, now I knew the road, I might next appear at the head of an army marching on Khiva. Many gave it as their opinion that the Russians might be at war with Persia, and that the Commander in Georgia was desirous of help from the Khan of Khiva. Some even asserted that the Russians had seized the Akkila fortress near Astrabad. Still they nearly all voted for my destruction either by execution or assassination, or, at least, for my enslavement. My arrival was a cause of great disquietude to the Khan, but from a dread of Russia he did not dare to take my life openly, however much he may have desired to do so. In this state of uncertainty and doubt, not being able to arrive at any determination, he thought it best to leave me in anxiety and suspense until he had procured further information or other means by which he might accomplish his purpose. Every day fresh deputations came to me to enquire about the object of my mission, but I remained perfectly reticent to all comers. This information as to the general desire for my destruction expressed by the members of Council, as also the secret scheme of the Khan's, gave me a great shock. I would not at first accept it as true, but further circumstances and additional reports convinced me very soon that it was no falsehood. Many schemes now began to flit through my brain. The idea of flight occurred to me, but thoughts of the disgrace of leaving my appointed task unperformed, whilst there was any hope, deterred me from this, and I determined to stay and defend myself manfully should I be set upon. Happily I found among my books *Pope's Iliad*, the perusal of which afforded me relaxation during my morning walks in the garden.

12th October.—This afternoon one of my Turcomans brought me some eggs and dried fruits, saying they were sent me by a Russian who was at the gate, and begged me to come out for a few words of conversation with him.   As I did not dare to do this, I had to dismiss him without seeing him. Three days passed without the slightest further enlightenment as to my fate, but the strict surveillance and rough treatment did not leave much room for doubt as to the Khan's designs. I was for 48 days altogether in this state of suspense, and what I suffered in body and mind during that period is impossible for me to describe.   I shall therefore occupy myself with other matters.

16th October.—Khwaja Margam's little son, of ten years old, who was a great pet of the Khan's, and had continually to play at chess with him, came to-day to Yal Kaldi, and brought me the news that his father would soon come to see me.   As, however, I had been so often before deceived, I did not believe this.   Khwaja Margam's brothers and many other officials often visited me, but bored me terribly instead of giving me any pleasure by their society.   At length I hit upon the thought that perhaps among all the people about me one might be found who would give me genuine and true information as to what was going on in Khiva.   I therefore assembled them all, presented each with as handsome a gift as I could afford, and endeavoured to persuade them one by one to do this ; but no one would dare to speak with me alone from fear of being betrayed by the others.   At last I found a poor old man, by name Bey Mahomed, a native of Bokhara, who wished to make the pilgrimage to Mecca.   He had left his country 17 years back and lived in this fortress, supporting himself by the manufacture of waist belts.   I presented him with a pair of scissors, and thereby won his favour to such an extent, that he ventured to come to me in secret and give me various scraps of information.   He could not, indeed, give me very much news, but he did me a great service by informing me of the quarrel existing between the Yuz Bashi and Att Chapar on my account.   I was really under the supervision of Yuz Bashi, a good, honest, unpresuming man.

To him had been entrusted the duty of keeping a keen watch over me, and therefore, when I invited him to visit me alone, he used to fear evil consequences, and always strove to

Portrait of Yuz Bashi Ash Nazar

avoid private interviews of that nature. Att Chapar never let him out of his sight, and always followed him when he came to me, dreading that I should give the Yuz Bashi a present. Noticing his greed, I one day (having given him cloth before then) presented him with a piece of linen, and conjured him to tell no one of it, particularly not the Yuz Bashi. His true character at once appeared ; he hastily seized the present, hid it like a thief, ran away from the place, and, coming back, sat himself down beside the Yuz Bashi as if nothing had happened. I enlightened the Yuz Bashi on this afterwards, and he enjoyed the joke with all his heart, and spoke contemptuously of Att Chapar and his whole family. On my arrival I had presented the Yuz Bashi as well as Att Chapar with a piece of cloth, which Att Chapar's steward had taken under his charge, but afterwards it turned out that half a yard of the Yuz Bashi's piece had been cut off, and Att Chapar insisted that he had done it himself. This was a bone of contention between them, and when I complained to the Yuz Bashi of the want and discomfort I was reduced to, and of the uncivil treatment I was experiencing, my confidence touched him, and he became my friend, severing himself openly from Att Chapar, who now no longer dared, as heretofore, to sneak about after him. Every day now I sent Petrovitsh secretly to foment their quarrel, and, profiting by their dissensions, to pick up true information. The latter managed once to persuade the Yuz Bashi to come into the garden and meet me alone, and then I received the comforting assurance that, although the audience day was not fixed, I might expect at any hour to be called before the Khan, and that the latter would most likely decide my case directly he returned, and not go out hunting again without doing so, as a rumour was current among his subjects that the Khan was overawed by a Russian Envoy, did not know how to answer him, and had therefore fled into the steppe, &c., &c.

In these conversations I often interrogated him about the Khan, his relations with neighbouring States, and the internal economy of Khiva, and acquired a good deal of information on those subjects. The Yuz Bashi resented the tyranny of the Khiva Government, and appeared to dislike the Khan, but never said a word against him. He said that all the people about the Khan stood in such dread of him, that they feared to allude to me even, but he nevertheless hoped that my affair would have a fortunate issue. The Yuz Bashi was related to the second Vizier, Kush Begi, and had himself fled to Bokhara some years before to escape the Khan's severity. He had remained there for two years, and returned only on the pressing solicitation of the Khan. After winning his confidence, my mind became much easier, and whenever I could not have a personal interview, I had only to send Petrovitsh to him : he took a sincere interest in my situation, and I could always tell by his countenance whether the news from Khiva was favourable or not.

When I subsequently met him at Tiflis as Ambassador from the Khan, he told me that the reports before mentioned with regard to the assembly of the senate and their vote for my death were not without foundation. When my Turcomans saw that things were going badly, they lost their respect for me, and, indeed, tried to abandon me from fear of having to share my fate. Directly they entered the market a crowd would assemble round them, asking on what day my execution was to come off, or if it were true that the Envoy had been strangled the night before, &c., &c. This gave their Chiefs a pretext for counselling them to desert me, and another thing that had great weight with them was the report that the Khan was much enraged against the Yomuds, because they had not yet paid the toll he had recently laid on all incoming camels. Said himself became disrespectful, as the following incident will show :—He had taken his female slave Fatima to all the villages and bazars about, but could nowhere get his price for her. This poor woman lived in the same room with all the rest of the party, but when they went out she used to be so ill-treated by the other people in the fortress, that I had frequently to send Petrovitsh to drive them off. On one of these occasions the ruffians behaved so badly to her, that Fatima fled, and declared that she would certainly take her own life if she were not sold soon. When Said returned I represented the state of things to him, and begged him to have it altered, and to sell Fatima, whose presence was a scandal to us all. He listened to me quietly, then rose up and said—" Farewell Murad Beg ! My service is at an end, for since this is to be your treatment of me, I leave you. Fatima is my slave, and I shall sell her whenever and to whomsoever I please." With those words he went away, but I called him back, and he came, probably supposing I would ask his pardon for my interference. " Look here," said I, " go back since you see my unfortunate situation, and fear that you may, perhaps, have to share it ; go back and tell Kiat Aga, who recommended you to me, that you have left me in this place. Know, however, that, so long as I have my weapons, I fear neither you nor any one else, and that without weapons no one shall ever see me. Now go, and do not come near me again." These words affected him ; he sat down and reflected, then began to weep, begged my forgiveness, and swore to stand by me and share my lot.

I made the matter up with him, and next day he sold Fatima. My food allowance became meanwhile every day scantier and of worse quality, and as I was not permitted to make my own purchases, I had to have recourse to stratagem, that is, I used to give Att Chapar's steward money to buy bread and mutton, and these, when they arrived, were passed off as a gift sent to me. Att Chapar was certainly a very eminent and rich individual, but so greedy was he, that he actually condescended to pilfer scraps of meat out of my store-room. He had seven Russian slaves in his service, of whom one was in Yal Kaldi, three in Khiva, and three in other places. The Russian at Yal Kaldi was called David, and had been kidnapped as a boy of 14 near the fortress of Troitsk on the Orenburg frontier, and sold as a slave at Khiva. He had already passed 16 years in bondage, and had changed hands several times. Quite a Khivan in manners and customs, he had nevertheless remained true to his faith. He was always kept away from me, but Petrovitsh once accidentally met him, and was immediately implored to get me to exert myself for his release. I sought every opportunity to get a word with him, and succeeded at rare intervals. I told him to try and find out from the Russians who occasionally came out from Khiva with their "Arabas" what was going on there, and what reports were current about me. David was easily able to get this intelligence, as he was intimate with four married Russians, who were favourites of the Khan, and always about his person. The news he brought confirmed what I have already given about the proceedings of the Council of State, and this was further corroborated by the ten Persian slaves who were in Yal Kaldi, and who did all they could to please me. Being very anxious to have a private interview with David, I managed to get him into my room one night, although he knew that it was death for him to be discovered holding communication with me. He gave me the very intelligence I had already heard from my Turcomans. I further obtained a deal of information from him about the Russian slaves in Khiva, and at last dismissed him with the present of a ducat. The Kirgis on the Orenburg frontier make it their business to catch Russians and sell them in

Khiva, but it is said that there are just as many Russian slaves in Bokhara as there are in Khiva. These poor people are all day set to perform the heavy labour, which neither Turcomans nor Khivans are capable of performing. For subsistence they each receive 80lbs. of meal per month, and no other remuneration beyond a cast-off coat (Caftan) now and then. Whatever they can save from their allowance of meal they sell, and by this means and pilfering on occasions they manage to scrape a little money together. When they have amassed the amount of their purchase-money (generally 20 to 30 Tillas), which seldom occurs under 20 years, they then purchase their freedom from their master, and are set at liberty, except so far as leaving Khiva is concerned, for the least suspicion of intended flight from the province is visited with capital punishment. A young Russian (up to 25 years of age) fetches from 60 to 80 Tillas. The Persian slaves are much cheaper. Of the latter there may be 30,000 in Khiva, but there are not more than 3,000 Russian slaves there. The Persians (caught by the Turcomans near Astrabad) come into the market in batches of five, ten, and even thirty at a time. Their captors do not trouble themselves about them on the road, and, if they get exhausted, leave them without compunction to die in the steppe. On arrival at Khiva their owner sets himself down with them in the market, and purchasers surround him, inspecting and examining the poor wretches, and haggling about their prices, as if they were buying horses. Sometimes the Turcomans kidnap them out of Khiva and take them back to their parents in Persia, who are often able to pay them handsomely. During my stay in Khiva several such batches were brought into the market, sold, and taken off to the villages. Att Chapar bought, when I was there, a boy of 16 years old, the son of a rich Astrabad merchant, for a pretty considerable sum, only in the hope, however, of being able to sell him back again at a great profit. The boy's sister, a girl of 14, was dragged through all the markets without a purchaser appearing, as the price demanded for her was 80 Tillas and sufficient good cloth to make a coat out of. Persian slaves are obliged to recant their doctrine and follow that obtaining in Khiva, but the Russians are not molested in this way. David assured me that they were even allowed a private place for their holy pictures, where they could say their prayers at night. On two festivals in the year they are permitted by their masters to go out walking and amuse themselves.

A view of the Yal Kaldi fortress

On those occasions they assemble together and intoxicate themselves with a spirit which they distil from a kind of berry.

The festivals generally terminate in murder or homicide. Masters have the power of putting their slaves to death, but seldom avail themselves of the right from economical considerations. They therefore punish their slaves, as a rule, by putting out an eye, or cutting off an ear.

In my own presence Att Chapar wanted to cut off one of David's ears, because the latter had been to Khiva and had stabbed a Persian slave in a broil. Att Chapar first struck him over the face with a whip, then seized a knife, and commanded that he should be thrown down and shorn of an ear, and it was with great trouble that Usbeg Mahomed Aga, his steward, could restrain him from having this carried out. I did not take David's part from fear of rather injuring than benefiting him by my intervention, and so left the scene, but David came to me the same night and said—" Did you see how they struck me and wished to cut off my ear ? More than that I received yesterday evening 500 cuts with a whip from the son, but nevertheless they fear me : just you see if they dont all fly before me when I get drunk ! "

20*th October.*—Said Nazar arrived from Arganj. He came to see me frequently, and whether it was that I was suspected of desiring to escape, or what, I do not know, but every time I asked him if the Khan would be back soon, he answered me angrily—" Perhaps, then, you think of running away ? " Well, just you try it, and you shall see what will then happen to you." I swallowed my anger, but answered him briefly that an Envoy never ran away, because his master was answerable for his safety. This conversation led me to speculate as to whether they had divined my intention of ultimately saving myself by flight should no hope remain ; so I went into the garden, looked at the wall, and perceived that a ladder which had stood at the furthest point, and on which I had been counting as a stand-by, had been removed, whereupon I complained to the Yuz Bashi of Said Nazar's rudeness, and declared that, in spite of Att Chapar's venerable white beard, I looked upon him and his whole breed with the deepest disgust. "You are right," said the Yuz Bashi, "a long beard has not much to do with the matter. Why, a he-goat has a long beard."

21*st October.*—Hakim Ali Bey called on me and assured me of his friendship, and said he was about to fly from Khiva with his caravan. "The Khan's eyes," said he, "are just now filled with blood; at other times every one might approach him : now, however, he listens to no one, but lays an unheard-of impost on each caravan that arrives, thereby quite barring the road to Khiva for us, and he has us hanged and impaled, &c., &c." This was no exaggeration, for he continually put his Turcoman subjects to death for theft and other misdemeanours, and by this means contrived to keep some sort of order in his territory. During my residence there five Turcomans were on one occasion all hanged at the same time.

Hakim Ali Bey begged me to give him a letter to Ponomarev, but I could not bring myself to trust him, so I gave him an old coin of Julius Cæsar, which all on board the corvette knew I carried on my person, and told him to give it to the ship's Chaplain, with the request that he would burn a candle for it before the holy picture, and said that, as this was one of our customs, I did not ask the service from him secretly, but he might make my commission known to every one. " Forgive what has passed," replied he, " and tell no one that I have behaved to you, Turcomanlike, so rudely. I have come expressly here to bid you farewell."

In spite of the strictness with which the Turcomans were forbidden to come near me, they always found means of gaining access. A few of them were of great service, but the greater number were simply a nuisance.

23rd October.—At length the Khan had returned from his hunting expedition, and arrived at the Canal Dash Haos. Every one looked on it as a certainty that I should soon be granted an interview. But five days passed, and I was still kept under surveillance ; so, seeing no means of escaping from my weary captivity, I determined to try the effect of threats as a last resource. I begged my keepers to go repeatedly to the Khan, and to say in my name that winter was now at hand, and that there was danger of the corvette's being icebound in the bay of Balkan, or of being wrecked, as she could not depart without me, and that, in case of her suffering any mishap, the Khan would have to render an account of it to the Russian Czar. Unluckily no one dared to carry this message to the Khan. Three of my Turcomans, seeing now how badly things were going, began to give themselves great airs, and one of them even asked me to discharge him. I did so, and perceived to my joy that he afterwards repented of his step, just as Said had done.

31st October.—To-day I invited Att Chapar and the Yuz Bashi to visit me, in order to learn for certain what the Khan's real designs were, and begged them again to represent the state of the corvette to him, and how he would be called upon to answer for any damage it might sustain; but they prayed me to wait only for one day longer until Khwaja Margam should come to Yal Kaldi, where he was hourly expected. Finding them determined, I wished to send Said or Petrovitsh to Khiva, but this was not permitted.

4th November.—I was to-day informed by a Turcoman that a Yomud, by name Niyaz Batur, had arrived in Khiva from the Krasnavoda coast with two letters from Ponomarev, one for the Khan, and the other for me.

6th November.—At daybreak I sent off Kuhlji secretly to Khiva to look up Niyaz Batur and to ask him for my letter.

The next day Niyaz Batur brought the letter to me himself. He said that the Khan had been greatly pleased with Ponomarev's letter, and had been formerly deceived by the false reports brought in by the Turcomans to the effect that the Russians were going to build a fortress on the coast, reports now contradicted by the letter. The Khan had therefore, as a mark of his favourable intentions towards me, sent him personally to deliver my letter, and to pray me to have a little more patience, as he would very shortly grant me the desired interview. Batur said a great deal more, but every other word was in his own praise, or about the deep obligation I was under to him, so I did not attach much faith to it all. However, I entertained him to the best of my ability as a messenger from the Khan, and old Att Chapar constrained himself to-day to be liberal, and spent about as much money as he usually did in a whole week.

Ponomarev's letter contained nothing of importance. He merely said that he would await my return until the 8th November.

I gave Niyaz Batur a considerable present, and told him that, as I had no wish to keep anything secret from the Khan, he might communicate this letter to him. Niyaz Batur swore that in two days I should certainly be summoned to the Khan, and that meanwhile he would send any news that might be of importance to me by his own special messengers. The more I reflected on the matter, the less I trusted this Niyaz Batur's words, but a man deprived of almost every means of rescue grasps at any scrap of hope that may turn

Plan of the
Yal Kaldi
Fortress

KEY

a Watch tower
b Gate into garden
c Workshop
d Praying area
e Guards' room
f My room
g My Turkomans' room
h Storeroom
i Room for guards' concubines
j Living quarters of Kirgiz family
k Room of the Russian slave David
l Stables
m Cattle pen
n Covered corridor
o Mill
p Servants' and slaves' rooms
q Huts occupied by Uzbeks
r Yards for storing grain
s Yard for keeping camels
t Mosque

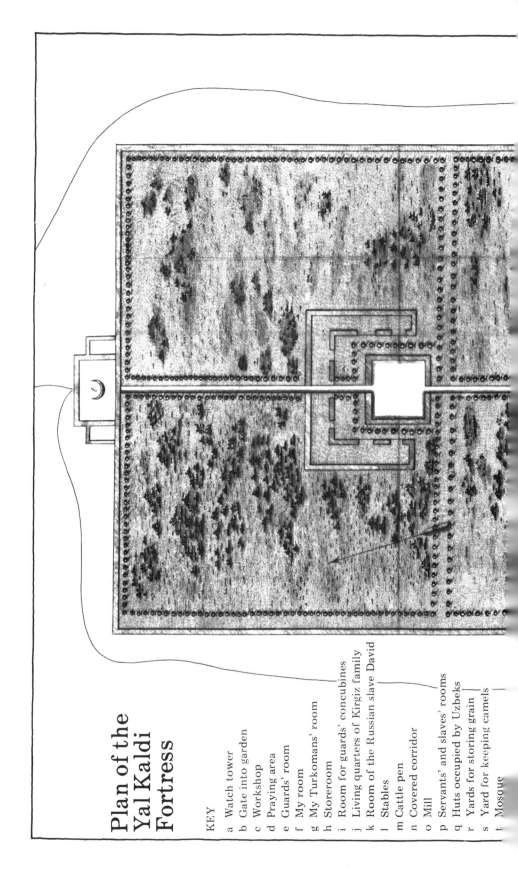

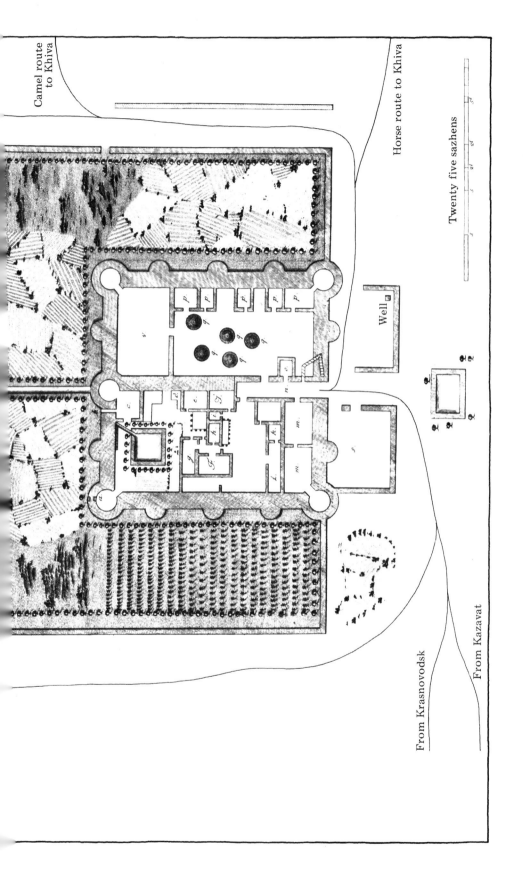

Camel route
to Khiva

Horse route to Khiva

Twenty five sazhens

Well

From Krasnovodsk

From Kazavat

up; so I abandoned myself to the joy that this conversation afforded me, and believed the assurances and promises to be true.

To celebrate the occasion I invited the relations of my Turcomans to the entertainment, bought two sheep, flour, &c., had a pilau made, and treated them and the inmates of the fort as well as I could.

This was probably the first time that those gloomy walls had echoed the sounds of mirth; but as the half-starved slaves and Turcomans began to fight over the viands and to snatch the meat from each other's hands, the festivities were soon over, and I dismissed Niyaz Batur.

9th November.—This evening he visited me again. He had found the Khan at Mai Jungle, whither he had gone for a few days' hunting. Five more days elapsed without the Khan's sending for me. Meanwhile David acquainted me that the Khan was preparing for my reception, and had already ordered dresses for presentation to me; that one door of my room was to be closed, behind which a Russian would sit and overhear my words, and that I should be dismissed with marks of honor, &c., &c. I could hardly believe all this; therefore I begged the Yuz Bashi to tell me if he thought I should have to pass the winter in Khiva, or should be able to depart soon after the audience, as I wished to shape my plans accordingly. He replied—"I cannot deceive you, and therefore confess that I do not myself know. It seems, however, that you may expect the summons hourly." I begged him again to carry my message about the corvette to the Khan, and he promised that, if no one should arrive from Khiva by the next day at noon, he would himself ride straight to the Khan. Three days went by, and he never took his promised ride.

I represented to him again that he had nothing to fear in the matter, as, according to Niyaz Batur, the Khan was very kindly disposed towards me. He replied—"You are mistaken. I did not wish to shake your confidence at first and to make you distrust a man in whom you had once trusted, but now I must tell you that Niyaz Batur is an arch traitor; in one word, he is a Turcoman, whose word no one should accept as true. We Khivans take the measure of these gentry very accurately, and, accordingly, it is here that they usually end their career on the gallows." He was right in the main, for Niyaz never sent me the promised messengers, and strove only to overreach me in making the purchases which he had undertaken for me.

14th November.—At last the Yuz Bashi having been much offended by Att Chapar in some matter or other, came to me, and said that he would immediately ride to Khiva and represent to the Khan both my plight and the situation of the corvette. Yes, he was resolved, he said, in spite of the dangers, to tell the Khan in my name that he would be responsible to the Russian Czar for the loss of the latter, and that, if he wanted to keep me, he might at any rate let the corvette go by telling me so. Two days hence the Khan was to go off into the steppe on a three months' hunting trip, and all his carts and beasts of burden had already been sent on ahead. "If things go well," said the Yuz Bashi, "expect me back to-morrow afternoon."

15th November.—He left me on the 14th, and the whole of the next day passed in fruitless waiting. I began to think that the Yuz Bashi had been called to account for conveying my message to the Khan, or that my affairs were taking an unlucky turn, so I determined to carry out my early project and save myself by flight. This project I disclosed only to Petrovitsh, for I feared to trust myself all at once to Said; however, I managed to lead the latter on to recommend the very thing I was driving at. At first I pretended that I could not possibly bring myself to run away, but at last assented to his (?) proposal, and then we settled down to consider the best means by which the scheme could be carried out. Eventually we concocted the following plan :—Said was to buy horses from his relations and to bring two Turcomans to go with us. These latter were Khan Mahomed and Janak, robbers who were leaving Khiva to escape the gallows. I promised to compensate Said for the loss of his camels, and further to make over to him and his comrades the presents intended for the Khan. Said, it was arranged, was to go to the market on the morning of the 16th and buy boots and furs ; he was to return by noon, go back to the village in the evening, and bring the horses to the fort at midnight, when I was to rouse my comrades, and we were then all to leave the place with our fire-arms loaded. In order that Said should run no unnecessary danger, it was agreed to wait for the Yuz Bashi until the evening of the 16th, and that, if he should arrive after Said had gone to fetch the horses, we should carry out our project all the same, however favourable the news might be that he brought, for without doubt the report of our intended flight would by that time have got abroad, and Said's ruin and our own would be the result.

16th October.—Said went off in the morning, as agreed, and Petrovitsh and I looked about us for the best place to effect our escape out of the fort from. After much reflection I found that the best method would be to get over the wall with a rope, although Said had expressed his strong dissent to this plan, saying that it would be much better to go out by the gate and take Att Chapar's horses with us. With them we could then go at full gallop to the frontier, and, leaving the exhausted animals there, steal fresh ones from the Turcomans.

When all had been settled for our flight, I waited impatiently for mid-day to see what fate had in store for me. If I had not wished to leave Yal Kaldi secretly, I could certainly have forced my way out, for there were only a few lads and armed men in the place, and besides, I could have counted on the assistance of David and the Persian slaves. If pursued, I would have defended myself to the last drop of blood, and would probably have had a fair chance of getting off safe and sound. Noon came, but with it no Yuz Bashi, and no Said. I began to fear treachery, and was not a little anxious about Said. The sun was sinking, and I was sitting meditating in a corner, when suddenly Said made his appearance and sat down beside me. "You are late," said I, "but perhaps your zeal and your many commissions are to blame. Is all ready for midnight?" "Hold, Murad Bey," he replied; "don't be in a hurry, but listen to what I have done. When I reflected that men are ruled by destiny, I thought that perhaps it would punish us if we should fly and try to escape it." I stood up on hearing this, and said—"Why did you not tell me yesterday that you could not keep your word? Destiny wishes us to fly, but you are a traitor. Have you bought what I told you to? I know what my course shall be." "I have bought nothing," said Said, "and here is your money back." I had given him 10 ducats, and he now gave me a handful of small coins and clipped tillas, worth scarcely eight ducats, because, as he pretended, he had lost heavily in changing the money. Depending so much as I did upon Said, who might betray me at any moment, I was much puzzled to know what to do—to make my escape alone, or to abide my fate. My visible grief went to Said's heart; he begged my forgiveness, wept like a child, and promised to arrange everything for our flight on the following day. I was reproaching him bitterly for his mean behaviour, when suddenly Kuhlji came with the news that the Yuz Bashi was

approaching. The latter came forward cordially and said—
"The Khan desires to see you, and to-morrow morning early
we must be off. At first he was angry with me for leaving my post by you, but when I represented to him the
circumstances of the case, the situation of the corvette, and
the responsibility he was incurring by his discourteous treatment of an Envoy, he determined at last to admit you to an
audience." I thanked him, and made him a handsome
present, and this was the happiest evening I had passed in
Yal Kaldi during my 48 days' imprisonment there. My
Turcomans paid me now all due respect, and Att Chapar,
formerly so rude and unbearable, condescended to all sorts of
flattery and self-abasement, begging me pressingly not to tell
any one how badly I had been treated during my stay.

17th November.—At night I sent to the neighbouring
villages for the horses I required. The report of the Khan's
favour had speedily spread, and towards morning friends and
acquaintances came round to wish me luck, really only in the
hope of getting something out of me, or of attaching themselves to my following, so as to come in for a share of the
gratuitous guzzling of pilau and tea at Khiva. Att Chapar
had promised the day before to provide horses, but the Yuz
Bashi advised me not to trust him, as although he was a
Mussulman, he had nevertheless all the deceit and treachery
of his native country. Before leaving I made Petrovitsh
distribute small coins among the inmates of Yal Kaldi, and rewarded all the servants and slaves who had tried to please me
with trifling presents. They all knew me very well now, and
came in a body to the gate to see me off; old men, girls,
mothers, and children followed me, and even my warder, a
surly dog, was civil for the first and last time.

We rode 29 miles to the N. E., and reached Khiva. After
passing through two tracts of steppe intersected by canals,
along the banks of which stood large villages and gardens
(the Khivans thoroughly understand irrigation), I came to
two canals, one crossing the other by means of an aqueduct,
over which again there was a bridge.

Five miles from the city the gardens begin. There are
roads running through them, and here and there appear places
like Yal Kaldi, the residences of the landholders. The city,
at a little distance, presents a very beautiful appearance. It is
surrounded by a high stone wall, over which towers the sky-
blue dome of the great mosque, with a golden ball at the top.
The numberless gardens, which prevent one's forming an idea

of the largeness of the town, help to make up a most charming picture.   Just in front of the entrance there are a number of ancient tombs, and a little canal, which runs right
through the high road, and is crossed by a handsome stone
bridge.

At this point there was a crowd of inquisitive people
waiting to see me, who accompanied me all the way to the
house set apart for my use.   The narrow streets I found
quite blocked up by a sea of people, pressing on every side,
and ducking under the very horses, and the Yuz Bashi had
to make a passage for us by main force.   In the crush I noticed several unhappy Russians, who humbly took off their
caps, and begged me in under tones to obtain their release.

After riding for about 500 yards between dwellings made
of wattle coated with mud, we alighted at a nice-looking
house in a *cul-de-sac*.   The Yuz Bashi led me into a fine
court-yard, clean and well paved, on to which opened several
apartments.   Of the latter a large one was allotted to me,
and a smaller one to my Turcomans.   My room was a very
elegant one, furnished in oriental taste, with beautiful carpets,
&c., but the cold was something intolerable.   The prying
crowd followed me even into my room, but the Yuz Bashi
drove them out, and then went to report my arrival to the
Khan.

During his absence the crowd again appeared, struggling
and scuffling up to the very door and completely stopping all
thoroughfare in the court-yard, the servants placed here by
the Farash Bashi being quite unable to disperse them, and I
was only relieved of my importunate visitors by the return of
the Yuz Bashi.   The gates and entrances were now securely
locked, and only my guards remained, who, however, never
presumed to enter the room without being asked to do so.
They took up their quarters in the Court, and only a few
went to their homes, first asking my permission.   Att Chapar
himself spent five full days in the court-yard, and was immensely
pleased with the title of " Father," which I occasionally addressed him by in irony, especially when I abused him.   The
Yuz Bashi now felicitated me on my arrival, and announced
that I was to be the guest of 'Mehtar Aga Yusuf, the Grand
Vizier of Khiva.   A cook was sent me, but independently of
what he prepared, great dishes of food, tea, and fruits came
every day from the Vizier.   These marks of distinction
are quite unusual among the Khivans, but in spite of them
all, during the five days I was entertained in this fashion

View of the town of Khiva

there was not the slightest relaxation in the watch kept over me. On the evening of my arrival Khwaja Margam came to make my acquaintance. He is director of taxation, and a very crafty person, but very sprightly in manner. A whole hour passed in mutual compliments, then he begged my permission to solicit the Khan to entrust the whole management of the negotiations to him. I replied that it was not my place to nominate the Khan's officials; but he arranged it for himself the very same evening, and informed me that the Khan had honoured him with the duty, and now requested that I would make over the letters and presents to him. I hesitated for a long time, and would not venture to comply with his demand until I had satisfied myself from the Yuz Bashi as to the truth of what he said. At first I gave him only the letters, but had soon to make over the presents as well, as they were called for the same night, Mahomed Ragim being in the habit of sleeping in the daytime and working by night. Yuz Bashi advised me to seal up the packet, so as to prevent pilfering on the part of Khwaja Margam and his subordinates. This I did, placing the cloth and brocade, &c., &c., in a large tray, and packing the whole in linen. I then made the package over to Khwaja Margam, whose servants carried it off with the greatest secrecy. I ordered Petrovitsh to follow them, but he returned in two hours, which caused me to dread that some *contretemps* had occurred. He came in dressed like an Usbeg, and immediately took off a huge head-piece, and, hurling it into one corner of the room and his coat into another, protested that this should be the very last job of the kind that he would ever undertake, for it seemed he had been kept standing in a corridor until near frozen to death. At last Khwaja Margam had appeared, made him take off his clothes, and presented him in the name of the Khan with this strange apparel, whereupon he was dismissed. By the way he sold the garments to Att Chapar the very next day. Dewan Baki Mehta Aga, from whom I had borrowed the tray before alluded to, came to ask me for it back. I asked the Yuz Bashi about it, but he said " Mehta Aga will never see his tray again, for the Khan is a strong man, and never lets go of a thing that once falls into his clutches." Among the gifts there was a salver on which were packed two loaves of sugar, 10 ℔s. of lead, 10 ℔s. of gunpowder, and 10 musket flints. The Khan had employed himself all night in gazing at his presents, but his curiosity had been greatly roused by this salver. He lifted it up, wondered at its weight, and asked the Yuz Bashi if he did not think it might contain the ducats he was expecting; but he was amazed, on taking off the linen covering, to find himself deceived. The Khivans put the following interpretation on this gift :— The two loaves of sugar stood, according to them, for an offer of peace and sweet friendship, whilst the ammunition signified that, if friendship were not agreed to, war would be the result.

18th November.—No audience granted yet. Being desirous of making a few presents to the Khan's eldest brother (Kutli Murad Inakh), I found that this was not allowed, unless the Khan gave his permission. I therefore sent the Yuz Bashi to obtain the necessary sanction, and despatched Petrovitsh in the night with some cloth, brocade, sugar, and other trifles. Petrovitsh had not been allowed to see the Khan's brother, but brought back five gold tillas which had been presented to him.

Among these gifts there was also a razor case, which was fitted with a tin soap box, containing a piece of black soap. Inakh looked at each thing separately, but when he came to the soap, an article he was unacquainted with, he began to suspect evil designs on him; so he called for his physician, and as that individual was also nonplused, he sent messenger after messenger in hot haste to ask me about it. I had quite forgotten what the case contained, and requested, therefore, that it might be sent for me to look at just for a moment, when I would at once explain the contents; but this was absolutely refused. I then desired that the small box containing the mysterious article should be sent; this also was refused, and I was reduced to asking for the article itself without its box; but here the Yuz Bashi replied—"Inakh is just such another strong man as the Khan; he also never returns what he has once got hold of. I shall, however, go and calm him. Of course it must be a piece of soap and nothing else." The same evening I remembered that I had 10 beer glasses for the Khan, which I had forgotten to send with the other things. I asked the Yuz Bashi to give them to him now, and to apologize for my forgetfulness. "That is of no consequence," he replied, "our Khan will *take* at any time; the only difficulty is to get anything out of him. With us glass is a rarity, and he will be much pleased with these; but don't send him ten, for that is considered unlucky among us. Send rather nine, which is our lucky number." He therefore took nine glasses to the Khan, and came back at midnight. The Khan had been immensely

delighted, and had examined each glass separately, repeating—
"What a pity! What a pity that they did not send me these
in the days when I drank brandy!" It turned out that he
had formerly been much addicted to this beverage, but had
now entirely renounced the use of spirituous liquors and
tobacco. He had even prohibited smoking among his subjects, and proclaimed that disobedience in this matter would
entail the delinquent's mouth being cut up to the ears. Nevertheless, in spite of this stringent law, smoking was very prevalent, and the Khan was forced to connive at the practice as
regarded some of his highest Ministers. Many Khivans
smoke, instead of tobacco, the leaves of a plant they call
"bang," which must be most injurious, as a beginner loses con-
sciousness on using it.

Among the Khan's gifts there was also a glass "Kaliyan"
(hookah-stand), which puzzled him much. The Yuz Bashi
did not venture to tell him the truth, so said it was a vessel
for holding vinegar, which he had a great fondness for. My
burning glass caused much astonishment, many coming to me
expressly to see it. The opinion was that its wonderful pro-
perties could not pertain to glass, and that therefore it must
be some sort of rock crystal.

18th and 19th November.—These two days were also
passed in close confinement. No one was permitted to visit
me without special sanction. I remembered what David told
me in Yal Kaldi, *viz.*, that a Russian would be posted behind
my door to listen to what I said, and truly I found everything turn out as he had foretold, and distinctly heard
some one at the door. I therefore took a seat close by it, and
spoke in a loud voice to the interpreter about the Khan's
warlike qualities, his great power, and the superiority of the
Khivans to the Persians, &c. For three successive days I
noticed that this eaves-dropping went on. The Prime Minister
and those who had charge of me did their best to win my
friendship, and, once when they saw me looking downcast,
sent for a certain Mulla Said to amuse me. This person was
about forty years old, was possessed of much intelligence, and
had all the gay humour and vivacity of a European. His
witty flow of talk was certainly most agreeable, and he
played chess (a great game in Khiva) better than any one
I have ever met. The Mulla lived entirely on the presents
given him by the high officials of the Khanate, with whom
he had frequently to pass his evenings. He played chess
with them, wrote verses, read aloud, related stories, and so on.

He thoroughly understood Arabic, Persian, and Turkish, and spoke distinctly and well : he was intimate with the ancient history of Asia, and spoke of it with enthusiasm, giving point to his words by frequent quotations from the best poets. He told me laughingly that he owned a house in the suburbs, which he had not entered for 14 years, as he had invariably to spend his nights with the Nobles of Khiva. He complained bitterly of the present *régime*, and lamented the severity of a Khan who would not so much as allow drinking and smoking in his realm. He stayed over two hours with me.

20th November.—At length, towards evening, Khwaja Margam sent me a message through Said Nazar to the effect that the Khan wished to see me. I dressed in full uniform, but put on a Khiva hat, and had a red facing sewn over my collar, so as to conceal my real rank from the Russians about court. The Yuz Bashi told me that it was not permitted to appear before the Khan with a sword on, but I objected to lay mine aside, and told him to represent this to the Khan.

"There you go spoiling everything," said the Yuz Bashi. The Khan is now well disposed to you, but I shan't give him your message. I shall rather tell him that you have not got a sword at all, but only a long knife," and, indeed, it was only a Circassian side arm that I had, and not a regular sword. Yuz Bashi, however, soon returned with the reply that the Khan begged me to appear without any side arm whatever, so as not to transgress the custom of the country. I gave in, hoping thereby to fulfil my mission more quietly. The Yuz Bashi and my warders now preceded me, and likewise some strong men armed with clubs to clear the way. There was a great crowd, the very roofs swarming with spectators, and here, again, I heard the imploring voices of some Russians among the multitude. Thus we passed through a narrow cross lane to the gate of the palace, where I was made to halt until I had been announced. I was soon invited to enter. The gateway is a handsome brick structure, showing considerable taste. The first court-yard is not very large ; it is sanded, and surrounded by a hideous mud wall. Along this wall 63 Kirgis Envoys sat who had only come to pay their compliments to the Khan, gorge themselves, receive the present of a coat of coarse cloth, and go home again. The second court is still smaller, and constitutes the arsenal. I observed here seven guns mounted on carriages, which quite resembled Russian pieces of ordnance. The third court is the so-called " Harniyush Khana," where

Councils of State assemble. From this court I was led into a covered passage (mud walls and thatch, the floor dirty and uneven), at the entrance to which stood the Khan's servants. On reaching the end of this corridor, we had to go down two steps into a fourth court-yard, larger than the other three, but surpassing them all in filth, and covered here and there with weeds. In the middle of this stood the Khan's Yurt. As I went down the steps, a man in a dirty sheep skin approached, whose slit nose betokened him to be a Russian convict, probably a refugee from Siberia. This fellow came behind me, and, seizing me by the sash, tried to drag me forward. At that moment the thought flashed through my mind that I was betrayed, and that I had been brought here unarmed, not for negotiation, but for execution. I turned round, and angrily enquired how he dared to pull me by my sash, but when I raised my hand the man ran off. The Yuz Bashi put my mind speedily at rest, however, by the information that it was the Khivan custom always to *drag* Envoys before the Khan. The Russian now drew near again ; he did not, however, venture to touch my sash, but only held his hand up behind me.

I remained standing before the Yurt, in the interior of which the Khan sat, wearing a red robe (made out of the cloth I had brought him) fastened at the breast by a little silver button. His head-dress was a turban, and he sat motionless with crossed legs on a Khorassan carpet. On one side of the entrance stood Khwaja Margam, and on the other Yusuf Mehtar Aga, an old man, whom I now saw for the first time.

The Khan has a very taking exterior. He must be six feet high, and they say that no horse can carry him for longer than two hours at a time ; his beard is short and red ; his voice pleasant, and he speaks distinctly, fluently, and with dignity.

I saluted him as I came into his presence, but without taking off my cap, and in order to adhere to the customs of the country, I waited silently until the Khan should address me. After a few minutes of silent expectation, one of the Khan's retinue uttered the following prayer :—" May God preserve this country to the profit and renown of its Ruler," whereupon the Khan stroked his beard, an action followed by the two at the entrance, and now addressed me in the following words :—" Khush Galub San ! Khush Galub San ! (*i.e.*, you are welcome.) " Envoy, wherefore art thou come, and what

dost thou wish of me ?" I answered in the following words :—
" The Governor of the Russian possessions lying between
the Black and Caspian Seas, under whose rule are Tiflis,
Ganja, Grusia, Karabag, Shusha, Nakha, Shekin, Shirvan,
Baku, Kubin, Daghastan, Astraccan, Caucasus, Lenkoran,
Saljan, and all the fortresses and provinces taken by force
of arms from the Kajars, has sent me to thee to express his
deep respect, and to deliver the letter indited in an auspicious
hour."

The Khan.—" I have perused his letter."

Muraviev.—" Besides this, he entrusted to me some gifts
to be delivered to thee, which I had the happiness to make
over some days ago. I am also commanded to make certain
representations verbally to thee, and only await thy order to
discharge myself of the message now, or at any other time that
may be suitable."

The Khan.—" Speak now."

Muraviev.—" The Governor desires to establish a fast
friendship with thee, and to enter into more intimate relations. It is therefore necessary that the trade between
the two nations be placed upon a firm footing to their mutual
profit and advantage. Our caravans going by Mangushlak
must now travel 30 days through a nearly waterless steppe,
and this wearisome journey is the cause that the trade on
both sides languishes. The Governor is accordingly anxious
that in future the caravans should come to the Krasnavoda
harbour in the Bay of Balkan, as by this new route they
would only have a 17 days' journey, and thy traders would
always find merchantmen from Astraccan lying in the
proposed new harbour, with all the goods and materials
for which thy subjects now come to us."

The Khan.—" Although it is true that the Mangushlak
road is longer than the Krasnavoda one, still the people
on that route are adherents of mine, whilst the Yomuds
inhabiting the coast towards Astrabad are subject to the
Kajars. My caravans would therefore run the risk of being
plundered, and for this reason I cannot agree to the proposed
change."

Muraviev.—" Taxir !* If thou wilt but ally thyself to
us, thy enemies shall also be our enemies. The renown of
thy arms is well known to me. But what reply dost thou

---

* Taxir, the Khan of Khiva's title, meaning literally "wine."

Reception of Captain Muraviev by the Khan of Khiva

command that I carry to the Governor, who desires thy friendship? He prays thee to send him a man who enjoys thy confidence, and who, on his return, will acquaint thee with his mind. For me, I shall, on reaching my own country, hasten to the Emperor and give him an account of my reception and thy answer."

The Khan.—" I shall send some trusty men with thee and give them a letter to the Governor. I myself desire that firm and sincere friendship may be founded between us. Khush Galub San!" The last words signified that I was to withdraw, which I did after bowing. I was then taken back to the " Harniyush Khana," followed by Khwaja Margam and Mehta Aga. Great dishes of sweetmeats and fruit were presently brought me, and I passed half an hour in this place, being questioned by Mehta Aga as to the relations existing between Russia and Persia, the strength of our forces in Grusia, &c., &c. To the latter question I replied that we could bring together in that province about 60,000 regulars, the same number of irregulars, and a formidable body of horse. The Yuz Bashi presently arrived with a servant, and gave me an embroidered turban from the Khan. This was tied on my head, whilst my waist was bound round with a rich Indian girdle, into which a silver-sheathed dagger was stuck, and a robe with short sleeves made of Russian brocade thrown over my shoulders; then, having exchanged my cap for a worse one, sent by the Khan, they led me back into the presence. Now came a repetition of the former scene. First I remained silent, then was ordered by the Khan to repeat my former words, which I did, receiving the same answer as before. I then said—" Khan, in what manner can I show myself worthy of the favours thou hast bestowed on me? I should, indeed, think myself fortunate if the Governor were to accredit me to thee next year, that I might prove my devotion."

" Thou wilt come if they send thee," he replied, " but let the Governor dispose of my representatives as he may think fit. He is quite at liberty to send them to the Czar if he likes." I went back to the principal gate, where I found a splendid grey horse of the Turcoman breed awaiting me. I mounted him and went off, my Turcomans, one on each side, holding the bridle, whilst two others walked beside my stirrups; but the crowd was so dense, that Petrovitsh, who was on foot, could not keep up with me. During the interview I had addressed the Khan in as loud a tone as I could command, and had stood erect and unconstrained in his presence, which seemed to the Ministers, accustomed to slavery and abasement, highly offensive, and they showed their displeasure by their looks at the time. The populace escorted me back to my quarters, and the Khwaja Margam came and had cloth coats distributed among all my people. Said was put out at only getting a coarse scarlet coat of the same quality as those given to the rest, and wanted to reject it, but did not dare to do so. Khwaja Margam also gave some further messages from the Khan, and informed me that a cannon founder from Constantinople resided in Khiva, and that the Khan had recently commanded him to cast an 80-pounder. He finally intimated that I was quite at liberty, and might go back when I chose.

All the servants now withdrew, and the people encompassed me in such a manner that without the Yuz Bashi's assistance I should never have been able to shake them off, or, indeed, to leave Khiva at all, as I had neither men nor horses at command.

The latter deficiency forced me to spend the night in the city, but thankful, indeed, was I to have discharged my duty. At the last I sent a petition to the Khan to be allowed to present something to his three most eminent Ministers.

Permission was granted, so I sent Mehta Aga, Khush Begi (who, however, did not reside in Khiva), and Khwaja Margam each a piece of cloth, some silk, and a watch. In spite of all my efforts I never contrived to see Sultan Khan, who had made a great name for himself in 1813 by uniting three Turcoman tribes, inimical to one another, under his standard, and leading them against the Persians. I asked the Yuz Bashi to allot the remainder of the presents according to merit. A glass "Kaliyan" took his fancy, and for a long time he pondered as to who was worthy of it. At last he asked me to cover my face with my cap and to make the allotment at random. This I refused to do, preferring to give the Kaliyan to himself, which made him very happy. Att Chapar kept bothering me for something, but I gave him only a scrap of cloth, with which he was much dissatisfied, and, going away in a rage, did not again give me the pleasure of seeing him. I heard subsequently that Khwaja Margam had sent in an enormous bill to the Khan for my expenses whilst at Yal Kaldi, charging at the rate of two tillas a day, whereas his father only received one tilla a day from him for my subsistence.

Chapter III
Return

21st November.—My wish had been to leave Khiva early in the morning and to go back to Yal Kaldi, there to await the arrival of the Khan's Envoys, *viz.*, the Yuz Bashi, Ash Nazar, and Yakoob Bey, a Sart by birth; the latter could read and write, and was a shrewd man, but bore a bad character. However, I had to postpone my departure until mid-day, and was meanwhile entertained again by order of the Khan, but was unable to eat anything, as cold pilau was all that was set before me. The Yuz Bashi went himself to the market and made a few purchases for me, and then, when all was ready and the horses stood saddled at the door, I suddenly remembered that the lock of my double-barreled gun was out of order, and asked for a gun-maker. A handsome young man of about 20, in a turban, but with unmistakable Russian features, presented himself to me as such. I asked him, if he spoke Russian, in that language, and he answered, "No," in Persian, and then proceeded to examine the lock, talking now Persian, now Turkish, all the time with the greatest fluency. In his conversation he showed much acuteness, and when he had discovered what was the matter, he took the gun and ran home with it. I now learned that his father was a Russian by birth, who had been kidnapped and sold as a slave at Khiva, where he had embraced the Mahomedan faith and married a Persian slave. The fruit of the marriage was this young man, who had made such rapid progress in his studies, that he was already a Mulla, and supported his poor family, having first had to purchase their freedom. I was in the act of starting when the young man, quite out of breath, brought me back the gun, but it was so badly repaired, that I could not use it. He also brought me some dozens of eggs and some white rolls, for which I gave him a ducat.

I gave the gun to the Yuz Bashi to examine, and asked him, should it appear necessary, to give it back to the gunsmith to put into thorough repair, and to bring it with him when he came to Yal Kaldi.

A Russian led my horse when I started, but muttered execrations on the awkwardness of the Khivans for their custom of being led in the daytime on horseback. On my way through the streets I saw many clusters of my unhappy countrymen at different spots, who greeted me affectionately, and addressed me as their deliverer. One of them walked for a long way abreast of my horse, and, when I turned to him, said,—"Oh! Sir, do not forget us poor people in the Fatherland."

In order to clear a passage for myself, I made Petrovitsh scatter small coins among the throng, which caused great fighting, but had the desired effect of making an opening.

To my horror, after we had been about three hours on the road, Petrovitsh discovered that he had dropped my money bag, containing 300 ducats. By a most lucky chance Said found it again, or I should have been reduced to the greatest extremities. Said asked the Yuz Bashi to request permission from the Khan for him to load 17 camels with grain without paying the impost. I tried to persuade him not to ask for this, but Said was obstinate, so I told the Yuz Bashi that he should refuse to have anything to say to such matters. Nevertheless, the permission was obtained, and Said and his comrades were let off the charge on their camels, and I supplied funds for the purchase of the grain.

At 11 P.M. we reached Yal Kaldi. The night was terribly cold, but David met me a long way from the place.

The native of Bokhara Mulla Bey Mahomed, and all the inmates of Yal Kaldi rejoiced over the happy termination to my affair, and wished me a lucky journey back; but alas! I was doomed to a further sojourn of six days in this place. My good reception by the Khan impressed every one most usefully, and my slightest word now sufficed to clear my room of inquisitive intruders when I tired of their society. My Turcomans also were most obedient; they had from intercourse with me improved much in manner, and always managed to command respect from the people who visited them. I was particularly satisfied with Abul Hossein and Kuhlji; they served me with the most obliging zeal, and I therefore promised to send them both to the Governor as Turcoman representatives. This pleased them immensely, for they were used to an indolent life and loved a well-supplied board. The intolerable Att Chapar was absent. In the meanwhile, however, he had seized the horse of a poor Turcoman entering the fort to buy some tobacco, and refused to give it back for all the unfortunate's tears and

Return journey of the caravan

prayers; indeed, he had had him kicked out of the place, and, changing his mind three days later, had turned the horse loose on the steppe.

I procured here all the necessaries for my return journey, past experience helping me to provide against the wants of the road. The cold was extraordinarily severe, so I bought furs, feet wrappers, and great Khivan boots.

For night wear I had large Kirgis caps made up, with long ear-lappets, so that by day I was a Khivan and at night a Kirgis in costume. I laid in also mutton and rice and purchased several Russian ambling ponies, which are common in the Khanate, and finally got all my weapons into thorough order, with the exception of the double-barreled gun which the treatment in Khiva had ruined. As I was preparing to clean this gun, I discovered a slip of paper in one of the barrels, on which the following was written in Russian :—

"We venture to inform your Honor that there are over 3,000 Russian slaves in this place, who have to suffer unheard-of misery from labour, cold, hunger, &c. Have pity on our unhappy situation and reveal it to the Emperor. In gratitude we shall pray to God for your Honor's welfare." The perusal of these lines deeply affected me, and I thanked God that I should, perhaps, have the fortune to serve as an instrument of help. And now I can say I have done my duty, for the Emperor is acquainted with the circumstances, and will certainly exert himself in behalf of the unfortunates to the best of his power. Almost at the same time David brought an old Russian to me, the same who had previously wished to speak with me at the Yal Kaldi gate, but whose request at that time the circumstances compelled me to refuse.

The old man's name was Joseph Melnikov; he had been 30 years in slavery, was the son of a soldier, and had only been married a week when he was seized by the Kirgis near the fortress of Pretshistinsk and sold as a slave at Khiva. After 30 years of bitter bondage, when by daily and nightly work he had at length scraped together sufficient money to purchase his freedom, his master cheated him by accepting his savings, and, instead of setting him at liberty, selling him to some one else.

During my first stay at Yal Kaldi I had seen several Russian merchant sailors from Astraccan, who had been captured near Mangushlak and on the Emba.

26th November.—The Yuz Bashi arrived to-day, but Ya-koob Bey is still at Arganj, detained there by domestic affairs.

27th November.—This day I departed from Yal Kaldi after receiving the hearty adieux of all. My first night's quarters was 11 miles from the fort, in the Yurt of a Turcoman, by name Aman, of the Bahram Shah race. Aman was a friend of Said's, had some kind of connection with the Court at Khiva, and had secretly acquainted me during my captivity with what went on there ; but in spite of all this, he was a thorough-paced scoundrel, and had so cheated me in some purchases I asked him to make for me on one occasion, that I had been obliged to drive him away. With Aman there dwelt an old Turcoman of 80 years, who in his younger days had been renowned for his robberies, and now in his old age assisted this family by his counsel in important matters. He was held in high esteem by all Turcomans, and his con-versation exhibited intelligence, experience, knowledge of men, and sagacity.

Joy at my departure kept me from sleeping, so I sat up all night, talking with this octogenarian. We did not adhere to our former route, but went back by the straight road from Khiva to the Tuar well, which passes by the Takka tribe. Travelling as I was with Khivan Envoys, I had now, of course, nothing to dread from the attacks of robbers : but with regard to the water scarcity, we heard that snow had fallen on the road, but thawed again, forming a puddle near the ruins of Shah Sanam, which was the only water we could depend upon obtaining until we reached the Ak Nabat well. We did not leave Aman's Yurt until the afternoon of the following day, as we had to wait for Yakoob Bey. I spent the morning in writing a letter to Ponomarev, which I intend-ed to despatch by the Turcomans Khan Mahomed and Janak as soon as we should have crossed the last canal in the Khanate. The caravan comprised 20 Turcomans, who had all looked forward to the happy conclusion of my negotiations, had waited for my departure, and now called themselves my servants in view to drinking tea and feasting at my expense on the road, and to secure continued immunity from the Khan's new impost. Many of them rode on horseback. They were, for the most part, friends and relations of Said's, and had probably all got off paying the tax. They were so utterly wanting in shame as to come and ask me for clothes for the journey, but I drove them all away. There was a certain

Ваше Высоко родие Осмѣливаемся сами Доношу Росписать люби нашотца
Всимъ юртомъ тоисста А призна плениковъ при штрцу нев ясносныи тербы Рдатъ
Ихолатъ виизыи Началъ при натки Заалтесь надиатмъ Стрныимъ ватамъ дик доне
сиит обз прому власство Зостав те вечно жили тъ До за взитъ

The original slip of paper discovered by Captain Muraviev in his gun barrel, see page 77.

Nazar Usta among them who had a young and very beautiful wife and two sons of eight and nine years with him. His laziness was so great, that he did positively nothing the whole way, his wife and children having to attend to the camels, as well as manage everything else. His sole occupation used to be to sit by my fire either to warm himself or to tell anecdotes. His wife also used frequently to come to me, and always brought me a piece of bread when she did do so, which I repaid in sugar. Their unaccustomed good living had now so told on my Turcomans, that they became as lazy as possible; only one man, by name Abul Hossein, did any hard work for me. He did everything, indeed; attended to the horses and camels, packed their loads, repaired the broken harness at night, and fetched the wood, kindled the fire, and cooked the food. We made much shorter stages now than on our upward journey, because the camels had all full loads : we seldom marched at night. But we had just as many hardships to undergo as on the former occasion, suffering from great cold and scarcity of fuel. I had at times to saddle my own horse, and almost every day to search for fire-wood and bring it in on my shoulder. Petrovitsh's duty, however, was to provide fuel for the whole of the caravan. When, therefore, we arrived at the place where we were to pass the night, he would assemble all the candidates for tea, and go out to forage for wood, amusing them with stories and praising the active ones, but not doing a hands-turn himself, for the good reason that he was so wrapped up that he could not move, that is to say, he had on six coats, a Kirgis cap completely enveloped his head, &c., &c. We always arranged our bivouac so as to have the baggage on one side and the fire-wood on the other, placed so as to leave only one means of entrance.

In the midst of this sort of redoubt blazed a huge fire, and outside the camels lying close packed formed a second breast-work. My fire was generally surrounded by a number of lazy Turcomans, and even the Khivan Envoys used to sit there cross-legged, inert and fuelless, not daring to order their own people to gather wood. They accordingly availed themselves of mine, and as they were too lazy to prepare food from their own miserable stock, they lived on me as well. This vice of indolence is prevalent in Khiva, both among the natives themselves and the Turcomans, to an extent that quite surpasses belief. They are quite capable of going without food for two days in order to lie in the same place and do nothing, and their avarice is just as enormous as their laziness. They would invite me to eat with them, whilst all the time I was treating them. For this consideration they, to be sure, accorded me certain rights of superiority.

The following is an account of my return journey in proper order :—

28th November.—After mid-day we left Aman's, and by evening reached the Canal " Buz Hioman," which is the last in the Khanate, after a march of about 17 miles. From this canal we crossed over into a tract of steppe as far as the eye could reach, single Yurts scattered here and there, but no cultivation of any sort. This evening I despatched my letter to Ponomarev. The cold was terribly severe, and I had to keep in motion all night without closing my eyes, and even then nearly had my feet frozen. Unluckily we could obtain no fire-wood whatever, and to make matters worse, three horses broke loose, and gave great trouble before they were recaught in the steppe. The Canal Buz Hoiman being frozen over, we carried off some pieces of ice for the way.

29th November.—We broke up our bivouac at a very early hour and pursued our course through the steppe. I was much struck by the large number of ruins.

30th November.—The road ran steadily through the flat steppe, very scantily clothed with brushwood here and there. From a distance we saw the ruins of " Daudan Kila."

1st December.—We passed the ruins of Kasil Kila, but did not halt here for the night, as our horses had not been watered since the 29th; we therefore pursued our march through the night of the 1st. The horses of these parts can go for four days without water,—a thing I should not have credited had I not witnessed it myself.

2nd December.—At daybreak we reached the dilapidated fortress of Shah Sanam, and this was the last ruin we came across for the rest of the road. We had a long search for the pool of water we had before been informed of. It was 30 × 8 feet in dimensions, and had only half a foot of water in it, but it is nevertheless the only stand-by for all the passing caravans. Here we all set to work, some fetching wood, others breaking up the ice with their daggers and melting it in kettles for tea, &c., &c. After watering our horses at this filthy pool, we again pursued our journey. The Shah Sanam ruin lies on the right hand side of the road, and is built on an artificial mound. The remains of some of the apartments are still visible. This place is celebrated for an event the memory of which lives throughout the whole of Asia, and is perpetuated in song and legend.

Shah Sanam was the lovely daughter of a very rich and eminent man. The young Karib, renowned for his song and his bandura, fell in love with her, and she, to test his faith, demanded that he should not approach her for seven years, but travel in foreign lands for that period. The singer now makes over his bandura to his old mother, enjoining that no one shall be allowed to play on it, and starts on his travels. Passing through many lands and encountering many adventures and dangers, from which he is rescued by the force of destiny and the help of good men, he at last returns after seven long years, his true heart burning with all the old love and cheered by the thoughts of home. His mother meanwhile has lost her sight from continual tears shed for his absence, and three months before his return Shah Sanam has been promised by her ambitious papa to a wealthy neighbour in spite of all the poor little creature's entreaties.

The unhappy Karib seizes his bandura, flies to the house of his beloved, and appears at the wedding feast. Time and travel have changed his features, and no one recognizes him. He touches the strings and pours forth a song descriptive of his love, his wanderings, his anguish, and is discovered by the magic tones of the bandura, his adventures, above all, by his voice and passionate fire. The joy of union now takes the place of the bitterness of separation. Shah Sanam falls into his arms, and papa agrees to confirm their bliss.

The numerous ruins and visible traces of ancient canals are strong evidence that the Amu Dariya once ran through this neighbourhood in the days when that river emptied itself entirely into the Caspian. This tallies also with the Khivan tradition, that the river altered its course to the northward in consequence of an earthquake which took place 530 years ago.

3rd December.—All the horsemen now hastened on ahead of the caravan, hoping to reach the well Ak Nabat by evening, but we were overtaken by the darkness, and forced to pass the night on the road with hardly any forage for our nags. The caravan itself went on all night, however, and caught us up on the morning of the 4th, having passed a great caravan of the Takkas, who were probably only deterred from violence by dread of the Khivan deputies.

4th December.—We arrived before noon at Ak Nabat.
The whole road right to Tuar was strewn with the bodies of
camels and horses lost by the caravans which had preceded us.
The cause of this was that the Turcomans had stayed longer
than usual in the Khanate, in the hope that Khan Mahomed
Ragim would remit the camel impost, and had only started
when the cold had actually set in, some of them having paid
the tax, others flying without doing so. Although not much
snow had fallen, still the frost had made the ground like
glass, and the camels, already enfeebled by want of forage,
could not get on. Among the dead camels we saw some human
corpses also. The Usbegs and Turcomans said that by
their long beards they must be Persians, who are continually
dragged from Astrabad to the Khiva slave market. They
remarked *à propos* of the corpses in the most cold-blooded
manner, that it was of no consequence whatever, and that
one-half of those "Kazil Bashes" generally died on the
way from hunger and cold. The water of the Ak Nabat
well is rather bitter. This well is situated in the midst
of a great steppe full of quick-sands. Only a few rises
in the ground are visible in the vicinity. Before reaching
the well, a road turns off to the left, which leads to the
Turcomans of the Takka tribe. We did not halt until
we had marched for an hour and a half after leaving
the well.

5th December.—At 2 o'clock in the morning we started,
and marched till daybreak. I rode on with Petrovitsh, but
as an irresistible drowsiness fell upon me before daybreak, I
got off my horse and followed Petrovitsh on foot, who unfortunately missed the road among the brushwood. It was
cold and dark, and I no longer heard the voice of Kuhlji,
who never left the caravan and always sang. I therefore
stopped in the hope that the caravan would pick me up,
and fell fast asleep, but, on awaking, found myself in the midst
of the steppe, with no trace of a human being to be seen. In
vain I shouted; no answer came : so, having the fate of the
Persians before my eyes, I began to search for a path, and, by
the happiest chance, came across Kuhlji, who was looking
for me, and who took me back to the caravan.

6th December.—Started on the 5th again, and went on
without halting until daybreak of the 6th, when we reached
a district called Tiyunakla. Here we found some caravans of
the Atta tribe : we rested on the steep banks of the old Amu
Dariya bed. The name Tiyunakla is applied to a great

sinking of the ground which is to be seen not far from the banks above mentioned. It is situated in the flat steppe, is about 80 yards deep, and 600 yards in circumference. In the bed of this hollow, on the north side, there is a small spring of salt, bitter water.

On maps Tiyunakla is shown as a great lake, but that is a mistake.

We had followed the left bank of the Amu Dariya for more than five miles before we could get across, when we found ourselves on a bald steppe, without a twig or a leaf on it. The river bed here is called Angiunj, and is not so deep as at Besh Dishik. In the river bed there is a little undergrowth. The night of the 6th we set apart for repose. The thermometer must have been down to 12° or 15°. The cold was terrible, and increased with the night.

7th December.—To-night also we had to bivouac on a perfectly bald steppe, not a symptom of vegetation to be seen.

8th December.—Towards morning we set out, and arrived by evening at the well of "Dali," which is looked on as the half-way house between Khiva and Krasnavoda. Beside this well stand the ruins of an old building. Here we found two Atta Turcomans with several camels, which they tried to exchange for the Khiva caravan camels, but their animals were in too bad condition to admit of this, for it was the "Atta" tribe whose caravans had suffered so terribly on the road, and their Yurts stood by a well in the steppe, parallel with the "Dali" well, but nearer the sea.

We wanted to water our horses and camels here, but there was a dead camel in the well, which had probably fallen in. From this place we found the climate much milder, and encountered no more snow for the rest of the journey.

Being impatient to get to the coast and the corvette, I determined to abandon the caravan and ride on ahead independently. I consulted with the Yuz Bashi, and, leaving him, Petrovitsh, and my servants with the caravan, started off on the night of the 8th in company with Said, Kuhlji, and Khivet (leader of a Turcoman caravan).

9th December.—At daybreak we rested for an hour, and saw several Atta caravans. The country was not quite so flat as heretofore. From here to the coast we rode straight on end, hardly resting at all, that is to say, we only halted for from three to five hours per diem, feeding our horses on a handful of "Jugan" and subsisting ourselves I know not how, for my companions devoured on the very first day all the bread and meat that I had laid in. For the two last days we neither ate nor slept. On the night of the 9th we reached the "Tongra" well. At a distance of one day's journey from here, on the left hand side, and four miles from the road, is situated the "Ak Kui," a well round which there is a settlement of the "Atta" tribe. Tongra is 74 miles from Dali. In the well we found the body of a drowned stag. From Tongra to the Tuar well we had only a ride of 23 miles.

10th December.—Before daybreak we reached Tuar, overtaking an Atta caravan in the act of watering their camels. As we had no leather buckets, we watered our horses from the water which the Attas had drawn for their camels. At first they opposed this, but we announced that we belonged to the Jaffir Bey tribe, and, in spite of their superior numbers, enforced our demands.

The Jaffir Bey tribe, from its numbers, its courage, and its extensive connection with other tribes, being universally respected among the Turcomans, the people of the Atta caravan at once gave place to us, lent us a wooden bucket, and begged pardon for their rudeness in opposing us in the first instance, saying that they did not know we belonged to the Jaffir Beys. The wells all along this route are foul. In the Dali and Tongra ones we had found a dead camel and a stag, and here, in Tuar, we heard the bleating of a sheep which had recently tumbled into one of the wells.

In the evening we took up our quarters in a ravine not far from the road. Here we found some heaps of dry sticks, and were about to utilize them as the materials for a fire, when we discovered several bundles of goods of sorts concealed under them. My Turcomans were highly delighted, and immediately set to work to open the bundles, which were found to contain raisins, tobacco, and "Jugan," and to appropriate the contents. This I, however, forbade in spite of Said's remonstrance. "This is a fine story," said he, "that we are to respect the property of these Attas, whom we hardly esteem so highly as our cattle and our slaves, and who would assuredly not lose a similar opportunity of despoiling us." "Do as you will, then," I replied, "but my horse shall not taste a single grain of the stolen corn. I do not want to lose the beast, and this ill-gotten forage would injure him." Said now represented that we had brought too little grain with us, but I answered that that circumstance gave us no claim on the property of others, and added—" If you hold the Attas in such great contempt as you declare, why did not you take what you wanted from them when we came across their caravan yesterday ?" Said now refrained from touching anything more, and the others brought back the articles they had appropriated, but Kaved remarked—" Of course it is disgraceful to pilfer other people's property, but you probably are not aware that these Attas formerly lived in the Balkan district, and that we expelled them 10 years ago for burning two merchant ships which had come from Astraccan to Krasnavoda, and selling the whole of the crews into slavery at Khiva. From that day to this no more merchantmen come to our coast, and we are forced to purchase in the Khiva and Astrabad markets. Judge now for yourself if the Attas do not deserve some punishment." As I saw that my orders were obeyed, I allowed them to take sufficient ' Jugan ' for one feed from the bundles, leaving in its place two Dollars in each open package. When the Turcomans saw this they left the money untouched, but appropriated all the tobacco and raisins, saying that they had now been paid for, and it was no longer theft. At noon we set out again, and reached the mountain chain Sare Baba. In the daytime I could distinctly recognize the Kuli Dariya lake, which I have described in former pages. We had a short rest, and then rode on throughout the night, watering our horses at noon on the 11th at the well of Damur Jema, from the vicinity of which the Yurts, which formerly existed, had been removed.

11th December.—Before reaching the well I had a strange adventure. Day had not yet broken and I was riding on ahead, my sleepy comrades lagging behind, when I suddenly came on a Turcoman leading two camels. I rode up to him and asked him whence he had come, and whither he was bound. On being thus accosted he took refuge behind his camels for a moment, and then sprang out with a naked sword in his hand shouting, " be off, or I shall cut you to pieces." He was so rapid in his movements that I had hardly time to draw my pistol, but when I did so, and pointed it at him, the poor wretch was so terrified that he dropped his sword and lost all power of utterance. Said coming up presently explained the whole mystery. The man had taken me for a Kirgis on account of my head-dress, and had thought himself attacked by a robber. From him I learned that the corvette still waited for me. We rode the whole day through, and only halted towards evening not far from the well Siyuli. On the night of the 11th I noticed two men riding, one on horseback, the other on a camel.

I pointed my pistol at the horseman, and asked him who he was. He took off his cap humbly and answered me in broken Russian. He turned out to be the young Yakshi Mahomed, son of Kiat Aga, who had picked up a few Russian words on board the corvette. He had left the ship nine days previously, and brought me a letter from Ponomarev. The intermediate time he had passed in Said's village, where dwelt a Turcoman girl, with whom he was in love, and whom he desired to marry. He told us that his father with all the notables had started on horseback to meet me, but had taken another road. Yakshi Mahomed's comrade was the Turcoman Vahl Usta who deserted Hakim Ali Bey, and came over to me on our upward journey. Seeing a fire off the road we went up to it in order to read Ponomarev's letter. By the fire we found two Turcoman families who were wandering northwards. On trying to return to the road we lost our way, and got back to the well of Siyuli with great difficulty at day break.

12th December —Being not very far from Said's Yurt, I sent Kuhlji on ahead to have food prepared. By evening we ourselves reached the Yurt, which now stood nearer the road, and were welcomed by Said's wife and the children of my other companions, who pressed round us on every side, together with some old men. Food was produced, and after writing to Ponomarev I fell into a sound sleep, the first I had enjoyed for some time.

13th December.—This morning I visited the wives of my other companions and started at about 11 A.M. accompanied by Said, his son, and three other Turcomans. We had only 29 miles now between us and the coast. At the distance of an hour and a half's journey from the latter we arrived at Mulla Kaib's Yurt, where I had been regaled with camel's milk on the way up. After this we ascended the mountain range, from the summit of which I beheld the sea and the corvette. I had already heard from Ponomarev, and had therefore no anxiety, but still this first view of the ship filled me with unspeakable joy. Sticking my cap on a long pole I tried to discover myself to my comrades on board, but no one seemed to observe my signals. However, shortly afterwards I saw a boat put off from the corvette, followed immediately by a second. The corvette lay a short hour's row from shore. As the boats always landed at a point not far from the Balkan well, I made straight for the latter and found some Russian sailors drawing water, who recognized me. Presently the first boat reached, and then the second, with Ponomarev on board. Our mutual joy at seeing each other safe and sound again may be easily imagined ; but the corvette had meanwhile had a bad time of it. Directly after my departure they had taken in all the available provisions from the merchant sloop, and then let the latter go altogether, not calculating on my long absence ; the consequence was that food became scarce, and the crew had been on half rations for a whole month. Out of the 140 men on board only 20 were effective, 5 had died, 30 were down with scurvy, and the remainder were so debilitated as to be hardly capable of dragging themselves about the ship. The stock of medicines were exhausted, so the Doctor could be of no assistance, Therefore, in the middle of November, Lieutenant Bassargin begged Major Ponomarev to let him make sail homewards, being further actuated by the frequent appearance of ice in the bay. Ponomarev said he would give me a fortnight's more law, and then when this term expired he added another week to my time of grace. When the week was up he added one day more, and on the afternoon of that very day a Turcoman boat came alongside, and Ponomarev by the greatest good luck received my letter. Universal joy at once spread all over the ship, the grumbling was at an end in an instant, and it was unanimously determined to await my arrival. Hakim Ali Bey, about whom I had several times informed Ponomarev, counselling the latter to arrest him, never showed himself on board the corvette.

The old coin I had entrusted to him he sent by the hand of another man, and in spite of my pressing invitations on arrival he invariably declined coming, making excuses on account of sickness, and so on. During my stay at Khiva all Turcomans returning thence used to make a point of going on board the corvette, and intimating that my return was imminent, hoping probably to obtain some reward for the good news. Continually deceived by false intelligence Ponomarev at last lost patience, and on a Turcoman's presenting himself and solemnly assuring him that I would return in four days, he detained him on board, promising him a reward if it should turn out that he had spoken the truth, but threatening him with severe punishment should his information prove false. On the fifth day, as I did not appear, the poor rascal in tears confessed to have invented the whole story in the hopes of a present. Kiat had always held himself aloof on board, carrying on whispered conversations with the returning Turcomans. But when the want of an interpreter and other causes compelled him to leave the ship and throw up the management of the Turcoman negotiations, he could never afterwards, without the greatest difficulty, be persuaded to go on board. As soon as the news came of my approach he at once started off to meet me, but, as before stated, we missed each other. His object was to have a private conversation with me. Other circumstances which I learned on my return made me resolve to avoid him, in order not to be obliged to enter into further explanations with him.

15th December.—It was determined to celebrate my safe return by a festival, so we went ashore and found a great assemblage of hungry Turcomans. Having divined Kiat's unfriendly sentiments, and fearing, consequently, hostile action on the part of the natives, I insisted on a guard being posted on the beach. We had horse-racing, boxing, shooting at the mark, and foot races, the winners receiving money prizes. Said and Kuhlji were not present during the amusements, as I had sent them to meet the caravan.

17th December.—Yesterday Petrovitsh announced the approach of the Khivan deputies, and to-day we recognized them coming over the hills with a body of horsemen. Their escort was composed of Turcomans, who rode in front, firing into the air from very joy. I immediately repaired to land, had a special Yurt erected for the deputies, and placed a guard at the door to prevent the Turcomans from intruding and pestering them with questions according to their wont. Directly the caravan arrived I took the deputies on board, many Turcomans also striving to accompany us from motives of greed. We were just going to start when Said came into the Yurt quite pale, fetched his saddle and his sword, and began to saddle his horse. I asked him the meaning of this, but he could scarcely answer me for trembling, and stammered out that on no account could he go on board the corvette, for he had dreamt to-day that as he was riding along the frozen margin of the sea, his horse's fore feet had gone through the ice, and that this must betoken that something evil would happen to him on board. As I could not drive this idea out of his head, I gave up trying to persuade him.

During my residence in, and journey back from, Khiva Said had given me great annoyance. I did not let him see this at the time, but determined to punish him on my return, by making his bad conduct known to the Chiefs, and driving him away from me in disgrace. But afterwards, when he acknowledged his faults of his own accord, I contemplated letting him off the disgrace, and simply intended to give him a private rebuke. Now, however, that he was going off as if nothing had happened, Petrovitsh detained him, and demanded that he should beg my pardon. Said replied—"May fate dispose of me as it pleases. I yield myself to its will, whatever may be about to befall me."

We now all went on board, and I introduced the Khivan deputies to every one in the corvette. Yakoob Bey had already made the trip from Mangushlak to Astraccan in a merchantman, and so did not show any particular astonishment, but the Yuz Bashi was amazed at everything he saw, and could not realize the idea of being actually on the sea. Ponomarev now distributed presents among my Turcomans. Said received a silver-mounted pistol, and then I took him one side and set his bad behaviour before him. He acknowledged it, begged forgiveness, and we became friends again. We passed this night on board.

18th December.—Towards evening we weighed anchor and steered for Baku. We had now two Turcoman and three Khivan representatives with us.

21st December.—After a calm we got a light breeze that carried us to the island of Shiloi, not far from the promontory of Opskheron. The islanders here support themselves by seal fishery.

24th December.—Owing to contrary winds we did not arrive in the Baku roads until this morning, and went ashore at noon.

30th December.—I had time to go and visit the so-called everlasting fire worshipped by the Indians. In Persian it is called "Atish Kad," and is situated 11 and a half miles to the north of Baku. The area containing naphtha is about two miles in circumference, and directly the smallest opening is made in the surface and fire applied, a flame bursts out, which it is difficult to extinguish. The fire-worshipping pilgrims who come here use this fire for cooking purposes, and also for lighting, by sticking a tube into the ground and igniting the gas at the end. Here there is a pretty clean caravanserai, in the interior of which are some inhabited apartments, some others set apart for idols (which, however, I could not get a glimpse of), and the remainder at the disposal of strangers. In the middle of the court-yard there stands a pretty large sacrificial altar, at the four corners of which burns the everlasting fire from high tubes. From 15 to 20 fire-worshippers generally reside here, but I found on my visit only six or seven. Their leader was an Indian who had formerly traded in Astraccan, and who besides his mother tongue could speak Russian, Armenian, Turkish, and Persian. The Indians whom I managed to see were nearly naked. They live and eat in solitude, each one having a fire burning in his room, before which he sits for hours at a time quite motionless with the hands up lifted or in some other position. However great the heat may be, they neither shift their ground, nor alter their posture. The emaciated countenances of these voluntary martyrs bear ample testimony to their sufferings. Among the seven present there was one who had served in an English regiment of sepoys.

January 6th.—The Governor, Jermolof, invited us to Derbent. We accordingly left Baku, and passed the night at Sugant.

January 9th.—We went *viâ* the Station of Kalisin to Khadersind, where we passed the night. Here we found a carriage in which we seated the deputies and then proceeded to Devitshi, where we passed the night of the 10th.

11*th January.*—We reached Kuba.

13*th January.*—Left Kuba.

15*th January.*—Reached Derbent, which the Governor also reached on the 17th, and four days after that the deputies were introduced to him, first the Khivan, then the Turcoman. The gifts sent by the Khan of Khiva consisted of two beautiful shawls, ten Bokhara dressed lambskins, two inferior saddles, and a few pounds of grapes. In return the envoys received two rings. The Khan had further sent two stallions to Jermalof, but they, together with the grey horse presented to myself, had to be left behind on the eastern coast of the Caspian. "You tremble on account of the Persians," once remarked the Governor to Kiat, who answered laughingly—"It is now winter time, when everything trembles." We left Derbent after the interview, went back to Baku, and thence to Tiflis, which we reached on the 24th February, and where we were cordially received by Lieutenant-General Welyaminov, the envoys receiving presents of cloth and silk stuff.

In the beginning of March General Jermolof received intelligence from Kislair, through the Governor of Astraccan, that Turcoman envoys had arrived representing the whole people. They made the same request as the deputation with us had proffered in writing, *viz.*, that the Turcoman races might be permitted to become Russian subjects, but with the proviso that a successor to the Sovereignty of Turcomania should be elected from amongst them. General Jermolof sent us over a copy of their petition, and on it we found the signatures of all the Chiefs, who here, however, styled themselves Khans, and among the rest that of Kiat ; the latter, however, denied all knowledge of the document, and said it was a forgery. On investigation it turned out that the leader of the Astraccan deputation was the brother of that Khwaja who in the year 1812 led the Turcoman levies against the Persians. His home was on the Chinese frontier, and he had visited the tribes in order to obtain from them the horses, arms, slaves, and jewelry of his slain brother.

As he was rejected with ignominy, he conceived the project of winning the rulership by the help of the Russian Government.

4th April.—To-day the Governor received the deputies with much distinction.

22nd April.—The Khivan deputies now wished to start homewards, so I gave them the following letter to the Khan of Khiva :—

" I have introduced the envoys, Yuz Bashi, Ash Nazar, and Yakoob Bey, sent by your Highness to the Governor who accredited me to you last year ; they will tell you how they have been received by us, and assure you of the Governor's friendship. I have also enjoined on them to convey to your Highness, the great ruler of the east, my most sincere thanks for the favour shown to me, as well as the confidence reposed in me by your Highness, and also to express the thanks of the Governor, who is now about to despatch me to my Emperor to acquaint him with the new alliance which has been concluded between the east and the west. May the rising and setting sun illuminate this bond of friendship until the end of time. May the splendour of this warm alliance shine like that orb, and be extinguished only with its extinction. Permit me further to say that having had the fortune to stand in your august presence, I cherish the hope that this letter may be received with favour and kindness in proportion to the veneration with which I am penetrated for your Highness. I would, indeed, consider myself fortunate if I could hope that you would from time to time think of me, whilst I pray for your immortal glory, and the uninterrupted continuation of all the prosperity bestowed on your Highness by the Most High."

Thus ended the task which had been confided to me by the Governor.

Supplementary Remarks

by the German Translator, Philipp Strahl,
chiefly derived from Voinovitsh's narrative

1. *Naphtha Island* (Cheleken *).—The Persians call this island "Chaharkan" (four mines),† and the Turcomans know it as "Naft Daga" (Naphtha Mountain). It lies in 39° 20′ N. Lat., and is conspicuous among the many other islands at the entrance to the Balkan Bay from its extent and elevation. It is visible from a considerable distance, and its abrupt coast line, especially on the S. and E. sides no doubt accounts for its Turcoman appellation. The character of the surface and sub soil is identical with that prevailing in the rest of the group. The soil consists generally of fine yellow sand, with here and there a little earth, the latter either mixed with yellow clay in combination with white mica, or with the *débris* of felspar, which is common on the coast. In these strata are found the naphtha springs at various depths below the surface. Here they are met with at a depth of two fathoms, there at a depth of ten or more.

The black naphtha found here (petroleum) is of two kinds, one of which is thicker than the other. Both kinds are, however, very thin, mixed with particles of earth, and possess a much fainter odour than the naptha found at Baku. The clay from which the naphtha is drawn is of the same nature as that on the surface, but is darker coloured by reason of its impregnation with the oil. The number of springs is uncertain, as they are frequently filled up by the sand, which necessitates new wells being sunk. Roughly estimated the number may be 20, but the sand interferes with their flow to such an extent that the annual yield hardly amounts to 1,600 centners. How trifling compared with the Baku annual yield! Besides this black naphtha there is also found

---

* Persian, Arabic, and Turkish words are spelt so peculiarly by the German translator that it is hard to trace them to what they are really meant to stand for, for instance, he spells جاي (Jai) "Tschai" يل كلوي (Yal Kaldi) "Ihl Hehldi," &c., &c., might not therefore his "Tscheleken" (which I have written "Cheleken"), perhaps, really be composed of the Arabic word جلاء and the Persian word كان and stand as "Jilakan," *i.e.*, the mine of brightness?

† (The German translator renders this four *wells*.)

(Sd.)   W. S. A. L.

Barbadoes tar (bitumen segne, crassum, nigrum, maltha, poix minérale, poix de terre ou malthe). This forces itself through the soil, forming a stratum of itself, which becomes hardened by the heat of the sun. The Turcomans free it from sand, &c., by frequent meltings over fire, when all the foreign particles sink to the bottom owing to superior specific gravity. The pure tar floating on the surface is then poured into pits prepared for it in the ground and left to cool, when it becomes more solid, and assumes a glossy black colour like "asphalt." This the natives call "Mumm," and carry it in its present form to Khiva, where it is mixed with wax and used for making up into candles and torches as in Persia. The salt found in great abundance on the island is not rock salt, but is obtained from a salt lake like those so frequently to be met with in Southern Russia, such as the Lakes of Elton in Saratovshen of Jenidja, Staroe, and Krasnoe in Tauria, &c. The lake from which it springs is very large, and is dry the whole year round, except just during the rainy season when water collects in it. When dry it is quite full of salt, which is very firm, and might therefore be taken for rock salt : unfortunately it is full of sand and earth and, consequently, very impure. Here also, like in Astraccan, there are a quantity of salt morasses. Indeed, the whole island is so impregnated with salt that fresh water is not to be found on it, and the water drawn from the wells is so brackish that the Turcomans only use it mixed with camel's milk, their usual resource when drinking water runs out. In conclusion, Naphtha Island resembles all those in its vicinity. The vegetable kingdom is represented by the " golden rod " (Solidago, Lin.), and in a few places by those kinds of grass which thrive in muddy or sandy soils, but these are all scorched up in the summer time, and the only verdure is then to be found in the swampy places, where reeds afford a poor means of subsistence for the camels, sheep, and the few goats of the Turcomans. Wild animals occasionally appear, such as foxes, wolves, wild goats, and pigs, and among the feathered tribes the most common are sea-gulls, cormorants (*pelecanus carbo*), mews, herons, and several species of snipe.

This is the only naphtha yielding spot on the east coast of the Caspian, although such places are not uncommon on the south coast, but it is worthy of note that the naphtha springs in the Balkan Bay Islands are exactly opposite to the springs at Baku and in the same degree of latitude. The traces of naphtha can be observed in the sea itself, for in the neighbourhood of the Island of Shilov the smell of it is quite perceptible, and it is even to be seen floating on the surface. Gmelin, in his *Book of Travels &c.*, has fully set forth the influence of naphtha on the Caspian, it being the principal cause of the bitterness of its waters.

Voinovitsh's Narrative.

2. *The Island of Ogurchin*—Is uninhabited, and only visited during Turcoman civil feuds. Seals abound here, as also the so-called red geese, and rose-breasted starlings fly about in clouds.

The Turcomans call the island Idak or Aidak. The name Ogurchin comes from Ogurjali (*i.e.*, pirates), a title bestowed long ago on the inhabitants of the coast and the islands of Balkan Bay on account of their piracies and their raids on the Persian provinces. All the Balkan Bay islands are known by this appellation to the Russians.— Strahl.

3. *The Bay of Balkan.*—So long ago as 1731 Soimonoff published a good and learned description of the Caspian Sea, together with a map, and did not omit this bay. In 1763 Professor Müller produced a fresh edition, his work is to be found in the Proceedings of the St. Petersburg Academy for 1762. In 1743 Captain Wudruff described the bay; in 1764 the eastern coasts of the Caspian were explored by Tokmatsheff; and in 1782 the bay was again carefully examined and described by Count Voinovitsh. Balkan Bay from its entrance to its innermost part is studded with islets, nearly all of the same area and elevation, some of them presenting the appearance of hillocks standing out of the water. At the entrance to the bay stands the Naphtha Island, to which the former islet of Dervish is now united, and to its south is situated the long island of Agurchin or Aidak. The former island of Darji, remarkable for its naphtha springs, and the so-called Naft Tapasi (Naphtha Hill) are both one with the land at the present day.

So shallow is the water behind Naphtha Island that only the smallest rowing-boats can venture into the middle of the bay, where there are a number of sand banks. There is generally a fine land breeze from the E. in the morning. Gales from N. E. fill the whole atmosphere with sand and dust, which sweep in clouds across the islands. The atmos-

phere in Balkan Bay is very dense, and on account of foul
vapours most unhealthy. The N. W. portion of the bay is
called Krasnavoda ("red water"), presumably on account of
the reddish sand shining at the bottom of the shallows and
on the surrounding mountains. The Turcomans called it
Kizilssa, also meaning red water. It affords a good
harbour for ships visiting the eastern shore of the Caspian,
for it is protected on all sides from the wind, and there
are excellent anchorages all over it. The only thing to
be careful of is the sand banks going in. The mountains
surrounding the harbour consist partly of the dark grey
granite characteristic of the rest of the Balkan range, and
partly of reddish coarse grained sand-stone. The country round about is a sandy desert, and neither trees nor
brushwood are to be seen on it. The little grass there is
is burnt up in summer, but nevertheless a number of nomadic
Turcomans (estimated by Voinovitsh at 2,000 families or
"Kibitks") inhabit this tract, and are often forced to drive
their flocks three or four days' journey into the steppe for
fodder. The necessaries of life they procure from Khiva or
from the Russian seal-hunters who sometimes visit them,
bringing flour, wooden vessels, and such like for traffic. In
later times many of these nomads have been driven away
by other tribes and have taken refuge in Khiva. In this
neighbourhood stood the redoubt which in the year 1716
Prince Bekovitsh caused to be erected during his disastrous
campaign against the Khivans, but very few traces remain at
the present day to mark its site. The Turcomans assured
Count Voinovitsh that both the other forts, one of which
stood on Alexandro Bay, the other on the Kargan promontory,
had been washed away and been covered by the sea, a proof
that the Caspian has encroached on its eastern margin since
the beginning of the 18th century.—STRAHL.

4. *The Balkan Mountains.*—This range, which embraces
the Balkan Bay, is of the same formation as the range round
Astrabad Bay which stretches away northwards along the
eastern coast in insignificant hills. It is a low range of
red sand-stone, here and there springing up into rocky
heights, the loftiest of which gives its name to the rest
of the chain. From a distance this mountain, the Balkan,
has the appearance of an abrupt promontory. Further
northward there are two other rocky heights not so lofty
as the Balkan, one the Kushama, the other the Bardshakla.
The rock composing these as well as all the smaller hills is

chiefly a kind of dark grey compact felspar or granite, called by the Turcomans " Karatash" (*ie..,* black stone). In the Balkan Mountain itself pure quartz-rock of various colours is found, and here the Turcomans quarry the ordinary millstone grit and carry it to the Khivan or Persian markets.

The whole coast is barren, producing nothing beyond reeds, a little bitter grass, and the golden rod (*Solidago Lin.*) ; but on the Balkan Mountain there is a better vegetation, a few trees (chiefly pomegranates) here and there, and where the soil is loamy and intermixed with good black earth, it is covered with rich and luxuriant grass. This fertility attracts wild animals to the mountain, and it is frequented by panthers, wild pig, wolves, foxes, wild goats *(Jairani)*, steinbocks, &c.

SECOND PART
Chapter I
Remarks on Khiva

Boundaries of the State of Khiva.—The limits of Khiva
admit of a two-fold definition ; that is to say, the name Khiva
may be considered as applying to the country occupied by
the Khivan race, intermingled to a certain extent with other
races which have settled down in their midst and accepted
the Khan's rule, in other words, Khiva Proper, or, from a
broader point of view, the name may comprise the whole of
that region the inhabitants of which are permanent or occasional dependants of the Khan's, either through conquest, or
through having sought his protection in time of need, or from
the requirements of their commercial situation.   Khiva Proper has no strongly marked natural boundaries, encompassed
as it is by vast unclaimed barren steppes.   It would, therefore, be easier to assign ethnographical rather than geographical limits to the State, by enumerating the various races
which surround it.   It lies in a bend formed by the river
Amu Dariya, and extends northwards on the left bank of
that river to the shores of the sea of Aral.   The Khanate is
therefore bounded to a certain extent on the north by the
sea of Aral, but it protrudes into the steppe lying to the east
of that sea, and which is inhabited by Kirgis nomads.

The Amu Dariya forms the north-east boundary of the
State, although the nomadic " Karakalpaks " (literally " black
caps ") on the right bank of the river acknowledge from time
to time the sovereignty of the Khan, as in their wanderings
they approach his frontier.

On the south-east a steppe separates Khiva from Bokhara, and on the south-west a vast sandy desert separates it
from the territory occupied by the Turcoman *Takka* tribe.

To the westward of Khiva an immense barren steppe
stretches right away to the Caspian Coast, a distance of
some 530 miles, and is bounded by the tracts inhabited by the
Yomud and Atta Turcomans.

Although the Khanate is thus surrounded by inhospitable wastes, it is nevertheless internally well supplied with water from numerous streams, which make the country wonderfully fruitful.

Khiva Proper measures about 120 miles from north to south, and 115 miles from east to west, but the Khanate, as before mentioned, has much wider limits if we reckon as part of the State the neighbouring countries which have become its dependencies, either through force of arms, political influence, or from the demands of a commercial situation. Under the first heading is to be classed the Takka tribe of the Turcomans, which has been subdued by the Khan, who, however, leaves the conquered country without a garrison.

The Atta tribe comes under the second category (*i.e.*, of those who, without succumbing to force, have nevertheless been induced, from motives of self-preservation, to acknowledge the Khan's sway). This tribe, it will be remembered, was expelled from the neighbourhood of the Balkan range by the Yomuds, and forthwith sought and obtained the protection of Khiva. Motives of commercial expediency have brought about the allegiance of the tribe Chobdur Essen Ili to the Khan of Khiva. This section of the Turcoman race dwells in the neighbourhood of Mangushlak, which is the mart of the Russo-Khiva trade, but the province is so remote from the Khan's capital, that the tie binding its inhabitants to the Government of Khiva is but a feeble and precarious one.

Ancient position of Khorassan.—The State of Khiva was in ancient days called Khorassan,* and had a different geographical position. It lay, namely, further to the westward along the banks of the Amu Dariya (a river known to the Greeks as the Oxus and Baktir, and to the Arabs as the Jaigun), which then flowed into the Caspian Sea. According to tradition the Amu Dariya (in its original course) formed the boundary between the great kingdoms of Iran and Turan, *i.e.*, between Persia of the present day, and the ancient Turkish fatherland.

Nature destroyed the frontier line which she had herself traced, and which separated countries and peoples from others of a totally different character and type, and it is apparent that since the migration of races brought westward so much fresh blood, the deserted regions have undergone tremendous changes. Frightful earthquakes have diverted rivers from their ancient courses, new basins have formed

---

* Chorasmia ?—W. S. A. L.

themselves, whilst whole kingdoms have disappeared, and once fruitful lands have been turned into barren steppes.

Seas and Lakes.—There is no important sheet of water in the whole of Khiva with the exception of the sea of Aral, which, moreover, lies only on the frontier of the State. This great lake is formed by the waters of the Amu Dariya and Sir Dariya. It contains fresh water, and, according to the dwellers on its banks, is very shallow; indeed, they say that a horseman could without difficulty pick his way across several of the friths of the two rivers by the help of the sedge which abounds in them.

Rivers.—The principal river in the Khanate is the Amu Dariya, which is a broad and deep stream. The natives say that a man on one side is hardly distinguishable to the eye from the opposite one, and that it is twice as broad as the human voice can reach, so that a conversation between people on opposite banks could only be carried on through the agency of a third person in the middle of the river. According to this, I believe, the breadth in Khiva to be about 600 feet. *

The Amu Dariya runs north and south through the whole length of the Khanate, and irrigates the remotest districts by means of artificial canals, carrying fertility to the most arid and barren steppes. The Sir Dariya was named the Jaxartes by the ancients. It does not run through the State, but the Kirgis nomads, who wander by its banks, are in some measure subject to the Khan. This river was once probably a tributary of the Amu Dariya, and like the latter has been turned from its original course by some convulsion of nature.

Ancient course of the Amu Dariya.—It appears from ancient history that the Oxus, when it flowed into the Caspian, formed the great commercial thoroughfare with India.

The obscurity which envelopes the history of Central Asia, particularly with regard to the period when two mighty realms perished, has also left us in doubt and uncertainty as to the stupendous volcanic activity which completely altered the configuration of a portion of the steppe in that region, and we are left to make our deductions from the awful traces to be seen to the present day. Among the latter preëminently stands the altered course of the Oxus, the ancient bed of which is still distinctly to be seen. Many, indeed, used to

---

* Yards?—W. S. A. L.

dispute the truth of this alleged deviation of the river, and were strengthened in their opinion by the results of Prince Bekovitsh's disastrous gold dust expedition in Peter the Great's time. Prince Bekovitsh, who was sent with an army to Khiva in 1716, built a redoubt on the promontory of Krasnavoda, and then, starting from the northern shore of Balkan Bay, advanced 80 miles in a due easterly direction, when, he asserted, he came to the mouth of the ancient river bed. He stated further that he had marched his men dry-shod up the bed for an hour and a half, when suddenly all traces of its course disappeared. Lieutenant Koschin, however, who served in the Prince's army, accused his Commander of treachery, and alleged that he had only brought forward the river question because he had no heart to measure his strength with the Khivans.

In the following year, 1717, Bekovitsh again set out with his force, intending to discover the dam, by means of which, it was rumoured, the Khivans turned off the Amu Dariya towards the north to protect themselves from the depredations of the Cossacks and of Stenka Rasin, who, it was declared, had ascended the river with his vessels and made inroads into their country. This expedition cost Bekovitsh his life, and further explorations in that region ceased. If Government had at that time the end in view of establishing the trade with India by turning the Amu Dariya back into its former bed, and thus conducting it to the Balkan Bay, we may take it for granted that they were acquainted with the size of the river. How then could the thought have been entertained that the rude Khivans were capable of damming up a stream of such volume, and overcoming the difficulties of the natural fall of the steppe, in order to lead the river northwards? The Khivans themselves laugh at the feat attributed to them, and their current tradition tells of a great earthquake that took place 530 years ago and brought about the change. My own researches make me conclude that the old bed of the Oxus commences where it is shown to do so in the annexed map, runs at first a short distance due west, then south-west, until it reaches a point due east of the Balkan Mountain, when it bends again to the westward and runs pretty straight in that direction until it separates into two branches, and thus falls into the Caspian, one branch dividing the Greater Balkan chain from the Lesser, while the other reaches the sea at the south-west horn of the bay.

I observed the traces of this bed on my journey from Krasnavoda to Khiva, *viz.*, at Besh Dishik, where it goes by the name of Uss Bai, is about 400 yards in breadth and 60 in depth. It is easily to be distinguished by reason of the deep track it makes through the level steppe, and its nearly perpendicular banks, which have here and there fallen in, and thereby facilitated the means of reaching the bottom. Its soil is very different from that of the steppe, producing plants and trees, and having fresh water springs. Rushes thrive in abundance, and among them it is usual for the Khiva bound caravans to bivouac.

The predatory Turcomans also use their friendly cover when lying in ambush to fall on a weaker caravan, sometimes going off with their booty southwards, keeping to the dry river bed.

In my return journey from Khiva to Krasnavoda when I took the south road, I again struck the river bed, and at a point nearer the sea than Besh Dishik. At the point referred to it goes by the name of Angiunj.

The banks and bottom of the Angiunj completely resemble those of the Uss Bai, but in the former the effect of the vegetation is more striking owing to the perfect baldness of the steppe on either side. The banks of the Angiunj are somewhat less lofty than those of the Uss Bai. A little further to the south the Angiunj takes a short bend eastwards, and then returning pursues its westward course to the sea. At this last bend the right bank recedes from the precipitous left one, and, gently sloping, blends with the steppe. To complete the evidence as to the river having once flowed in this bed, I may add the following :—The Khivans, as well as the Turcoman inhabitants of the Caspian shores, are unanimous in declaring that in ancient days a vast stream flowed here which fell into the Caspian ; that its name was not then Uss Bai or Angiunj, but *Ami Dariya*, and that it was identical with the river which now waters Central Asia and falls into the sea of Aral. They say further that the dwellings of their ancestors stood on the banks of this vanished stream, a statement which is borne out by the yet visible traces of canals and ruins of buildings. A Turcoman tradition has it that the mouth of the river used to be farmed out by the Ruler of the country and a great revenue derived from it. This mouth is here and there quite choked with sand, but scattered mulberry trees mark the banks, a tree nowhere else to be found in the neighbourhood of the Balkan, and whose presence here we may attribute to the water having carried down the seed from Khiva or Bokhara.

Canals.—Khiva is rich in canals. They lead the water from the Amu Dariya and spread prosperity and fertility all over the land.

The chief canal is the "Gyuiktam On," which flows by a village of the same name, past the upper part of the city of Khiva, and makes the chord of the arc here formed by the Amu Dariya. From the 'Gyuiktam On" three other large canals branch off to the north-west, *viz.,* the Buz Hioman in the south, then to the north of the Buz Hioman the Ak Serai, and to the north of that the Dash Haos.

There are two other canals, one, the most southerly, the Khisarist, which is fed direct by the Amu Dariya, and another, the most northern, the Arna Canal. These canals are laid out with great skill and feed many lesser ones, and thus irrigate the whole country.

At certain places they form artificial lakes which serve the inhabitants as reservoirs against times of drought. The main canals are 20 yards broad, and their water is occasionally kept at a high level by means of dams. Here and there a canal is conducted across another one by an aqueduct. The wells throughout the country contain bad water, which is consequently seldom used.

To my thinking, what I am now going to point out is worthy of particular attention. When I had accomplished two-thirds of the distance between Krasnavoda and Khiva, I perceived, not far from the old Oxus bed, a steep declivity falling about 80 yards down from the steppe above.

This wall of rock is uniform in height throughout, has a yellowish tinge, and the fragments of stone that detach themselves from it are brittle and triturable, and contain a quantity of marine fossils. The natives here believe that this was once the sea coast, and appearances certainly support their belief, but if they are right, the wall can only have been the margin of a bay in the Caspian, which disappeared long before the period when the Amu Dariya fell into Balkan Bay. The supposed sea coast is everywhere equally precipitous, and at the Besh Dishik well (in the old Amu Dariya bed), which is close to it, one loses it in the far distance both towards the east and the west. The shore corresponding to the one just described is met with two days' journey from Besh Dishik in the Khiva direction, on the right hand side of the road, and the Utin Kila ruins stand near (see map). It would therefore appear that the road passes up an inlet of the ancient sea, whose coast line it would be no uninteresting study to trace through all its bends. A traveller by the south road from Khiva to Krasnavoda does not touch this coast line, but it runs parallel with his road at a distance of three or four hours' ride for some days before he reaches Angiunj, as the map will show. The precipitous rock line is seen from the south road to be crowned, in places, with towers.

Steppes.—The steppes which encompass the State of Khiva are for the most part sandy deserts, perfectly barren. Only at rare intervals is a symptom of verdure to be seen, and the most prevalent plant is the so-called " Golden-rod," *(Solidago Lin)* which bears scarcely any leaves, but is useful to make charcoal of. Charcoal burners find plenty of fuel to their hand in the old dry logs continually to be met with. Here and there even the traces of forests remain, the decayed trunks and black soil testifying to the great revolutions which have passed over the land in days gone by. Caravans and robber gangs depend for their fuel entirely on those old *débris*. It is vain to look for fresh water in the steppe. The springs are all more or less brackish, with the exception of those in the old bed of the Oxus. A journey in summer through these sandy wastes is attended with no small degree of danger and hardships, for dust storms are of frequent occurrence, which turn the brightest day into darkness for the hapless traveller. In spots, where there is no sand, the ground is firm, dry, and of a whitish grey colour.

The unextensive but well-watered state of Khiva may be regarded as an oasis, a rich and fertile island in the midst of a vast expanse of dead nature. There are other spots in the steppe presenting a similar fertility and cultivation, among which the country inhabited by the Turcoman tribe of Takka may be reckoned, a tract lying to the south of Khiva. The natives say that the further one goes to the east, the more populous and better cultivated the country will be found, and that caravans going by the eastern route are never more than two days without water.

Although I discovered no forests in Khiva, I am nevertheless inclined to think that some important ones must exist in the northern portion of the country, on the Kirgis frontier, for the Kirgis are well supplied with timber, and go up the Amu Dariya into Bokhara on rafts of their own construction.

Mountains.—Khiva and its surrounding steppes form, south-west from the Amu Dariya, a great plain interrupted only by the unimportant chain of Sare Baba, and the long rocky line of the supposed ancient sea coast before mentioned. To the east of the Amu Dariya lies the Sheikh Jeri range, which stretches away to the north of Khiva along the sea of Aral; and to the west of the same river and north of the Sheikh Jeri stand the Kuba Mountains, apparently an isolated range, but most probably connected with the Mangushlak chain.

Metals.—It is difficult for any foreigner to obtain information respecting the produce of the mines of Khiva, and the difficulty increases in the case of a Russian, owing to Peter the Great's attempt to discover gold dust in this country, the memory of which still lives with the people. They fear a renewal of an expedition which would combine the original object with that of wreaking vengeance on the descendants of the murderers of Prince Bekovitsh (known in Khiva as Dowlat Harai). It nevertheless came to my ears that the Sheikh Jeri Mountains are well known to contain rich veins of gold and silver, a very little copper, and a large amount of lead and sulphur. The people work only for lead and copper, and show little acquaintance with the mining art. The idea should be dispelled, which I find is freely entertained, with respect to gold dust being brought down in quantities by the Amu Dariya. The Khivans themselves deny the fact, and the absurdity of the idea is shown by the circumstance that this money-loving people are entirely dependant for their gold on Russia and neighbouring States, whereas, were there really gold dust in the country, they would long ago have profited by it, seeing that the operation of washing for gold is one demanding no great skill and few preparations. Another current belief is that gold dust abounds in the neighbourhood of the Amu Dariya beyond Bokhara. This probably also is only a groundless report.

Beasts.—The following animals are to be found in the Khivan steppes, *viz.*, wolves, foxes, jackals, and rats. Of the last named there are several species, and the most remarkable one is that called by the Khivans " Elingirj." This rat is as large as a large tom-cat, has short fore-legs, and a spotted skin, yellow, marked with black. They all live in the sand. Jackals abound, and their howls at night terrify travellers unaccustomed to the sound. There are also many deer and wild goats (Jairan).

The Natives state that these animals can exist for two months without touching water, but I imagine that when no other means of satisfying their thirst remains, they keep themselves alive by licking up the dew which falls so plentifully here. The same kind of story is told of the Turcoman sheep, *viz.*, that on their way to the Khiva market they go for days without water. I have not heard for certain that beavers and others are to be found in the Amu Dariya, but do not doubt that such is the case.

Birds.—The most noteworthy of the birds of prey are the great eagle and some kinds of hawks. The Khivans prize the latter very highly, and train them to capture birds and wild goats. Ravens are very numerous. They attach themselves to caravans and clear the bivouac grounds of all *débris* directly the party has started on the march, then overtaking it they hover about in expectation of a fresh halt. Among the artificial lakes in the neighbourhood of canals there are plenty of snipe (called " Kish Kaldaka "), which have an excellent flavour and afford a very favourite sport to the Khan and his highest officials.

Fish.—There are carps in the canals and fish of different kinds in the Amu Dariya.

Roads.—Made roads are unknown in the State ; foot prints and cart-tracks, which the wind frequently obliterates, are the only signs to indicate the way. Where there are no dwelling-places for land marks, the sun is the traveller's only guide, wells mark the halting grounds, and when such are missed, the caravan halts and bivouacs when the sun goes down.

It is noteworthy that the children of the desert, the natives of the steppes, never lose their way, although they may have absolutely no signs to guide them. Camels also have this gift, and many instances are known of those animals straying off the road at a distance of from 300 to 400 miles from home, and returning safely by themselves.

Climate.—Khiva, from its limited area, has pretty much the same climate in every portion of the country. In summer the heat is for several months quite intolerable, but strong winds from the east, south-east, and other quarters cool the burning atmosphere frequently. It seldom rains, even in autumn, but at that season continual gales blow off the steppes and fill the air with impalpable dust, darkening the face of the land like a dense black fog, whilst the appearance of the desert completely changes in a few hours, new sand hills rearing themselves in every direction, and old ones vanishing. Winter is never of long duration, and the cold is pretty moderate, still the thermometer falls at times to from 16° to 18° below zero, and then the weather is very trying, especially if the lowness of the temperature be aggravated by a piercing and persistent east wind. There is seldom any snow, but black frosts are continual, and those operate most unfavourably on the caravans, either keeping them back altogether, or if they have started before the frost has set in, committing ravages among the camels on the road. The latter are unable to make their way over frozen ground, owing to the formation of their feet, and should frost overtake a caravan, *en route*, many animals succumb and have to be left to die in the wilderness. Nearly all the year round the sky is serene and cloudless, which I ascribe to the flat surface of so vast an area of steppe, &c., offering nothing to attract the clouds to it. The clearness of the atmosphere makes every object look unusually bright, and charms the stranger, until his eye falls on the human beings of this shining region, and he is forced to think of their detestable character. The pest never shows itself in Khiva. The air is healthy, and both foreigners and natives thrive in it. Free indulgence in fruit, looked on as hurtful in all other countries, is here considered conducive to health.

Races.—Khiva is inhabited by four different races, *viz.*—

I.—The Sarts, who are the aboriginal inhabitants of the country.

II.—The Karakalpaks, nomads, who wander in the neighbourhood of the Sarts, and are greatly under their influence.

III.—The Usbegs, foreigners who have conquered and possessed themselves of the country.

IV.—The Turcomans, who are divided into many tribes, and have been tempted by motives of profit (commercial and other) to settle or live a nomadic life in the State.

The relation of the four races to one another used at first to be as follows:—I., Noble; II., Servant; III., Conqueror; IV., Guest. By-and-by, however, as the nation grew more closely welded together and became one great whole, the old distinctions disappeared and the classification became as follows:—I., Merchant; II., Agriculturist; III., Noble; IV., Warrior.

The Sarts.—The Sarts or Tatas, aboriginal inhabitants of the land, dwell in the towns, and chiefly employ themselves in trade. Their character is deceitful, cunning, and truckling.

They are most abject, and capable of any self-abasement in times of distress or when they can gain anything by that means, but proud and domineering in prosperous days. They are for the most part wealthy and well-to-do, owing their riches to trade or to cheating.

They are cowards, have no acquaintance either with arms or horses, never keep a promise, and are invariably false to their engagements. Their disposition is malignant, and their own interest is the only thing they give a thought to. In the foreign countries to which their commercial business sometimes brings them, they readily yield to every excess, gambling and drinking to an unheard-of extent. The Usbegs despise them for their mode of life, saying "we live by our arms and our courage, but they by their yard measures and their cheating." Their number is reckoned at 100,000 families, but it is probably higher than that.

The Karakalpaks.—The Karakalpaks partly lead a nomadic life on the other side of the Amu Dariya, partly cultivate land to the south of the sea of Aral. The warlike Usbegs and crafty Sarts exercise a powerful influence over them.

They are fond of agriculture, do not engage in trade, and live in poverty and distress. They number something over 100,000 families.

The Usbegs.—The Usbegs, who wrested the country from the Sarts, came from the country beyond Bokhara, where a great portion of their race dwells to the present day. " Us " in Turkish signifies " self " and " Beg " master, so Usbeg may be translated as " Own Master." The name was appropriate enough up to the time of the reigning Khan, Mahomed Ragim, who, by ability, craft, and force, established himself as uncontrolled Ruler, since when his countrymen in Khiva style themselves " Khidmatgar " (servant) instead of " Usbeg." They may number about 30,000 families, and are divided into four different tribes. They generally dwell in the towns, filling the highest offices of State. To them belong the little strongholds to be seen scattered throughout the Khanate, and theirs also is the land, which they rent to the landless Turcomans and Sarts to till for them. The Usbegs are proud of their name as conquerors, but for 200 years they have been resting on their laurels, and since the conquest of the Sarts have become so effeminate as to be incapable of carrying out any great enterprise, or one demanding endurance. Idleness is their God, repose their highest bliss, nevertheless, in spite of this propensity, they frequently go out on plundering excursions, and then they are indefatigable, the profession of a robber being in their eyes a most honourable one.

They consider the extirpation of unbelievers to be a duty they owe both to themselves and their religion. They fall upon caravans on the high roads, but never dispute among themselves in the division of booty. They never pay for a night's lodging, and if they do not consider their host sufficiently hospitable, do not hesitate to carry off all his property by force. Revenge is their ruling passion, and feuds are considered hereditary, generally ending in the extermination of the weaker clan when a reconciliation has not been brought about. In their revenge they consider all means admissible to obtain their end; therefore assassination and open attack are equally legitimate in their eyes. On the whole, they possess much warlike spirit, but they are best qualified for short expeditions. They delight in hearing tales of war, and revere stubborn endurance, whence they are frequently prompted to give a slave his freedom, who has steadfastly undergone his punishment of torture. They surpass all the other races in Khiva in magnanimity and honesty, hating a lie and every meanness, and the lust for money or place. "We are simple people," say they, "our business is only with our crooked simitars, but life is pleasent under us, if folks will only follow our trade, and be honest." War alone they esteem an honourable calling, every other mode of gaining a livelihood mean and despicable; hence their hatred for both Sarts and Karakalpaks.

The Turcomans.—Under many different names the Turcomans populate the vast tracts of Central Asia. We find them north of India and Thibet, west of Khiva, in the vicinity of Bokhara, as well as in the country by the Caspian. All those scattered tribes have a common origin, but the tie which once bound the numerous family together has now been snapped owing to several causes, such as the sandy deserts which separate the several cultivated settlements, the patriarchal system with its segregation of tribes, each under its own elder or Chieftain, and the immense distance intervening between the remoter sections of the race. This people has been most incorrectly denominated the Tartar race by several European authors. The term was probably borrowed from Tatar, the Chief who founded the tribe of that name, existing in the remoter steppes to the present day. The fertility of

Khiva and the profitable trade to be driven in kidnapped slaves enticed Turcomans from every side, and belonging to the most diverse tribes, to settle here, and they are acknowledged as a distinct order in the State. At first they were treated as temporary sojourners, but gradually became permanent settlers, and now form the soldier-class from which the Khan's war army is drawn. Their innate predatory tastes well qualify them for this distinction. Among the settlers the Yomud tribe of Bairam Shah is the most largely represented, who formerly inhabited the country by the Caspian, but have now settled round the Arna Canal. In outward appearance the Turcomans much more nearly resemble the Usbegs than they do the Sarts, but they are far superior to all in fight, in warlike stratagems, and in horsemanship. They love gold, are cruel and treacherous, and the main features in their character are plundering and thievish instincts and dishonesty. They are much more apt for warlike enterprises than the Usbegs, and, although they do not possess the virtues of the latter, they have all their vices and passions intensified by their own vile nature.

The number of the Turcoman warriors and freebooters is always fluctuating, for their wish is to be regarded as merely temporary residents, encamping in the Khanate to-day and leaving it to-morrow. Many of them have squatted in the desert between the tracts of cultivation, suffering the severest hardship from want of water, designedly selecting such sites so as to escape having to work in the fields. Of actually domiciliated Turcomans there may be about 50,000 families, who engage largely in agriculture and dwell in villages.

Slaves.—To the above enumerated four classes, or orders of the State of Khiva, we must add a fifth, *viz.*, the foreign slaves, whose numbers are very considerable. For them no laws exist; their lives are in the hands of their masters, and their lot is the saddest in the whole world. The slaves are by birth either Russians, Persians, or Kurds. The Russians are reckoned at 3,000. They are generally kidnapped by the Kirgis on the Orenburg frontier and brought to Khiva. The Persians are ten times as numerous as the Russians, and there are said to be 30,000 of them. The Kurds also muster very strong, and both of these classes of slaves are supplied by the Turcomans. Persian slaves frequently regain their freedom, and then some of them become wealthy, and receive posts of emoluments. Such persons are called by the Usbegs " Kisil Janow," *i.e.*, " Gold snaffles."

Jews.—There have always been Jews in Khiva, but it is remarkable that they profess the Mahomedan religion. Members of no other nations are to be met with here, as foreigners avoid a country where plunder, tumult, and violence reign supreme.

Since the commencement of the present reign, a much greater equality has prevailed among the four component races of the Khanate (who are all members of the Suni sect), and although, as a rule, a man adheres to the peculiar calling of his order, he is all the same at liberty to abandon it for that of another. One therefore occasionally sees a Sart filling a Government appointment, a Turcoman farming, a Karakalpak turned robber, and an Usbeg engaged in trade. Mahomed Ragim introduced this system, so as to give equality to the orders and to put a stop to the quarrels arising from the superior privileges enjoyed by some over the rest.

Population.—If we count the inhabitants of all the territories directly subject to the Khan, we may assume an aggregate of over 3,000,000 souls ; but this calculation must not on any account be accepted as absolutely accurate, for it is based only on the results of my own enquiries and suppositions. The Khan himself has no knowledge of the extent of population in his dominions, and it was difficult for a foreigner to extract information from a suspicious people, loth to speak on this topic. This much is, however, certain, that the population is always on the increase, owing both to the fresh conquests of the Khan, and the increasing immigration of Turcomans, attracted by grants of land and sites by canals.

Towns.—There are only five important towns in the Khanate : these are :—

I. Khiva.—Here the Khan resides. The Natives declare that the ancient name of this town was Khivak, and that it was in existence before the Amu Dariya changed its course. It is of considerable dimensions, is surrounded by a wall, the east face of which abuts on the Gyuiktam canal, and the north on the Dash Haos. The principal buildings are the great mosque, with its dome of turquoise-blue (a colour revered by Mussulmans) ; the Khan's palace, which is, however, an insignificant structure, and several smaller mosques. Mud is the material in general use for building purposes. The streets are narrow. Here and there stalls are set up, but there is a regular market two days in the week. The town is said to contain 3,000 houses and 10,000 inhabitants. Like all other towns in the Khanate, Khiva is surrounded by a broad belt of gardens, among which stand many castles and villas.

II. New Urganj.—The proper capital of the country. This is the Khan's Deputy's permanent place of residence (Kutli Murad Inakh, brother to the Khan, is the present Deputy); it is a much larger town than Khiva, and is the centre of the whole trade of the Khanate.

The inhabitants are chiefly Sarts. In the shops and booths are sold all the costliest wares of oriental luxury, market is also held here twice a week, and crowds come in to attend it. This is the depôt from which goods are exported to foreign countries, or to the other market towns in the State. Malte Brun fixes the houses and inhabitants of new Urganj at 1,500 and 5,000 respectively, but this estimate must be far below the mark, as the town is more populous than Khiva. Like Khiva, it also is surrounded by a wall.

III. Shevat.—A small town of 2,000 inhabitants.

IV. Kett.—A still smaller town than the above. 1,500 inhabitants. Both Shevat and Kett are walled, and both engage principally in trade with the Kirgis.

V. Giyurlan.—Here dwell many of the rich traders. The buildings in all the above towns are very mean (the only ones approaching to anything like size being a few mosques), and mud is the almost universal material of the houses, as it may also be said to be that of the town walls, * which are only faced with stone at intervals. In spite of this perishable material, the buildings stand for many years, owing to the very scanty rain fall. The Khanate is not divided into provinces, neither have the towns their particular districts allotted.

Besides the five towns enumerated, there are also some villages which are not surpassed by the towns in commercial importance. To the latter belong Khisarist on the Bokhara high road, and some villages in the neighbourhood of the Khan's country seats, which are all walled. Among the most important are Kipjak-Konrad, Ak-Sarai, Khan-Kalassi, Mai-Jegil, &c., &c.

In some of those villages markets are held on certain fixed holidays, when the merchants from the five towns

---

* The town walls are about 36 feet thick at the base, and 48 feet high. They are protected here and there by a half " contre force," and towers occur at certain intervals.

attend, and supply the hamlets and Yurts with the goods they require. Besides the walled residences of the Khan's there are many other single castles and mansions round which villages have also collected.

Ruins.—New Urganj does not occupy the same site as Old Urganj. According to the inhabitants the ruins of the latter are still to be seen. The whole steppe stretching away to the west of the Khiva is thickly covered with the *débris* of buildings, with brick fragments, stone vessels, &c., and occasionally gold coins are picked up. This would seem conclusive evidence that in former days cities flourished on the banks of the Old Amu Dariya. The most prominent ruins existing at the present day are Daudan Kila, Kazil Kila, Shah Sanam, Utin Kila, &c. The further one leaves the towns behind, the more scattered and badly constructed are the dwelling places, and the more uncouth the people.

Chapter II

Internal Disturbances. Change of Constitution.
Establishment of Despotism. Character of Ruler.
Present Form of Government in Khiva

As Khiva within a short space of time underwent many political changes owing to the repeated endeavours of ambitious Chiefs to establish themselves as absolute Sovereigns, I find it expedient, before proceeding to a description of the existing state of affairs in that country, to give first a *résumé* of the various attempts of those Chiefs, and then to point out the helplessness of the people, which, having given private interests the preference over public ones, now languishes under the iron sceptre of the cruel tyrant, Mahomed Ragim. An account of the internal agitations of the country, of the several attempts to introduce despotic rule, and, finally, a sketch of the reigning despot's personal character, will aid the reader in forming an opinion as to the present condition of the Khanate.

The Usbegs, who conquered the land of the Sarts, and took the name of Khivans from the great town in that country, came originally from beyond Bokhara, and are divided into four tribes, *viz.*, the Kiat Konrad, Wigar Naiman, Kanglu Kipjak, and Niogus Mangud.

Each of these tribes was governed by its own elder or Chieftain, who bore the title of Inakh, but the Chief of the Kiat Konrads enjoyed a preëminence and certain privileges over the others, partly owing to the antiquity, partly to the superior numbers of that clan. This had for long been the form of Government obtaining with the Usbegs. The neighbouring powerful and enlightened State of Bokhara meanwhile exercised a weighty influence over those freedom-loving warriors, and the Khan of the not distant Kirgis hordes, taking advantage of their weakness and their internal dissensions, sent his Deputy to Khiva. Diversity of race now gave rise to endless quarrels, outbreaks, and lawlessness among the Khivans. The feudal system prevailed, and the feudal lords, each proud of the independence he had won, and being himself a despot engrossed only in his own interests, did not trouble themselves about the common welfare. The idea of legislation, and of a firmly established form of Government, was never entertained, as no one wished to be shorn of any of his undefined powers and privileges. Violence, robbery, and murder were therefore the order of the day.

Ambitious Chiefs assembled their bands and tried for supremacy over the rest, not hesitating to appeal for assistance to the Rulers of neighbouring States, who willingly joined in the strife, in order eventually to establish their own deputies at the capital. The latter, however, had a most precarious tenure of office, and it was not uncommon for the Kirgis deputies to be expelled time after time in rapid succession : no sooner in than out again. For several centuries was this unhappy country torn by civil wars, which killed trade and undid the results of all the Sarts' labours for the improvement of their land.

In Prince Bekovitsh's time, 1717, Inakh Ishmad Bi, of the Klat Konrad tribe, ruled in Khiva. He was succeeded by his son Mahomed Amin Inakh, who again was succeeded by his son Awas Inakh, father to the present Khan.

During the three reigns above mentioned no events of any great importance occurred. Ahltasar, the eldest son of Awas Inakh, became Inakh on the death of his father. He was a man of warlike spirit and great ambition, and not to be satisfied with the insignificant province of his ancestors. He sought to be the uncontrolled Ruler of the nation, and to that end made use of every intrigue and every cruelty imaginable. Backed by his troops of adherents, he overturned the former order of things, brought all the other tribes under his sway, imposed heavy restrictions on them, and made himself the first Khan, or sole master over the whole of Khiva. Ahltasar inaugurated his new career by an infringement of the law of Mahomed, which prohibits the union of a " Said " woman (*i.e.*, one descended from the Prophet) with a man not descended from Mahomed's tribe. He married a woman of the sacred race, and the Usbegs saw with pain how their holy religion was being contemned, not daring, however, to show outward signs of disapprobation from dread of the Khan's terrible power.

When Ahltasar had by this step raised himself above the laws of the Prophet, so cherished by all Mussulmans, he felt he had shaken off the last trammels on his actions, and perceiving the muteness of his subjects under such circumstances, his boldness and his might increased, whilst the people groaned under his dreadful yoke. His next step was to throw off the control hitherto exercised by Bokhara over his nation, as the moral influence of that country was galling to him and dangerous to his supremacy in proportion to its weight with the people of Khiva.

A great number of Usbegs have settled in Bokhara and became subjects of the Governor, and these are bound by the closest ties of blood and friendship to their Khivan fellow-countrymen. They originally took refuge in Bokhara to escape oppression in their adopted country, and the Rulers of Bokhara gained thereby a pretext for interfering in the internal quarrels of Khiva. This produced a feeling that Bokhara was the superior of the two nations, and the feeling was heightened by the rigorous manner in which the Bokharian authorities punished marauders on the mutual frontier. Ahltasar accordingly considered a brilliant victory over his neighbour to be the only means of destroying that moral ascendancy which was the last impediment to his undisputed rule. He therefore assembled a powerful army, and intentended to invade Bokhara suddenly and without warning. However, he was drowned when crossing his force over the Amu Dariya, and his project came to nought. The people attributed the Khan's death to the hand of an offended Deity, as a punishment for his defiance of the laws of religion and his disregard for the customs of his subjects. The event caused universal joy, and the Khivans hoped that the old *régime* would now be restored, the elders reinstated to authority over their respective tribes, and their independence recognized. They were encouraged in this dream by the quiet and unambitious character of Kutli Murad, the deceased's successor. Kutli Murad Inakh did, in fact, adopt the system of Government of his ancestors, not from any consideration for the welfare of his people, but from cowardice, dreading an insurrection of the Usbegs. He therefore contented himself with the title of Inakh, and the Khivans abandoned themselves once more to their feuds. This was not to last : a storm cloud was gathering over their heads, which soon burst with terrible fury. Two near relatives of the new Inakh, and the nearest in succession to his office, stirred up a civil war and strove for the upperhand over one another. These were the Inakh's cousin, Mahomed Niyaz Beg, and his own brother, the present Khan, Mahomed Ragim, both of them crafty, ambitious, and cruel men. Kutli Murad took no part in the strife raging between his ambitious relatives, perhaps from a desire not to add to the number of innocent victims, but most likely in order the better to ensure his own safety. The dreadful bloodshed lasted for long, every method of execution being practised, and incredible cruelties perpetrated, but neither side appeared to gain any advantage over the other. A false peace was therefore concluded, and both cousins had recourse to cunning and treachery. Mahomed Ragim profited by this cessation of hostilities to strengthen his force, simulating the while good-will towards his cousin, who was imprudently striving to win ascendancy in spite of the Treaty. At length Mahomed Ragim's rival fell into his hands by a treacherous stratagem, and his captor showed no mercy, causing him to be put to death in his own presence, and massacring all his most eminent adherents and his relations, together with their wives and children.

Thus, after putting his chief rival out of the way, did Mahomed Ragim become the most powerful man in the country, and he declared himself Khan of Khiva in the year 1802.

Striking awe into the hearts of all by the number of his executions, the new Khan speedily reduced the Usbegs and other Khivans to submission ; and in order to keep them in subjection and at the same time gratify his own tigerish ferocity, he stained his hands daily with the blood of fresh victims. Those of his own relations who fell into his hands were, with the exception of two persons, put to the sword. Eleven of his kinsmen thus perished, all either his brothers or cousins. Kutli Murad was one of the two whose lives he spared for having stood aloof during the struggle, and he permitted him to retain the title of Inakh, and made him Governor of Urganj. Inakhs were also selected for the three other tribes from among the Chiefs who had not taken up arms against the Khan and had acknowledged his supreme authority. A period of false tranquillity succeeded the sanguinary contest, but the blood of suspected persons still continued to flow, and freedom departed from the land where so recently the term " slave " had been applied only to foreign captives.

Mahomed Ragim surpassed Khan Ahltasar in ferocity and cruelty, and as if to show that he too was free from the restraints of divine law, he took his predecessor's (" Said ") widow to wife, and soon after married two other women of the same race.

During the reign of terror which followed his assumption of the Khanship, two of his brothers, Turri Murad and Khwaja Murad, had effected their escape, with a small band of malcontents, into the Karakalpak country on the coast of the sea of Aral, and there built a fortress. The neighbouring tribes allied themselves with the brothers, and the Khan's enemies were increasing in numbers. Mahomed Ragim, beside himself with rage, marched against them, but sustained a defeat and had to retire ignominiously to Khiva, where his presence and a series of executions soon crushed the revolt which had taken place among his subjects.

Turri Murad and Khwaja Murad did not follow up their victory. Discord, which had proved of such service hitherto to their bloodthirsty enemy, now separated the brothers, and Khwaja Murad sent messengers to Mahomed Ragim begging for forgiveness and favour.

The Khan pretended to be pacified, granted the pardon, and invited Khwaja Murad to Court, but about a month after he had his unsuspecting victim assassinated whilst sitting at table.

A similar fate awaited Turri Murad. Mahomed Ragim knowing his inability to overcome the latter in the field, had again recourse to craft. He corrupted one of his brother's servants, who soon carried out the Khan's wishes, by murdering his master during a hunting expedition. Turri Murad's death caused the disbandment of his followers, but Mahomed Ragim required more blood; he seized the wives, children, and other connections of his two unfortunate brothers, and had them put to death in his presence with frightful tortures, whilst he taunted them in the vilest terms during their agonies.

Among other atrocities he caused the pregnant women to be ripped open, and the embryoes torn from their wombs.

Although these abominable and nearly incredible barbarities enraged the whole nation, they were allowed to pass without remonstrance, for no one dared to raise a hand against the monster. The Khivans were mute in their terror, indifferent to the calamities of the unfortunate, each hugging himself in his own precarious immunity. Thus the Khan's power waxed greater, the people by their cowardice contributing to their own ruin, although a few, less submissive, but not less spiritless than the rest, sought safety in Bokhara.

At length after a long course of continual slaughter the number of executions began to decrease, not because the Khan's appetite for blood was appeased, that was as keen as ever, but because victims were becoming scarce. All those who were capable of withstanding his authority had now disappeared, having either lost their lives or fled the country, and his subjects were crushed and subdued.

Finding himself completely master of the Khanate, he next turned his attention to its interior economy, and sought to make himself respected by neighbouring States.

He accordingly abolished anarchy, appointed a Council of State, prohibited theft and robbery, increased the revenue by strict taxation, and established tolls and customs.

He instituted a mint, and was the first introducer of gold and silver coinage, besides founding many other useful institutions. In a word, after spilling rivers of blood and sacrificing many thousands of innocent lives, the Khan, for his own security, power, and renown, created an entirely new nation, so to speak, out of the original elements of the State, a nation which must now be counted as one of the most powerful of Asia.

Formerly the Khans of the Kirgis Kaisacks, availing themselves of the weakness of Khiva, used to exercise a powerful influence over it; to such an extent, indeed, that it had become an established custom for one of the horde to be sent at times to the Khivans, with full powers, whom in proof of their subjugation, the latter proclaimed their Khan; the Kirgis plenipotentiary used then to be feasted, presented with robes of honor, and at last dismissed with the greatest marks of respect.

The mock Khan, however, lost his lofty title as soon as he crossed the frontier, and went back to his own people in his original position.

This extraordinary custom bore evidence to the weakness of the Khivans and to their servile dependence on the Kirgis Kaisacks. The extent of this dependence used to be greater or less according to circumstances, but Mahomed Ragim put an end to it at once, and not only that, but he raised his country to such a height of power by the success of his arms, that Sherghazi Khan, the Kirgis Ruler, pays him. tribute at the present day, and has to yield to Khiva one in every hundred head of the numerous Kirgis flocks and herds.

The Kirgis have to bring the tribute every year to Khiva, and this humiliation affords the Khan a much higher gratification than the actual gain that accrues to him.

Besides the tribute deputation, many Kirgis Envoys are sent every year with gifts to Mahomed Ragim, indeed,

Sherghazi Khan (to whom the Khan of Khiva is now related by marriage) occasionally brings them in person.* Mahomed Ragim inflicts rigorous punishments on any Kirgis caught marauding in his territories beyond the Sir Dariya.

The state of dependence in which Khiva stood in relation to Bokhara was very galling to the Khan, and he attempted to free himself from it by force of arms, but fortune did not favour him, and his army was routed. Among many other prisoners who fell into the hands of the victors was Kutli Murad, and in order to redeem him the Khan acknowledged the Bokharan claim of superiority, pledging himself, under certain circumstances, to conform to the orders of Mir Hyder, the Ruler.

But after his brother returned from captivity the Khan never exactly fulfilled the conditions agreed upon, and if he still acknowledges a slight authority on the part of Bokhara over his Khanate, it is merely on grounds of policy. For the present he conceals his plans and awaits a favourable opportunity, and, in order to hide his weakness from the people, he has spread it about among them that a war between Khiva and Bokhara is not permissible, owing to the Rulers and subjects of the two nations professing the same religion. In order to strengthen belief in his imaginary scruples he has commanded the priesthood to exert themselves in preserving a friendly feeling between the States. The priests are elated at their important commission, and believe themselves to have weight with the Khan, who gladly allows them to cherish the illusion, and only consults the Chief Priest or Cazi on the subject, invariably punishing any Khivan caught plundering on the frontier of Bokhara.

With all this, however, Mahomed Ragim no longer pays the tribute which up to his time was rendered by Khiva to Bokhara, and was so oppressive to his subjects. For this he has not to thank the power of his arms, but rather the peace-loving character of Mir Hyder, whose sole aim is to keep his people in tranquillity and obedience, shunning aggression, and only taking up arms to chastise the freebooters who from time to time venture into his territory. He is therefore content with the moral influence he possesses over a nation which he regards as a band of robbers, kept in check solely by the awe in which they stand of their ambitious Khan.

---

* When I was in Khiva in 1819 I found Sherghazi Khan there, and he died during my stay. Mahomed Ragim nominated a successor from among the sons of the deceased, and the Kirgis had to accept the nomination as indisputable.

Mir Hyder may be set up as the model of a good Governor, for he prefers the fame of a legislator to that of a conqueror. His sole thought is for the welfare of his subjects, and his sole desire, the proper regulation of the affairs of the nation and the administration of justice, hence his surname of " Adal," or the just.

In spite of the miscarriage of his expedition against Bokhara, Mahomed Ragim armed once more, partly to give his subjects something to do, partly in the hope of a rich booty, and threatened the Persian province of Khorassan, trusting to rouse its warlike inhabitants to revolt against the Persians whose yoke they disliked.

He accordingly marched into the steppe with 12,000 followers and his whole artillery (7 guns of different calibres). A great portion of his force was attached to the caravans with the baggage, or as servants to the different officers. The army passed through the districts occupied by the powerful Turcoman tribes, Takka and Kaklan, and Mahomed Ragim, relying on their friendship, asked them to make common cause with him against the Persians. To this they would not agree, and moved out of the Khan's way.

The latter concealed his resentment, but meditated vengeance. He next sent messengers with the same proposals to all the Yomud tribes on the eastern coast of the Caspian from Astrabad Bay to the Balkan, and further into the steppe to those dwelling on the banks of the Giyurgan and Atrak, and on the Astrabad frontier. These tribes did not reject his proposals in direct terms, but temporized, for they were much weakened by their disastrous campaign of the previous year (1812) against Persia, and had become to a certain extent the vassals of that power.

When Mahomed Ragim found he could get no satisfactory reply from the Yomuds, he marched into Bussrahn, a district lying near the Giyurgan river, which (the Giyurgan) forms the boundary between the Yomud country and Persia. Here he encountered a Persian force, of strength equal to his own, commanded by six Khans of different ranks. The Persian army occupied some high ground, and the Khan of Khiva drew up on the opposite heights and opened a fire of artillery ; but his guns were in bad order, and were badly served, and the distance intervening between the two armies was too great, so the cannonade made no impression.

The Persian guns were better served, but they also failed to inflict any damage on the Usbegs.

For four days the opponents faced each other in this manner, the artillery wasting their ammunition and the archers their arrows, only a man or two being hit by a stray shot, and a few captives made on either side; and then both armies retreated.

On his march homewards Mahomed Ragim bethinking him of the revenge to be inflicted on the Kaklans for their withheld assistance, fell upon them unawares, defeated them, and carried off all their property and numerous prisoners of both sexes to Khiva. He lost nearly all his horses in the great steppe, but no sooner did he reach the capital than he remounted his cavalry, and marched against the Takkas, who had also refused him their support.

He routed them as he had routed the Kaklans, securing an immense booty and many prisoners, and annexing all their arable land to his own Khanate.

The members of this tribe, who had escaped, took refuge with their Chief, Murad Sirdar, in inaccessible and barren hills, but were soon compelled by hunger to purchase grain from their conqueror, who not only put an exorbitant price on their supplies, but charged them a heavy toll as well. This induced them to settle in Khiva, where Mahomed Ragim received them kindly and encouraged them by gifts and grants of land near canals.

Mahomed Ragim was at the same time shrewd enough to win the friendship and alliance of a stronger power. The Afghans had revolted against their Sovereign, Shah Mahomed, and driven him from his dominions. From Cabul the Prince fled to Bokhara, but, finding Mir Hyder inclined to deliver him up to the brother who had usurped his throne, he was forced to look elsewhere for safety, and threw himself under the protection of the Khan of Khiva. Mahomed Ragim received him with the greatest hospitality, and paid him the highest marks of respect, hoping to secure in him a future powerful ally. A second revolution in Cabul caused a reaction in Shah Mahomed's favour, and he was reinstated, but carried back with him lasting feelings of gratitude towards Khiva. The two nations now wage a common war against Persia, and the Kajars live in hourly dread of Afghan inroads.

The terrible war against Mir Vaiz, the extirpation of the reigning family, and the devastation of Persia by the Afghans still live in every recollection. At the present day

Khivan traders carry their goods to Cabul safely and without hindrance, and are treated by the Prince with special kindness.

Mahomed Ragim next sought to extend his sway over the Turcomans dwelling on his frontier. His attention was especially drawn to the Chobdur Essen Ili tribe (of 8,000 families), who lead a nomadic life about the Mangushlak promontory.

An important trade is carried on at that place between Astraccan and Khiva, the Sarts carrying thither not only articles of home manufacture, but the products of India and Bokhara ; and the Chobdur Turcomans, who are masters of the place, used frequently to be obstructive, until the Khan succeeded in winning them over by flattery and important concessions. The tribe has very little grain of its own, and depends mainly on Khiva for supplies, a circumstance Mahomed Ragim turned to account, by allowing them to make their purchases under advantageous conditions, and thereby gained their good-will so thoroughly, that now-a-days his caravans resort to Mangushlak in perfect safety, and pass months there without the smallest annoyance.

Besides this, several Chobdur families have settled and become naturalized in the Khan's dominions, and the whole tribe now obeys his authority, partly because some of the settlers are related to the most eminent of its members, and are, as it were, in the position of hostages, partly because the increasing intercourse with Khiva has rendered a good understanding with the latter indispensable to the Chobdurs.

It is manifest that the Khan of Khiva never lets slip a favourable opportunity for increasing the numbers of his subjects and his political influence over other States.

One may therefore safely predict that in course of time Khiva will rank among the first of Oriental powers.

Mahomed Ragim is of lofty stature (about six feet in height), and has a robust and powerful frame ; his age is about fifty. The ferocity of his nature is not betrayed by his rather taking countenance. His features are regular, the eyes small but fiery and piercing, and his beard is short and foxy. It is strange that his eyes should be the only part of his face at all characteristic of his nation, and that otherwise he much more nearly resembles a Russian than a Khivan ; his red beard adds to this effect, as all other Usbegs are black-bearded.

From what has gone before, the main features of his character may be summed up as follows:—A clear intellect, quick perception, ambition, monstrous cruelty, love of power, enterprise, intrepidity, extraordinary determination, covetousness, and suspiciousness. At the time of his struggle for supremacy he was much addicted to drink and fond of women, and in his cups would devise new methods of torture for the unhappy victims of his ambition. He is now quieter and more temperate, and has only seven wives in his harem. Intoxicating drinks he has altogether abandoned, and uses vinegar instead of wine; he has, moreover, issued an edict prohibiting the use of strong drinks and tobacco in his dominions, under a penalty of all offenders having their mouths slit to their ears. In comparison with his countrymen he may be called a learned man, for besides his mother tongue he both speaks and reads Arabic and Persian, and has studied astrology and medicine.

He affects simplicity and frugality in all things; dressing himself in a quilted robe of Bokhara silk, and a turban or cap surrounded by a white band; whilst never more than two or three dishes appear on his table, such as pilau, greasy saffron soup, or meat roasted without butter. His mode of living is quite nomadic, for he occupies a felt tent all the year round, keeping his houses for his wives only. The greater part of his time is passed in the steppe, hawking or hunting, snipe and wild goats being his favourite game. During his absence he generally makes over the Government to his brother, Kutli Murad, or to one of his favourites, and peace and order are never disturbed. His habits altogether are totally dissmilar to those of other Asiatic potentates. He sleeps but little, and that only in the day time, which may be attributed either to the suspicious fear which haunts all evil-doers, or to other causes concealed by his strange disposition. He thoroughly understands, and likes the game of chess, and often makes the children of his favourites play whilst he looks on, but he never takes a part in the game. He keeps Friday (the Mahomedan day corresponding to our Sunday) very strictly. On this day he assembles all the Chiefs, the priests, and his friends, and they dine together and offer up their prayers in common.

The Khan's family at present consists of his two brothers, Inakh Kutli Murad and Mahomed Nazar Beg, and three sons, the eldest of whom, Alla Kuttura, is 17 years of age, and the 2nd, Raman Kulla, 15. The latter has inherited

Mahomed Ragim's physical and mental qualities to a much greater extent than the elder brother, and when he plays with the sons of his father's favourites, he beats and maltreats them in the cruelest manner (being extraordinarily powerful), whilst the Khan rejoices in him as a worthy successor to his honors. The third son is still very young, and I cannot give any particulars with regard to him.

From their tenderest years these children are trained to gaze on sights of barbarity, and, instead of being moved by the reeking blood at an execution, they eagerly witness the tortures of condemned victims. This kind of education is usual in nearly all Asiatic reigning families ; the children are hardened by brutal spectacles, and thereby prepared to be the curse of the people entrusted to their rule by fate.

The name of Raman Kulla may yet resound terribly throughout Central Asia.

There are several established terms for addressing the Khan by, *viz.*, "Taksir," (*i.e.*, "fault") the significance of which probably is that the Khan is the punisher of crime, or that he who ventures to address him admits his own guilt beforehand, "Khan Hazrat" (equivalent to your Highness) and "Khan Khwaja."

From the foregoing it is to be seen that the present system of Government in Khiva is despotic, the Ruler being absolute and untrammelled by laws or customs, but regarding the Khanate as his private property, to be governed solely for his own benefit. All laws are accordingly framed to this end, and the Khan looks on the Khivans as his own, his slaves, whose happiness is but a secondary consideration to his own profit and that of his favourites. Naturally there is no public spirit, and all conceal their wealth lest their master should deprive them of it. Commands are obeyed, but obeyed unwillingly. The subjects living near the Khan are obedient from fear of summary punishment, but those in more remote districts, in proportion to the weakness of the Government at the time, strive to evade orders, and only give in when they see immediate danger in further disobedience.

As a rule, the Khivans regard their Khan in the light of an enemy. Patriotism under such conditions is, of course, an impossibility, but to the Khivan the word "country" or "fatherland" means no more than the ground covered by his own tent of felt, or occupied by his family.

With a view to giving his tyranny the colouring of justice, Mahomed Ragim has organized a Council of State, to which he has committed the duty of deciding disputes, trying criminals, and carrying out sentences. At first sight this institution would appear to be in favour of the people, shielding them from the arbitrary violence of the Ruler, but on investigation it becomes evident that Mahomed Ragim, whilst seemingly abstaining from despotism, has made the Council a means of confirming him in his tyrannical power.

This Court of Justice consists of members appointed at will by the Khan from the number of his creatures, who must strictly adhere in their decisions to the orders of their master; for if they dare to set up an independent opinion, they are at once dismissed with insult and disgrace. Through this arrangement Mahomed Ragim is enabled to stop the murmurs of the people, for when the latter are roused by his unjust decisions, he shifts the whole blame on to the shoulders of his Council.

The Khan is President of the tribunal, and the number of members is indefinite, being dependent on the number of Court favourites. The Grand Vizier, Yusuf Mehter Aga, has at present a seat among the members.

This person possesses the Khan's highest esteem and confidence; he is a Sart by birth, of a gloomy and suspicious character, but cringing and obsequious to his superior. He is over fifty years old, and *ex officio* has charge of the Khan's treasury, and control of the revenue and expenditure.

His also is the duty of receiving and entertaining foreign Ambassadors.

During the Khan's absence he conducts the affairs of State, and is sometimes entrusted with full powers. Mahomed Ragim's selection of this Minister from the Sart population has brought about the union of the Usbegs with that race, which they had formerly oppressed.

The selection was certainly a good one, for a Sart from perpetual oppression is more patient than an Usbeg would be under the changing humours of his master, and is the more subservient if he only sees his way to bettering himself. Since Yusuf Mehter Aga's elevation the Sarts (*i.e.*, the trader class) have gained access to the Khan, and although, like the rest of his subjects, they have gained no *rights*, still they have profited by the temporary favour in which they stand to win many concessions from him, which have improved their business.

The second Vizier, Madra Kush Begi, is also a Member of Council, and is highly respected by all. He is an Usbeg of the same tribe (Kiat Konrad) as the Khan, and assists the people of his tribe in their suits and petitions. He is considered wise, resolute, good-hearted, and obliging; whence he would appear not to have the Khan's full confidence.

He is, indeed, obedient, but detests Mahomed Ragim's imperiousness, and loves his country or rather his tribe, but still never dares to oppose him, always behaving with circumspection, and apparently awaiting the time when the Khan and his foreign favourite shall be overthrown. His office is nearly identical with that of the Grand Vizier, and he is actually the latter's junior colleague, but the reins of Government are never entrusted to him when the Khan leaves Khiva.

The third among the high officers of State is Khwaja Margam, whom the Khan holds in great favour. His father was a Persian slave, who renounced the tenets of his sect and married in Khiva. Khwaja Margam received his freedom from the Khan for the great services he rendered during the expedition against Bokhara, and was loaded with special marks of favour and granted lands and canals. He was made Director of tolls and customs, in which appointment he has attained to great power, and surrounded himself with his friends and relations, all manumitted slaves.

He purchased his father's liberty, and the Khan took the latter (Alla Vardi by name) into his service, gave him the title of "At Chapar"* i.e., "swift horse," and uses him as such. Perhaps Mahomed Ragim's object in elevating Khwaja Margam, a born Persian, was to show his subjects that he looked more to services than to descent in selecting individuals for his preferments.

Khwaja Margam is, like all parvenus, loved by many and hated by many. The Sarts and slaves are among the former, the Usbegs among the latter. His disposition is evil; he cringes to his master, and obeys him obsequiously; imperious and domineering to the weak, he lowers himself in the dust before the great, servilely officious when his own interest demands it, and zealously careful in any matter from which advantage can accrue to himself. He flatters the low passions of the Khan, and has thereby won his entire confidence.

---

* Muraviev explains this apparent nonsense in his diary. Alla Vardi was employed to proclaim the Khan's edicts throughout the country, which gave him a good deal of hard riding; hence his nick name.—W. S. A. L.

He tries to intermeddle in every matter, and to make himself of importance. Although not an actual Member of the Council he contrives by underhand cunning to mix himself up with the affairs, and none of the counsellors are able to put a stop to his interference. The wealth, which he owes to the liberality of the Khan and to the extensive bribes derived from his position, enables him to make valuable presents several times a year to Mahomed Ragim, who accepts them with pleasure, plunder and presents constituting the main source of his income.

Thus Khwaja Margam keeps himself in favour. He is about forty years old, with an expressive and intelligent face, fine features, dark complexion, and a long black beard.

He dresses himself in a more cleanly and expensive manner than the rest of his countrymen, and his manner is easy and indeed pleasant.

The above three persons are therefore the Khan's chief favourites, and fill the most important offices in the State.

Each one has his amanuensis (or Mirza) and an official establishment (Diwan Beg).

The duties of the latter are not laid down, but the officials are employed on different missions, and some of them have the task of attending to foreign Envoys.

Inakh Kutli Murad occasionally takes a seat in Council, for the Khan, his brother, is fond of him, and sometimes follows his advice. The Cazi, or Chief Priest, is also a member, but his spiritual rank gives him no precedence at the board, and the Khan treats him as he does the rest, *viz.*, abuses him and drives him away from the assembly on the slightest symptoms of independent opinion on his part.

The ancient institution of a Council composed of the Chiefs of tribes is retained in name, that is to say, the heads of the four Usbeg tribes sit in the Khan's Council of State as inferior members, but the privilege is an empty one, and is only conceded as a sop to the Usbegs.

Those Chiefs have hardly any voice in State matters: they are particular about the order in which they sit (according to age), but do not take a part in the transaction of affairs, of which, indeed, they are totally ignorant. As Mahomed Ragim overthrew the authority of the Inakhs, he now holds aloof from his own person and from a participation in the Government all those who pride themselves on their descent, or who might, perhaps, be desirous of a return to the old state of things.

When the Inakhs ruled the country, each tribe used to have 32 officials of different degrees for the settlement of disputes. Among them were the Inakh, the Bi, the Sultan, the Yuz Bashi, &c. Their posts conferred certain privileges and advantages, and imposed certain obligations on them, and there was a good deal of dignity attached to their position. The Khan stripped them of their jurisdiction and attached the titles to the possessors of certain estates, which are hereditary, unless the Khan be pleased to confiscate them and make them over to other families.

The Council assembles every Friday in a building set apart for the purpose in one of the yards in the Khan's palace. It is only a rough enclosure, without floor, roof or window, and very dirtily kept. The rush matting covering it in has a large hole cut in it to admit light, but unfortunately snow and rain intrude by the same aperture. The hole serves also to carry off the fumes of the charcoal at which the counsellors warm themselves. This filthy apartment, or rather stall, is dignified by the high sounding name of "Harniyash Khana," or Hall of the Privy Council.

The Khan ordinarily presides, but before deliberations commence his servants set great dishes of pilau before the Counsellors, and nothing is done until they have stuffed themselves full. The Khan listens attentively to the opinion of each member, but should it not coincide with his own, he storms and rages and turns the speaker out of the hall and all other members who may concur with the views of the latter. Neither the counsellors, nor, indeed, any of the Khan's officials, receive fixed salaries, but are rewarded from time to time by presents, or the concession of some favour, such as permission to cut a new canal or reclaim some waste land.

With the exception of the body I have described, there is no other Court, Civil or Criminal, in the whole Khanate, and the kind of justice that is administered can easily be imagined, for there is no written code of laws, and decisions depend on the caprice or passions of the Judges, and must invariably subserve the Khan's interests.

Every town has its priest or Cazi, who is under the immediate orders of the chief priest, and whose duty it is to watch over the observance of municipal and religious laws, every breach of the same being reported to the Khan. The Cazis have no power to judge a case or to settle a difference, unless the latter be one of the most trifling nature, and the opposite parties agree to their deciding between them. They derive great emoluments from their office.

Under the administration of the Inakhs the chief priest had a much higher position and more extensive powers ; for, besides dealing with infringements of the laws of Mahomed, he was the principal judge in lawsuits and family quarrels, and his decisions and sentences were considered just and sacred, as being founded on the precepts of the Koran.

Executive power rests with the Khan alone, whilst his favourites see to the carrying out of his orders. The most zealous of those is the " Nasakchi Bashi," or head executioner, who forms one of the household. Another great favourite is Sultan Khan, who fled to Khiva for protection from the Turcomans in 1813. His native country is on the Chinese frontier. He enjoys the partial confidence of the Khan, and is entrusted by him with a cavalry command in war time.

Among the Khan's subordinate executive favourites there is a Russian, who has long since embraced the Mahomedan religion. This man has been enriched by his master, and has his own private attendants and slaves. His duties are various, but he does not possess so much power as Khwaja Margam. His name is " Tangri Kuli," or " the servant of God." We must further include in the executive the Turcomans, who are the Khan's stand-by in the way of an army, and are employed by him in many other services.

It will be seen, then, that since Mahomed Ragim forced himself on to the throne, he has drawn his Ministers and other public servants from the ranks of the Sarts and Turcomans, sometimes even employing foreigners, whilst he excludes the Usbegs from office as much as possible. By this means alone has he been able to establish and increase his power, for his servants, having suffered at the hands of the Usbegs, rejoice to see the tables turned on their oppressors, and vie with each other to win the good opinion of the Khan, and to carry out his orders to the letter ; whilst, on the other hand, the Usbegs detest their Khan and curse his knavish foreigners, as they term the Sarts and Turcomans.

All the officials are the Khan's obedient slaves ; their fortunes and their lives belong to him. Sometimes he and his Grand Vizier, whom he prizes for his ability, spend the whole night together in familiar conversation and jesting, and the Vizier rarely fails to profit by the Khan's good humour by furthering his own private ends.

The towns of Khiva are not without a police; that is to say, some men, armed with thick copper-bound clubs, are appointed for the purpose of preserving order among the crowd on gala days and at large meetings. They are styled " Asaul."

When one of those persons strikes in the name of the Khan, the proudest Usbeg moves on; but he nurses his revenge, and not unfrequently assassinates his striker, then flies into Bokhara, where his countrymen receive him with open arms, and where he is safe from punishment. A Sart, on the contrary, receives the blows patiently and contentedly, nay more, with a certain amount of satisfaction; for he knows that slavish submission is his path to the Khan's favour, and feels himself in a way honored by this thrashing. The Turcoman does not care about the disgrace of the beating, but dislikes the pain, and will try to be revenged on the " Asaul," and wrest his club from him for the sake of the copper on it.

It is a difficult matter to define the rights and privileges of the different orders which compose the Khiva nation; for as there are no fixed laws, everything depends on the will of the Khan, or on a few customs which have taken root during the lapse of time. There are no such things as political rights, but the Usbegs, as the conquering race, have a sort of general precedence, and domineer over the other classes. The Sarts, as the subjugated race, again, are patient and cringing, as also are the Turcomans, who, however, add to those qualities a marauding disposition. The Karakalpaks are the patient tillers of the soil; and the slaves groan under the most frightful oppression.

One privilege only is enjoyed by the four orders, and that is, that they can be tried and punished by the Khan and his Council, but by no one else. The slaves have no rights at all, and are not permitted to complain against their masters.

Mahomed Ragim never shows mercy. In his judgments he does not discriminate between a wilful and an accidental offence, but only sees the bare deed, and is quite inexorable, neither the intercessions of his favourites nor compassion for the family of the condemned can move him a hair's breadth from his decision.

Treason, infringement of the laws of religion, murder, robbery, cheating, and other offences are all punished by the most frightful deaths; even petty theft is a capital crime.

There are two ordinary modes of executions, *viz.*, hanging and impaling. A man condemned to be hanged is generally brought to the Khan's palace, in front of which, or the Privy Council Hall, the sentence is carried out; but the execution sometimes takes place in the market or some other public resort. The body remains hanging on the gallows for the people to look at for several days, and not till then is it made over to the relatives for interment. Criminals are sometimes hanged by the feet instead of by the neck, and in this case their agonies are protracted until apoplexy relieves them.

Impalement is carried out in Khiva with still greater cruelties than attend it in Turkey. The stake is of wood, and has a rather blunt point, and, in order that the victim may not die too soon, his hands and feet are firmly bound; as soon, however, as the stake has entered pretty deep into his body, they are released again, when the tortured wretch increases his sufferings by his violent struggles.

Sometimes an impaled man will live for two days on the stake, only dying when the point comes through his shoulders or back.

Robberies in the interior of the Khanate are generally perpetrated by the Turcomans, or the slaves when they go into the steppe to burn charcoal.

The charcoal trade is very remunerative, therefore many Khivans send their slaves into the steppe to prepare and bring in that article. The charcoal-burning gangs not unfrequently attack and rob each other, or plunder the merchants' caravans that they come across. The Khan reserves to himself the right of committing the last named act of violence, and when he perpetrates it, dignifies the robbery by the name of "war," or "an act of policy," or "a necessary chastisement" for some offence on the part of the merchants, which he invents for the occasion. It is interpreted, however, as highway robbery directly a subject ventures to commit it, and the punishment is impalement.

Offenders are sometimes punished by the loss of all their property, which the Khan then appropriates to himself. The ruined man must then go a begging or trust for support to his relations, who, however, often withhold assistance from dread of evil consequences to themselves.

There are two other kinds of punishment, which Mahomed Ragim describes as "Domestic Discipline;" the first consists in merciless flogging, the second in slitting the mouth to the ears. The latter punishment is usually inflicted for tobacco smoking, but the Khan is aware that many of his subjects smoke, and he connives at this breach of the law, except in cases where he wishes to be revenged on some one whom he cannot bring otherwise within his grasp.

During Mahomed Ragim's struggle for power, he used to put his victims to death by decapitation, but that method is now obsolete. The Inakhs in former days used to fine for every offence, but that punishment also has been abandoned now-a-days.

Foreign Envoys who may be condemned to death, and unbelievers, are buried alive in the steppe, as they say the blood of an infidel spilt on the soil would dishonor the latter.

This was the death that was in contemplation for me, but Prince Bekovitsh, who perished in 1717, had a more dreadful end, for he was flayed alive, and a drum head made out of his skin.

The slaves are subject to many other forms of punishment, for they are in the hands of their masters, who devise all kinds of torture for them. The masters have full powers of life and death, but as the death of a slave is a direct loss of property, they generally chastise light offences by cutting off an ear, or thrusting out an eye, or by stabs with a dagger in some not vital part.

The sufferer, under those circumstances, is immediately driven to his work without time being allowed him to bind up his wounds. The very tasks slaves have to perform make their lives a prolonged torture, and they frequently sink under overwork. The minor punishments enumerated above are inflicted for meditated desertion, but should a slave be suspected a second time of the intention of running away, he is nailed by an ear to a post or to the house-door, and left for three days without food or drink, exposed to the jibes of passers by. Few survive this, as they enter on the ordeal with frames exhausted by toil and hardship.

Chapter III

Current Money. Taxation. State of Finance.
Trade and Industry

Since Mahomed Ragim came to power he has established a regular mint at Khiva, where coins are struck with his own stamp.

Tilla.—The most valuable current coin is the tilla, a round gold piece without much alloy, and pretty distinctly marked. Its value is about 12 shillings and 6 pence of English money. On the obverse side the name Mahomed Ragim is inscribed in Turkish characters, and on the reverse, the year, the mint where struck, and a passage from the Koran are written in Arabic, round the inner edge there are dots showing the value of the coin in silver.

Abass.—The tilla contains 14 " Abass," and the Abass is worth about 10·75 pence. There is no such coin really ; it is an imaginary one to facilitate calculation.

Tenga.—Two tengas make a Khivan Abass ; one tenga is therefore worth about 5·375 pence. It is a well struck, very pure, silver coin. On the obverse side is the Khan's name in Turkish, and on the reverse there is the same inscription as on the tilla, *viz.*, the place where struck, the year, and a verse from the Koran in Arabic characters, the whole surrounded by dots showing the value in the next lower piece.

Karapul.—A tenga contains 40 Karapuls. This is a copper coin, badly stamped, and unsightly. The Karapul is worth about ½ farthing.

Foreign money.—The foreign coin most commonly in circulation is the Bokharan gold tilla, called " Padshah Tillassi," or royal tilla.

Dutch ducats are popular, and one that has not been clipped is valued at 10 Abasses or 800 Karapuls. The Persian silver "real" is also current ; 5½ reals go to one Dutch ducat. Foreign pieces never circulate very long in Khiva, as the Khan carefully collects them and melts them down for his own mint.

Ancient coins.—Among the ruins of the old town of Urganj, on the banks of the former bed of the Amu Dariya, gold and silver coins are often discovered, some of which date so far back as the time of the Chorasmii. They are never circulated, for every one must give them up, on discovery, to the Khan under severe penalties, and they are all melted down.

The Khivans are very expert in changing money, and from practice can tell at once the exact intrinsic value of a coin. The commonest individual will at once detect a clipped ducat, and know how to fix its worth; and will immediately recognise a false tenga, which is the prevalent counterfeit coin in the Khanate, and which is palmed off extensively on strangers.

They are adepts at clipping tillas, but as they have no knowledge of alloying the precious metals, their money is struck from nearly pure gold and silver.

Revenue.—The public revenue and expenditure, and the private income and disbursements of the Khan are in no way separate, but form one account. I must, therefore, in enumerating the public resources, include the items which accrue only to the Khan himself.

The sources of income are : poll-tax, gifts to the Khan from the four classes, proceeds from the sale of the Khan's private crops, farm rents, tolls, share of plunder, charge on incoming caravans, and extraordinary war-taxes.

Not all subjects are liable to taxation however. Born Usbegs are exempt, for they are almost all soldiers or hold public offices, and are bound to equip themseves at their own expense and follow the Khan whenever and wherever he may choose to wage war. Only those Usbegs, therefore, who engage in trade are liable to be taxed.

The Turcomans who have settled in Khiva, and who form the war army, are also exempted from paying taxes. They never intermingle with the Usbegs, for the origin of the two races is quite distinct, and their interests are at variance.

They form a sort of mercenary force, which the Khan maintains by numerous gifts, partly as a safeguard against outward hostility, and partly as a menace to the unruly Usbegs; and as he cannot exist without their support, he does all in his power to attach them to himself and increase their numbers.

Poll-tax.—The main source of revenue is the so-called "kettle-tax," corresponding to the capitation or poll-tax of other countries. It is remarkable that in an uncivilized State like Khiva the incidence of this tax should be regulated according to the means of the payers. The day-labourer, or any one else who can prove that he does not possess a felt tent of his own, and that he does not cook his food in a special pot of his own, is exempted from the tax.

The Khivans being all divided into tribes and septs, the weakest of which contains 200 families, each section is taxed in proportion to the value of the land it occupies, the number of years it has been settled, and the lucrativeness of its trade.

Each body elects some one to assess and collect this tax, and he assesses it in such a manner that the poorer families do not pay very much, whilst the wealthy contribute a proportionately larger quota. As a tribe makes its own selection of this officer (and can depose him at will, should he fail to give satisfaction), the choice is generally made from among the most respected Chiefs, and a person appointed who possesses the confidence of the community; the tax is, therefore, as a rule, allotted considerately, and in accordance with fairness and justice, and to the satisfaction of all parties. The maximum annual tax on each kettle is £1·75, the minimum £0·4375.

This tax falls chiefly on the Sarts and the Karakalpaks about the sea of Aral, who are the Khan's subjects.

The Khan's private Estates.—A nearly equally lucrative source of income is the sale of the crops and other products of the Khan's private estates.

Although Mahomed Ragim calls the whole of Khiva his own, he has certain estates which he has inherited from his ancestors, and which he has supplemented by the land confiscated from the unfortunate Usbeg families which he destroyed on coming into power.

His estates are full of canals, and are carefully cultivated by slaves, and by Sarts and Karakalpaks, who have settled and built villages on them, and whose contribution to the kettle-tax has in consequence been remitted. This remission of tax takes from his income on the one hand, but he is amply compensated on the other for the decrease, as he grows wheat, rice, sesame, jugan, &c., in great abundance on his property, and disposes of his crops at a high price to the Turcomans who stream in from all quarters to purchase it. In order to enhance his profits he has prohibited the Khivans, on pain of death, from selling grain to any one whomsoever, until he has disposed of his own at a certain price.

Considerable sums are further derived from farming out canals, &c. The great canal Gyuiktam and many minor ones are the Khan's private property, and he lets either a portion of the former, or several of the smaller ones which are fed by it. The soil, being chiefly sandy and unproductive, requires great culture, and alluvial deposit is therefore much prized. To obtain this the fields are flooded from time to time, and an extraordinary fertility is the result. All the labours of the agriculturist are accordingly devoted to the construction of water channels, and the land is valuable in proportion to the number and quality of the latter rather than to its extent of area.

The octroi tax and the tolls are very remunerative; the latter are established in every part of the Khanate, and a thirtieth part of the value is levied on all goods entering the country; the same charge being made on all cattle driven in. A moderate sum is paid by every one setting up a booth or shop, and the right to hold a market or fair must be purchased in money from the Khan.

Income derived from booty.—The Khan never lets slip the smallest opportunity of making a profit, however slight.

He accordingly imposes many taxes, quite regardless as to the effect they may have on trade.

He has ordered the robbers (chiefly Turcomans) who live in Khiva to give him up a fifth share of their booty after each raid into the Persian provinces.

The booty consists generally of slaves, concubines, horses, camels, cattle, and merchandise, none of which the robbers are able to conceal from him.

Impost on caravans arriving in Khiva.—In 1819 the Khan imposed a charge of half a tilla per camel on every Turcoman caravan arriving in Khiva.

This may bring him in from £23,000 to £29,000 per annum.

Income derived from presents.—Besides the sources of income which have been mentioned above, the Khan makes a good thing out of his Sart and Turcoman subjects in the shape of presents.

The Sarts, ousted in a great measure from a voice in politics, have thrown themselves now-a-days entirely into trade. Their transactions might be termed *cheating* with much more accuracy than *trading*, but they have to purchase immunity from the usual penalties of rascality by valuable offerings to the Khan. The gifts must be of frequent recurrence, and the Khan gladly accepts them, and in return leaves the donors for a time to pursue their nefarious practices in peace. The Turcomans bring him also handsome presents, especially when his hunting excursions take him into their neighbourhood, but they are actuated by quite different motives from those of the Sarts, expecting to receive *quid pro quo* either in the shape of some new privilege, or a return present of greater value. They are seldom disappointed in their expectations, for the Khan is obliged to keep this race in good humour, as they are the mainstay of his power. On the whole, however, the value of the gifts he receives from all the Turcomans is far greater than the value of those he makes in return from time to time, so that this item must come under the heading of income, even although it be not a very large one.

Extraordinary taxes.—When the Khanate is threatened by an attack, or when the ambitious Mahomed Ragim wishes to wage war on a neighbour, the Sarts and Karakalpaks are called on to furnish a special contribution in money, which is, however, devoted to the end for which it is levied.

Amount of the revenue.—It is difficult and nearly impossible to determine the exact amount of the Khan's revenue. It is probably about £150,000 ; for if we reckon the Sarts at 100,000 and the Karakalpaks at 70,000 families, and allot one tax-payer per family, then taking the mean between £1·75 and £0·4375, each family would pay £1·09375, and the sum realized by the kettle-tax would amount to £92,968·75.

The camel toll may bring in £29,000, and the other items of revenue as much more, which gives us a total of over £150,000.

Expenditure.—There is a popular belief in Khiva that Mahomed Ragim possesses an enormous treasure in gold and silver, but this is certainly not the case, for he does not bury his money ; true, he lives frugally, but he applies his income to the payment of his troops, the rewarding of his Ministers and servants, the forming of new canals, the construction of buildings, and the remuneration of the various artificers whom he collects round him from foreign lands. His treasure really consists of different kinds of arms, a number of splendid stallions, and a few jewels. Warlike glory he prefers to all articles of " luxe." The maintenance of his Turcomans alone costs him a great deal; for every Turcoman who goes on service receives from him a sum varying from 5 to 20 tillas for his equipment. Presents to his officers form a heavy item of expenditure. In the days of the Inakhs public officers received fixed salaries, the money for which was levied by a tax; but this has all been changed now, and Mahomed Ragim rewards officials, or those about his person, according to their merit or his inclination towards them.

Industry.—The inhabitants of Khiva are chiefly engaged in agricultural and horticultural pursuits, from which they derive large profits.

The Sarts, original lords of the soil, turned their attention from the earliest days to the irrigation of their country by canals conducted from the Amu Dariya, and with incredible toil and trouble they at last converted the most sterile wastes by this means into rich fields, which now-a-days yield a superabundance of grain. The interior of the Khanate has a most pleasing appearance ; everywhere there are fields of waving corn, vineyards, orchards, &c., spreading out between the canals. The landowners live in affluence, and the produce of the soil is far beyond the requirements of the people, so the surplus forms an important object of trade ; for the neighbouring races, such as the inhabitants of the Balkan and Mangushlak districts, a portion of the Kirgis Kaisack tribe, and the Atta and Takka Turcomans are eager grain purchasers.

The Khivans sow chiefly wheat, which yields good crops and commands a ready sale. Rice is also grown, but not to the extent it would be did it require less water, which is an expensive article in Khiva ; it is therefore regarded as an article of luxury for home consumption.

Where sufficient water can be supplied it thrives very well. Sesame is grown to a great extent, and oil manufactured from it, which forms a staple commodity of trade with foreigners. The oil is much used in the Khanate, and is burned by the poorer classes.

Barley and hemp do not thrive, and there is but little cultivated of either. Sesame oil takes the place of hemp-seed oil, and is superior to it. Rope is spun from wool.

Horses are fed on jogan, of which an abundance is grown.

The grain of this cereal is very firm, and resembles a pea; it grows very like maize. The poorer classes some times eat it, but it has to be cooked for a long time before it becomes fit for human food; when thus cooked it is called " Kuja."

Nature has not made Khiva a wooded country, but the industry of the Sarts has covered it with orchards, which produce the most delicious fruits. Several kinds of vines are cultivated, the grapes being dried and sold under the name of " Kishmish." These raisins are round, small, and transparent, and extremely sweet. The orchards produce apples, pears, almonds, cherries, mulberries, pomegranates, &c., in great abundance.

All the vegetables grown in Russia are to be met with in Khiva, with the exception of cabbages, radishes, potatoes, and turnips.

Onions attain to a great size, often equal to that of a large apple, and have a much milder flavour than the ordinary European kinds.

Melons deserve especial notice on account of their enormous size and excellent flavour. Some of them attain to $1\frac{1}{2}$ foot in length and 1 foot in thickness; they are very sweet and have a charming aroma and a thin rind. The sandy soil of Khiva is peculiarly favourable to this fruit. Water-melons also abound and are remarkably good.

Cattle breeding is carried on to a great extent, and herds of camels, horned cattle, and sheep are to be seen everywhere.

Besides the pursuits which minister to the primary requirements of human life, the Khivans engage in sundry handicrafts; but their manufactures are only for home consumption. They spin silk both from Bokharan and indigenous raw material, and turn out several kinds of stuff, which, if not exactly beautiful, is nevertheless very durable : they spin cotton in the same manner.

The Turcoman settlers manufacture felt tents, camlets, and handsome serviceable carpets. The Khivans are also very expert in making up silk waist girdles. The home demand for all these articles equals the supply, so there is no export trade in country fabrics.

The wealth of the people does not consist in articles of luxury or large sums of money, but in the profusion of articles of every day use, which serve to keep them in affluence and enable them to pay the Khan's taxes. On the whole, they are bad handicraftsmen, and their manufactures are in a state of infancy; they do not work in iron to any great extent, and Russian slaves are their only smiths, neither do they understand working in copper, so instead of utilising that metal as it comes from their own mines, they prefer purchasing the ready made articles from Russia. They have no acquaintance with the art of making glass, many of them, indeed, have never seen that commodity, and it is very rare and expensive in Khiva.

It is strange that in spite of their wealth of grain they neither employ water nor wind-mills, but grind their corn in hand-mills, or in larger ones turned by camels.

Trade.—Trade, both home and foreign, is in the hands of the Sarts; that of the country, is very unimportant, confined only to the sale of grain and hardware at the different fairs, and to dealings in slaves. Business cannot be transacted at all times and places in the Khanate, for the Khan has fixed certain days for markets to be held in different parts of the country. The industrious inhabitants of Urganj and other towns accordingly hasten with their goods from place to place, and market days resemble the ordinary fairs in small European towns.

Weekly markets are, however, held in the five chief towns; in Khiva, for instance, the market days are Monday and Friday. The Khan confers the right of holding markets on those places where there is a considerable population; and there shops are erected, for which ground rent is paid to the owner of the land, who, again, is responsible to the Khan for the payment of the established market tax.

The Turcomans buy their grain at the markets, and dispose of slaves, so useful in the cultivation of the land, as they are generally the ploughmen; were the trade with the Turcomans to cease, Khiva would lose the chief source of its prosperity, and probably sink back into insignificance.

In home products, then, Khiva is very deficient, and is unable to carry on a trade of any importance with other States, but its situation in the midst of barren steppes, on the thoroughfare of Russian commerce, almost in the centre point of all Asia, causes it to be the great depôt of the numerous Asiatic goods, and to the Russian market, and renders it a place of great importance to Russia.

The trade with Russia induces now-a-days the money-loving Sarts to repair to Bokhara and other Asiatic countries, where they purchase the required articles, and carry them to Orenburg and Astraccan. This traffic, which enriches Khiva, and brings a large revenue into the Khan's coffers, would be greatly extended, had the cruel tyrant only true notions of trade, but he regards merchants as merely the instruments for increasing his own immediate wealth, and oppresses them with heavy imposts, deterring them thereby from investing capital in goods or from making their prosperity apparent in any way whatsoever. Were Khiva only under the influence of some well-regulated Government, the commercial enterprise, which even at present so benefits the country, and which in spite of all restrictions has so spread itself, would be widely extended, and would raise the Khanate into a most flourishing state, for Khiva would then attract the entire trade of Asia, including even India, to the Caspian Sea, and be the means of pouring the wealth of the East into Europe, through Russia.

Trade with Bokhara and Russia.—The wares which the Khivan merchants bring from Bokhara consist partly in Bokharan goods, partly in those of other eastern countries, such as different kinds of linen prints, blue calicoes, spun cotton, silk, and silken or half silk stuffs, Cashmeer shawls, China porcelain, silk waistbands, woollen stuffs, Bokharan black lamb skins (reputed the best in the East), tobacco, &c., &c., all of which, after deducting for the requirements of Khiva itself, are carried into Russia through Orenburg and Astraccan.

The great emporium for imported goods is Urganj, and they are passed on from that town, which, as the commercial centre, is a place of bustling activity. Its countless shops dazzle the eye with the brilliancy and rich colours of the costly Asiatic fabrics which they contain, whilst the ear is deafened by the unceasing clamour of buying and selling. Innumerable traders of all nations surge through the streets, and above the roar of human voices resound the groans of camels reeling under their heavy bales. The Sarts' love of gain is made apparent by a visit to Urganj, for there it is seen what long and difficult journeys they are ready to undertake for the sake of profit.

Like all other Asiatics, the Khivans employ camels to transport their goods through the steppe. From Urganj the caravans take six or seven days to reach Bokhara, but besides this land route they also employ rafts to bring their merchandise down the Amu Dariya. These rafts are dragged by ropes; they are large enough to hold fifty horses, are constructed of thick logs and furnished with rudders. Most of the articles purchased in Bokhara are, as before stated, disposed of in Russia, where they realize large sums. In return the Khivans buy articles of European manufacture, such as English cloth, fustian, gold and silver thread, needles, razors, scissors, fine linen, looking-glasses, writing paper, honey, lead, copper and iron vessels, &c., &c. Mangushlak is the usual rendezvous for Russian and Khivan traders, the Russians sending their goods to that place from Astraccan; but caravans also go through the Kirgis steppes straight to Orenburg. Russian merchantmen arrive at Mangushlak at certain fixed seasons; and as soon as they appear the Turcomans give notice to the Khivan merchants, who immediately start off their caravans, the latter generally taking 29 days to perform the journey.

The exchange of goods takes place at Mangushlak, but many Khivans pass over to Astraccan, whither a favourable wind carries one in 24 hours. From Astraccan some of the more enterprising penetrate with their choicest wares into Russia, and sometimes go as far Moscow, St. Petersburg, and the chief market towns such as Nishni-Novgorod, Erbit, &c.

The Sarts who go to Orenburg have first to come to an agreement with the Kirgis Kaisacks, through whose steppe their route lies. They generally hire their camels from the latter, paying 10 ducats per head for the trip to Orenburg.

Each camel must carry 670 pounds. From Urganj to Orenburg a caravan takes about 33 days.

In spite of the Sarts' astuteness and cunning, they are frequently cheated by the Armenians in Astraccan, and instances have occurred of Sarts returning home quite empty-handed from the over-reaching of those people.

It sometimes happens that a Sart who has gone on business to Astraccan marries a Turcoman woman there and enters into partnership with an Armenian merchant. With their united capital they then fit out a ship and trade to Astrabad and Ghilan, the Sart returning to Khiva after a few months' profitable sojourn.

The Khan has strictly prohibited gold or silver being taken out of Khiva, and the Khivans themselves prefer retaining their money at home, so mercantile transactions take chiefly the form of barter.

Another article which has not been mentioned is also brought by the Khivans to Astraccan. This is madder, which they recently learnt how to prepare from a native of Derbent, now in Khiva, by name Lexin Meshedi Novruss; but very little business is done with it, as it is quite a new article to the Khivans, and Daghestan supplies the Astraccan market with it every year in greater quantities and at a lower price. The Khivan soap, however, is an article of export, which is well known for its good quality and cheapness.

Russian merchants do not venture to visit Khiva, where they certainly could establish their trade on a better footing, and their fears are well-founded, for on the occasion of the least difference between Russia and Khiva, or of one of their number coming under the Khan's suspicion, they may rest assured that they would all share in the most cruel punishment. Armenians, however, in the pursuit of gain, venture to Urganj, but not into the town of Khiva. The last Armenian who was there visited Khiva in the reign of Catherine II., and is now living at Kuba, a town in Daghestan.

Trade with Persia.—The feeling of hatred existing between the Khivans and Persians makes their mutual trade of very trifling importance.

But rarely does a Persian dare to visit Khiva, and then only when he has an acquaintance there. Under any circumstances, he makes his purchases as fast he can, or, as more often happens, buys the freedom of some of his relations or friends in slavery, and remains concealed during the whole of his stay, only showing himself to his friends.

Trade with Nomadic tribes.—A very lively traffic is carried on between Khiva and the surrounding nomads, especially with the Turcomans, the independent Karakalpaks, and the Kirgis Kaisacks. From them the Khivans purchase sheep, camels, camlet, &c. The Turcomans supply them more particularly with blankets and felt, and those who dwell by the rivers Giyurgan and Atrak bring horses renowned throughout the East for their beauty, size, and strength.

The Kirgis Kaisacks bring in a number of small steppe horses for sale to the town of Ket. They are chiefly broken into amble, and are greatly prized by Khivans, who use them for long journeys, reserving their Turcoman stallions for times of need.

The Kirgis horses endure hunger, thirst, and fatigue, have great courage, and do not readily lose condition.

Slave trade.—These nomads also supply the Khivan slave market with Russians, Persians, and Kurds. Many a fortune is made by this nefarious traffic.

The Turcomans capture Persians and Kurds in Astrabad and Khorassan, whilst the Kirgis kidnap Russians on the Orenburg frontier. The unfortunate people are dragged to Khiva and set up for sale in the market like so much merchandise.

Russian slaves are in highest demand, both on account of their physical activity and strength, and their intellectual superiority. A young and healthy Russian fetches from 60 to 80 Tillas.

Persians are sold at much lower rates, and Kurds at the lowest of all; but on the other hand a Persian female slave commands a far higher price than a Russian woman. Khivans not unfrequently sell their slaves again in Bokhara, or give them in exchange for merchandise.

Persians belonging to rich families fetch very large sums, as a high ransom may be expected from their relations.

The practice of catching human beings and selling them to the Khivans has become an absolute necessity to the nomadic tribes; that is to say, the latter have to depend for grain on Khiva, and grain cannot be grown there without extraneous labour, so that this abominable trade has become an institution for the mutual benefit of Khiva and the predatory tribes, without which neither could exist.

From the above remarks on the trade of Khiva it has been shown that the Khanate contains no wealth. The natives have not sufficient industry, and are too much oppressed by their Khan to search for the treasures, perhaps hidden underneath the soil. On the other hand, the climate and land are of such a nature as to favour the growth of plants indigenous to warm countries.

If Khiva belonged to Russia, the whole trade of Asia, including India, could be directed through the Khanate to Astraccan, and the country itself would benefit in every way by the change of masters.

Chapter IV
Military Resources, Mode of Warfare &c, &c

KHIVA has always had a warlike population. Its position, like that of a fertile island in the midst of a sea of sandy wastes, made it from the earliest days a place of refuge for runaways and marauders, who, as their numbers and sense of security increased, became in time peaceful and industrious citizens. The nation formed in this manner had, however, to succumb to the Usbeg invaders, but the predatory and nomadic inhabitants of the surrounding steppes maintain a warlike spirit equal to that of the conquerors themselves, to whom, indeed, they are, in a great measure, allied and whose actual army they constitute. This warlike spirit is the leading feature in the Khivan character, and taking it and the position of the country into consideration, it seems likely that Khiva will go on extending its limits and increasing its power until it may become a dangerous neighbour to the adjacent States.

Strongholds.—The continual feuds which tore the Khanate before Mahomed Ragim seized the reins of Government, and which were kindled by the conflicting interests of the different races of the nation, compelled individual landed proprietors to protect themselves from plundering raids by the erection of strongholds. These strongholds stand generally in the midst of fields and gardens, and are provided with granaries, water tanks, dwelling-places for masters and servants, mills, slaughter-houses, cattle sheds, in short, with all that is necessary for the support of 100 or 150 persons for a limited period and for repelling a sudden attack. The buildings are in the form of a square, and are surrounded by walls generally of mud, but sometimes of masonry. The walls are 8 feet thick at the base, diminishing to 3 at the summit, and are from 18 to 20 feet high.

They are supported on the exterior faces by round buttresses, also of mud, and are crenelated, but the battlements are merely for show, as there are no means of getting up to them. The faces are from 300 to 500 feet long, and have commanding towers at the angles with domed roofs.

These mud forts have no ditch, but they are only intended as a shelter from the attacks of cowardly robbers, who have no ladders, and who, if they had them, would never have the heart to venture into such a confined space, where they would be deprived of their horses, and consequently their means of rapid flight, and would assuredly fall into the hands of the defenders. No fort of the kind would hold out for two hours against 50 regular soldiers.

There is only one gate to each fort, but that is a pretty large one, and is secured every night by a strong padlock. Above the gate there is a small balcony. The walls sometimes collapse of themselves, but this does not occur so often as one might expect, owing to the small amount of rain that falls in Khiva.

These strongholds quite fulfil the object for which they were erected, for the Turcomans and Kirgis regard them as impregnable fortresses, and the occupants, who are mostly armed, believe themselves to be perfectly secure within their walls. The slaves and domestics live generally in felt tents pitched in the court-yard, and the horses stand there also, so that a night *sortie* on the besieging body is no difficult matter.

Forts of this description are very prevalent in Khiva, and they give their owners a great sense of personal security.

Fortified towns.—As the five principal towns before mentioned are surrounded by walls, they are looked on in Khiva as fortresses, but the walls are built without science, taste, or regularity. They are about 36 feet thick at the base, but have only a height of 48 feet; they are constructed of mud and have towers at certain intervals, in short, they entirely resemble the private forts, except that they enclose a much greater area.

The towns also are without ditches, and have no heavy guns and no garrison, so that in the event of an attack their defence would be left to the citizens.

Castles belonging to the Khan.—As the Khan spends most of his time in hunting, away from the town of Khiva, he also possesses some fortified country houses which completely answer to the description of the others, only they are rather larger.

The principal ones are : Ak Serai, Mai Jangal, Khan Kalassi, &c.

War Army.—The Khan of Khiva has no real standing army. In the event of a war an army is raised from among the Turcomans and Usbegs, who form the military order exclusively. When the Khan summons them they are bound to arm and follow him at once, all being mounted. There are no degrees of rank in this force, but the bravest warriors who have distinguished themselves in forays or other warlike enterprises form the Khan's body-guard, and always accompany him. Now when the Khan entrusts the charge of an expedition of any sort to one or more of this *élite*, Usbegs and Turcomans detach themselves from their respective bands and come forward as volunteers for the raid in the hope of plunder, and form the expeditionary force under the leader, who is now called "Sirdar." They follow the latter to whereever he will lead them, but otherwise he has not the slightest control over his band.

Mode of attack.—When they meet their enemy, immediately the bravest warriors dash to the front with terrible shouts and throw themselves on the foe, the remainder of the force acting each as his amount of valour may dictate ; should the first onslaught succeed, then the battle is decided, for the leaders of the worsted side immediately fly the field, and the victors spur after them, cutting down all who resist, and carrying off the disarmed as slaves. Such are the battles sung with so much spirit by the bards of Asia.

Their heroes are men without honor, greedy only for spoil, who muster sufficient spasmodic courage at the moment of onset, but thousands of whom would show their backs to a few hundred regulars.

Strength of the Khan's army.—The largest number of well armed troops that Khiva can furnish does not exceed 12,000, but when the Khanate is menaced by any great danger, the Khan forces the Sarts and Karakalpaks to bear arms ; now although this supplement doubles or trebles the strength of the army, it does not make it in reality more formidable, on the contrary, it acts rather as a drag upon it, for neither Sarts nor Karakalpaks have any liking for war, or aptitude for warlike exercises, and they are badly armed besides.

Equipment of the army.—The Khivan troops must pay for their own equipment, with the exception of the Turcomans, who receive an equipment allowance of from 5 to 20 tillas per man from the Khan.

Supplies and Baggage.—The soldiers must subsist themselves during the whole campaign ; therefore every one who is well off starts with a heavily laden camel carrying his supplies, while the poorer individuals have one camel between two. It can easily be imagined what a huge baggage train this must entail, what a host of attendants and slaves, and what an unwieldy and cumbrous thing a Khivan army moving on active service must be. The consequence of these impediments is that the army never makes a longer march than ten miles in one day.

In spite of the supplies brought from home, all go out plundering, and carry off everything that the country through which they are passing contains. Such a force can never be kept together in the field for more than six weeks at a stretch, for there is absolutely no discipline, and when bad weather sets in, or there begins to be a scarcity of provisions, or should the first attack fail, every man turns homewards.

No one is punished for this desertion, but can leave the ranks whenever it seems good to him without any further enquiries being made, for there is no martial law, and the soldier is not paid for his services.

The different arms. Cavalry.—The Khivans have no infantry; every soldier is mounted. Their operations are therefore strictly confined to the level plain, and they are baffled by the most insignificant field work. Those who have seen Asiatic troops assert that a few companies of regulars could rout these great masses of irregulars with ease. The only difficulty would be in getting at them, and in provisioning one's own force. The Turcoman horses are very fleet, and no broken cavalry horses could possibly keep up with them; besides the uniform of an European dragoon puts him at a great disadvantage to the active Turcoman in his easy dress.

Artillery.—The Khivan artillery consists of 30 pieces of ordnance of different calibres, according to their own account; but at Khiva I saw only seven guns, which stood in one of the court-yards of the Khan's palace.

They were all in the worst possible order, the wheels and carriages broken, but otherwise resembled Russian pieces. For my own part I do not believe the story of the 30 guns; had they been in existence, they would certainly have been drawn up for my edification. It is most likely that the Usbegs felt their own weakness in this arm, and tried to veil it by a false statement. They assured me that they had a few pieces of extraordinary size. As the Khan has a gun foundry of his own, it is not impossible that he may possess a few more guns than the seven I saw, but if he does, I should say they were in a very bad state, and hardly fit to be used.

Casting Guns.—The first attempt at casting guns in Khiva was a complete failure, for they were cast hollow, and generally burst at the first discharge. The Khan then followed the advice of a Russian slave, and had them cast solid, and as no one knew how to drill out the bore, Mahomed Ragim sent to Constantinople for a gun-founder, who actually did turn him out some pieces of artillery. The scarcity of the metal in Khiva makes it improbable that more than a very few pieces are cast in the Khanate.

Service of the Guns.—In an expedition the artillery accompanies the Khan, horses dragging the guns. Russian slaves serve the latter, for the Usbegs consider them more skilful than themselves or any other race in the Khanate. Notwithstanding, however, that they have Russian Artillerymen, selected for being the best gunners, eye-witnesses declare that the Khivan artillery is of no use.

Besides the heavier pieces the Khivans have a few falconets.

Gunpowder.—Powder is manufactured in the country, and to a considerable extent. The Sarts are the principal manufacturers.

The soil yields plenty of saltpetre, and sulphur comes from the Sheikh Jeri mountains.

Gunpowder is very cheap, but it has no strength, for the Khivans are ignorant as to the proper proportion of the ingredients.

The possibility of conquering Khiva.—Although Prince Bekovitsh's expedition failed, it yet demonstrated the possibility of subjugating Khiva ; for he penetrated into the interior with only a very small force, and even with that would certainly have been successful, had he shown greater courage and capacity.

At the present day a determined and independent leader with 3,000 brave Russian soldiers could conquer the country —a country so important by reason of the influence it exercises on the trade of Asia. We could utilise the knowledge we have now acquired of the Khanate and of the individuals holding the high State offices, and could turn to account the disaffection of the Usbegs towards the reigning Khan and the friendly spirit of the neighbouring nomad tribes. The latter adhere to Khiva solely, because they are dependent on the Khanate for their grain supply, and would come over to us at once if we were to make Russia their "land of Egypt," which could easily be arranged.

Once in Khiva, the invading army would be increased by 3,000 Russian and 30,000 Persian slaves, the latter race being particularly anxious to ally themselves to us. The only difficulty appears to be the march through the steppe, but this would be readily overcome, for the route from the Caspian to Khiva is now well enough known ; and with regard to provisions, it would be unnecessary to take more than would be sufficient for the actual journey, as Khiva itself abounds in supplies. The transport arrangements would be entrusted to the Turcomans of the Caspian, who would gladly undertake them, and give their general support to the expedition. The Turcomans would supply horses accustomed to the steppe for the use of the force. The feasibility of this enterprise is already proved by the circumstance that Mahomed Ragim has himself made the march to the shores of the Caspian with 12,000 horse. We could therefore penetrate to Khiva with a small army without difficulty, provided ordinary measures of precaution were taken. I consider the present moment to be the most suitable one for the undertaking, as the political state of the country favours us. The Khan is not yet quite established on his throne, and there are now malcontents among his subjects who will subside in time, when the despot shall have increased his power and become a dangerous neighbour to surrounding States.

Ascendancy of the Khivans over their neighbours.—However unworthy of respect may be the troops of Khiva as compared to a regular army, they are nevertheless dreadful in the eyes of the neighbouring nomadic races. The Kirgis have several times been defeated by them, and Mahomed Ragim has overthrown the Takkas who opposed him ; but the Khivans do not owe their triumphs to a better organized army, but to their superior numbers and to the awe inspired by the harmless thunder of their cannon.

The Khan is fond of being present at a battle, and incites the combatants to deeds of valour, rewarding the brave, and inspiring all his troops with an honourable spirit of emulation.

He does not, however, expose himself to danger, but finds his greatest enjoyment in beheading those captives who have enraged him by a courageous resistance.

His rank exempts him from risking his life, but it is said that in his youth he displayed great bravery, never sparing himself, and venturing all to gain the object immediately before him.

Fortune has since then spoiled him, and his valour has degenerated into the fury of a wild beast.

Khivan arms.—The arms of the Khivans are the sword, dagger, lance, bow and arrow, and musket. They sometimes wear coats of mail and helmets, and when they are opposed by an enemy thus protected they attack him with the mace.

Swords.—Their swords are curved and some of them are of excellent Khorassan steel. They form their favourite weapon, but they do not understand the art of making them themselves, and employ Russian slaves for the purpose. Swords are sold for large sums and have often handsome leather scabbards.

Their daggers are huge knives, but they do not often wear them.

Lances.—Only some have lances, and those who have, seldom use them.

The lance shaft is thin, not more than nine feet long, and headed with good iron.

Bows and Arrows.—Bows and arrows are used by those who have no fire-arms. The bows are small and have little spring in them, sending an arrow only a third of the distance that a native of Kabarda shoots up to with his bow. The blame is, perhaps, with the bow strings, as the Khivans do not understand the manufacture of good ones.

Fire-arms.—They have but few muskets, and those they have are very long and heavy, with a small bore. If loaded with good powder, they carry fairly, but are very unwieldy. They cannot be used from horseback, as they must be fired from a rest, so they are only employed in sieges. The barrels are often inlaid with silver, and some, but very few, have locks like the Persian muskets. The Khivans are good shots at a fixed mark, but their preliminary arrangements are so multifarious and slow, that their fire-arms are hardly worth the trouble they give. The marksman has to lie flat on his stomach and take a long aim, in the course of which he often lets his match go out, and when all goes well he cannot be sure of hitting anything at a greater distance than 60 or 80 paces. This description applies more or less to all Asiatic nations, and yet we hear travellers loud in their praises of Asiatic marksmen.

Pistols are hardly known in Khiva, owing probably to the difficulty of getting locks.

Helmets and Armour.—Some Khivans wear helmets and armour, but those can only be of service against an enemy without fire-arms.

Maces.—The mace is a common weapon. It is like a hammer with a head pointed at one end and blunt at the other, and a long handle.

Horses.—The swift, strong, and beautiful Turcoman horses are of the utmost value to the Khivans.

The hardship and fatigue endured by this breed are hardly credible. A Turcoman horse will hold out during an eight days' journey through the desert without grass, and supported only by a little jugan, and will go without any water whatsoever for four days on end. Turcomans feed their horses when they are quite heated and then give them a long gallop.

Saddles.—The Khivan saddle slightly differs from the Persian one. It has the same high seat, but the cantle is much broader. The head gear is sometimes very costly, the cheek leathers, &c., being covered with silver plates and precious stones.

Marauding.—We may lay it down as a fact that the Khivans are not adapted to the carrying out of any warlike enterprise which demands time and endurance. Their favourite trade is that of a robber, and their favourite resort for pillage the Persian frontier.

The "*fainéantise*" of the Government of Persia and the deserts lying between that country and Khiva account for the frequent recurrence of Khivan inroads and for their remaining unpunished.

A young Khivan, arrived at man's estate, must signalise his entry into the grown up world by a deed of rapine, until when he has the regard neither of his father nor of his friends. The more successful robberies he commits, the sooner will his name reach the ears of the Khan, who will stimulate him to go on by appointing him to his guard and making him a few presents. Mahomed Ragim encourages marauding on principle, for he gets a fifth share of all the booty. The Usbegs seldom or never engage in plundering forays, but leave the robber trade to the Turcoman inhabitants of the Khanate. The following is the *modus operandi* of a Khivan robber gang. They collect in a band of from

50 to 300 horsemen, and make straight for the Persian frontier by some familiar route, taking with them a considerable number of camels to bring back the spoil.

At a day and a half's journey from the frontier they halt at some secluded and easily defended spot, and send forward those of the band who have friends or relations among the Turcomans on the border. The latter, although sometimes in vassalage to Persia, joyfully welcome the robbers, and indicate to them the best points to attack in order to make a profitable raid. When they have obtained all the necessary information, the marauders fall unexpectedly on the villages or caravans they have been directed to, and pillage them, carrying everything away. They are careful not to take the lives of their victims, each person killed being a slave the less, but drag them off without respect to age or sex, to be disposed of in Khiva, where a terrible fate and cruel bondage await the unfortunate beings.

Many of the captives sink on the road and are left to die of want or to become the prey of wild beasts.

On their return to Khiva the band must give up a fifth share of their booty to the Khan, who thanks them for the same, and presents them with clothing, &c.

When they capture a prisoner of good or wealthy family, they take great care of him, and on no account send him into the market, in the hope that his relations will come forward with a large ransom. It often happens too that Turcomans from the Giurgan repair to Khiva for a bribe, and kidnap Persian slaves there in order to return them to their people.

Favourite resorts of the marauding bands.—The Turcomans make their inroads into Persia from several points. If their numbers be inconsiderable, they remain in the neighbourhood of the sea, and pillage the Astrabad District, but if they are in force, they go up the Giurgan River and ravage the Khorassan border. Those wooded districts serve their purpose admirably, for they can with ease conceal themselves among the trees and await a good opportunity to fall on the passers by. They make their expeditions generally in the autumn, when they have got their harvest in, and feed up their horses beforehand for the purpose.

Warlike character of the Khivans.—The Usbegs are much less adapted for war than the Turcomans; they are a handsomer and richer race, and look upon themselves as noblemen, but they do not care to go out into the steppe. Their dress lies nearer to their heart than their weapons do, and they comfort themselves with the thought that the Turcomans are bound to protect their country for them, and to sell them booty.*

The Sarts possess no warlike qualities; like the Jews, they love money and hate the smell of gunpowder. A weapon in their hands makes them ridiculous, and the Usbegs say of them that the yard measure becomes them better than the sword. For the rest, the valour of both Usbegs and Turcomans is renowned throughout the East.

The wealthy Khivans generally keep a bard in their service, who entertains them with stories and songs, and airs played on a sorry kind of lute. Sometimes they compose ballads relating the deeds of ancient heroes. The applause accorded to these bards frequently raises them to a pitch approaching ecstasy, when they elevate their voices yet higher, and strive by their gestures to bring home to their audience the valour and lofty deeds of the departed warriors. This singing is kept up the whole night not unfrequently, during which the host and his guests sit attentively listening, motionless, and apparently buried in meditation.

The white bearded bards sometimes sit before the door, celebrating in their songs the days of yore, the feats of their master's ancestors, &c.

---

* This is one of several conflicting statements made by Muraviev with regard to the Usbeg character.—W. S. A. L.

Chapter V
Character, Religion, Customs
and Enlightenment of the Uzbegs

Character and physique of the Usbegs.—The Usbegs are on the whole sensible, agreeable, and witty. In their undertakings they show steadfastness and determination. They are upright and abhor a lie, despising the cheat and the time-server. War is their passion, and they prefer it to a life of quiet; it and marauding, therefore, are their principal employments. Their frames are powerful, well proportioned, and large, their complexion suggests the Calmuck, but has something agreeable about it; their eyes are large and piercing, and their beards black. They lead a lazy, careless life, despising all work except war; but although they are good robbers, they are only warriors by name, and do not like going far from home on an expedition; once in the field though, they are indefatigable, ardent, and audacious.

They have extraordinarily good constitutions, sometimes possessing great muscular power, and numbers of them live for upwards of 100 years.

Costume.—Their clothing consists of three or four padded coats, one over the other, no matter how warm the weather may be. The coats are made of silk stuff, striped, and chiefly of a lilac colour. Their shirts are like those of the Russians, *viz.*, cut out at the neck. In winter they wear wadded shirts and pantaloons, over which they draw great yellow boots with high heels and long pointed toes. They shave their heads, and wear large black hats of Bokharian lambskin, over a skull cap corresponding in colour to the coat. The wealthy sometimes have their coats made of cloth, but that is very rare. They delight to sit with bare-feet, and the best welcome to a guest is to ask him to take off his boots. In winter furs are brought into use. The Turcomans wear coats of yellow camlet, made of camel's hair.

Women.—The women are very beautiful, although there is a dash of the Calmuck about their faces also. Their eyes are piercing and their complexion brown, but pleasing. They dress in a very strange costume, and generally go about veiled. Like all Asiatics, the Khivans are very jealous. They shut their wives up in harems and make them one of the chief objects of their existence, but the ladies are often the cause of feuds and murder. No one, not even the nearest relation, is permitted to enter the female apartments, and the women are condemned to a life of the strictest solitude and most dreadful *ennui*. They are slaves, and on a man's death, the son has a right to sell them at pleasure.

Education of Children.—The Khivans pay hardly any attention to the training of their children, and confine their exertions in this respect to corporal punishment irrespective of age, so that the children lose all respect for their parents and are sometimes to be seen stoning them. Religious teaching is unknown, and the most that a father cares for is that his children shall observe the outward forms. Sometimes reading and writing are taught. A boy of 12 or 13 left to his own devices educates himself entirely by his own experience.

The father takes him into his service like a common attendant, and he must strictly obey his master until his 18th year. Then he marries, but it happens often that the bridegroom has not seen his bride until the wedding day. The state of servitude in which these lads are held by their parents almost surpasses belief. They are not permitted to sit down in the presence of their fathers, much less eat with them, and occupy a lower position than the domestic servants, for, if the servant be an Usbeg like his master, he is permitted to sit down with him, and sometimes to eat out of the same dish even.

Usbeg avarice.—The Usbegs are very avaricious, and conceal their money, sometimes burying it in the ground, but this is probably from fear of the Khan.

Usbeg hospitality.—Although they are very hospitable, they neutralise this virtue to a great extent by their avarice. They certainly never refuse their hospitality, but they exercise it in as narrow a manner as possible, and make up for any extra outlay by stinting themselves on the following day, or by sponging upon a neighbour.

Diet.—They are as greedy and gluttonous when feasting at another's expense, as they are frugal at home. Their favourite dish is "pilau," but they seldom indulge in it, and substitute for it a small wheaten loaf, some milk, soup, some mutton, &c. This meal they call "Mustapha." If they want to entertain any one in a better style, they add to the above items a greasy soup and a joint of mutton roasted over charcoal without butter. They do not despise camel's or horse flesh, and are often to be seen, when on their travels, devouring the flesh of animals who have sunk on the road. They are very fond of sweetmeats, especially sugar and comfits, and gorge themselves with those dainties when they can do so without paying for the treat, but the richest will grudge himself the smallest piece of sugar if he has to stand the cost of it himself.

The Usbegs hate all strong drinks and abhor drunkenness, but the latter is a common vice among the Sarts and Kazil Jilams, who look on drinking as their greatest pleasure, and cannot practise moderation in it.

Tea is the favourite beverage of the Khivans. They make it very strong, and prepare it in a copper kettle, which they say improves the flavour. They do not use sugar, but drink it as it is from morning to night, and eat the leaves. So fond are they of tea, that they would rather endure hunger for several days than go without it when on a journey. Besides tea in the ordinary form, they also use the so-called Calmuck or brick-tea, which is boiled with milk, butter, and salt, a combination most distasteful to those who have not accustomed themselves to it.

The diet of the slaves and servant class is very bad, the latter have to be content with what is left from the tables of their masters, and they struggle and fight amongst themselves for the fragments. The slaves, however, receive from their owners a fixed quantity of grain, of which they sell a portion, and save the proceeds, either to buy their freedom or provide themselves with clothes. These wretched creatures frequently go a whole day without a meal, and keep soul and body together by what they can beg or steal.

The Khivans are extraordinarily dirty in their habits. Like all Asiatics, they eat without knife, fork, or spoon, and their frequent ablutions before and after meat have only the semblance of cleanliness. They do not shrink from the filthiest person, if he only attend to their superficial forms, but look with disgust on the cleanliest if he neglect the smallest conventional usage, and hold him to be impure.

Dwelling houses.—Their dwelling houses are devoid of windows and flooring, and of furniture of any sort.

They sit on carpets and eat out of great bowls, round which they squat. This custom is universal, common to the beggar and the Khan.

Their dishes are of stone, perfectly plain, or sometimes they use wooden Astraccan ones. Tea they drink out of China cups. Their cooking pots are generally of cast iron.

There are two meals in the day, the one soon after sunrise, the other before sunset. Before eating they generally say a prayer and stroke their beards. Their board presents a ludicrous but at the same time a digusting appearance. They are fond of ginger-bread and of all aromatic herbs, and throw pepper and ginger into their tea.

They take opium several times a day, and smoke Bokharan tobacco from a "Kaliyan" made out of a gourd. They also smoke the leaves of a plant called "bang," which has an intoxicating effect on those who are not accustomed to its use.

The houses are very bad and wretched, and a great portion of the people live in felt tents all the year round. Even the wealthy do this, although they possess houses, because they are so accustomed to a nomadic life. The houses are of mud, cost very little, are speedily constructed, and last for a considerable time owing to the paucity of rain. The interiors are narrow, dirty, cold, and dark ; the fire is made in the centre of the room, and the smoke finds egress from a small aperture in the roof, which is stopped up at night with hay or rags.

The thatch consists only of rushes or dried boughs. In most houses all the members of the family inhabit one, or at most, two filthy rooms. Their stables are kept much cleaner, for they love their horses, although they do not feed them very abundantly.

Buildings.—Several of their mosques are handsome edifices enough, the handsomest being the great one at Khiva with its turquoise blue dome. Their tombs are pretty neat.

Bridges are numerous, and are constructed of the burnt bricks which they get from old ruins.

There are no other buildings of any importance. Canals and tanks are unscientifically dug. In general, buildings, &c., are only built to last a short time, as there is no security of property in the country. Even those works whose solid construction in the first instance would contribute, not to their comfort, but to their real profit, are run up in the same flimsy manner. The houses are generally provided with roofed verandahs, where the occupants take their ease during the heat of the day.

Pastimes.—One of the chief pursuits and certainly the chief amusement of the Usbegs is hawking wild goats and different species of birds. They do not like hunting with dogs, for they despise those useful animals. They are fond of racing, and show a good deal of skill in that sport. They nearly all play chess, and some of them have acquired great proficiency at it. They also play draughts and a sort of game of tables called "Etel" in which 32 pieces of equal value are used, and drawn up as in chess. The moves resemble those of draughtsmen, only instead of being oblique they are direct, either to the front or the flank.

Music.—The Khivans love music, that is to say, they are ignorant of both time and harmony, but they love a great noise, and call it music. For instance, drumming, shouting, or a man bellowing with might and main please them much more than the finest harmony of the sweetest instruments. When they sing, two voices never go together, but, on the other hand, they pay great attention to the words which are generally those of their best poets. Their musical instruments are a two-stringed lute, played either with a pin or the fingers, and a kind of rustic fiddle with four strings, and the most abominable tone, which is planted on the ground like a violoncello and played with a bow. The Usbegs look down on musicians and players, saying that their vocations only become those who have to live for the amusement of others, but would disgrace one of the warrior class. Some of them hold music to be a profane amusement, and would sit with folded arms for weeks together rather than have anything to do with it.

Religion.—The Usbegs, like all the other inhabitants of Khiva, are Mahomedans of the Suni sect. They believe in one God and in Mahomed as the latest and greatest Prophet who was sent to inculcate the doctrines of a true religion. They are very careful to repeat all the prayers laid down by the Commandments, and never put off a night prayer for longer than the following evening. Their hours for business are regulated by their hours for prayer, which they know so well by habit that they never make a mistake.

Like all Mahomedans, they count their hours from sunrise or rather from the first prayer until the last. It is ordained that ablutions should be performed before prayers, and in the arid steppes, where water is not procurable, travellers purify themselves with sand instead.

Altogether they reverence God, and never allow anything to distract their attention whilst they are at worship.

The Sunis fold their hands at prayers, whilst the Shias let them hang down by their sides, therefore the Khivans say of them "these infidels do this, in order not to stain their clothes with the innocent blood, in which their hands are imbrued." This animosity against the Shias is much fiercer than their aversion to Christians, for they consider that we adhere to the doctrines laid down by our faith, whilst the Shias infringe the laws of theirs every hour by their unbelief.

The Sunis, more especially the Usbegs and Turcomans, consider it a noble and praiseworthy act to injure the Shias in any possible manner, and rejoice in shedding their blood, particularly if they are Persians.

Every Persian captive is forced to become a follower of Omar, but still he must remain a slave, as it were in punishment for having ever been a Shia.

During their wars in foreign territory they put their opponents to death with the greatest cruelty and carry off the property of their co-religionists, the Turcomans, but on their return home they do penance for the murder and ravages committed on their Suni brethren by fasting, prayers, and ablutions. Those acts of penance are a source of great profit to the priesthood.

No other religion but the national one is tolerated in the Khanate, but the Russians seldom change their faith, and even hold private meetings for prayer in spite of the stringent orders against this. Their good qualities, bodily strength, and industry have won them the respect of their oppressors even in their state of bondage, so that the latter, bigotted Mussulmans, as they are, waive in their favour those laws of the Mahomedan faith which prohibit the tolerance of any other. Russian slaves are even allowed to cele- brate the festivals of the birth, baptism, and resurrection of our Lord, and on those days are excused from all work. On the holidays mentioned they meet together and amuse themselves with national games, or drown the thoughts of their suffering in deep potations of a kind of brandy which they make themselves.

There are Jews in Khiva, but they have long ago re- nounced their religion, and are now as ardent Sunis as any other Khivans.

A Mussulman is allowed to have four wives, but the number of concubines is unlimited. The usual custom in Khiva is to have two wives and one concubine; but the rich are not so moderate.

Mahomedans worship Saints and frequently call on them in time of need. The Usbegs have also their own particular Saints or Imam, whose tombs are scattered all over the Khanate, but who do not enjoy an equal celebrity. The Yomud Turcomans adore a Saint over whose tomb they settle their differences by an oath. A false oath under those circumstances is unknown, for it is firmly believed that whoever forswears himself over the tomb can only save himself from eternal punishment by dying on the spot.

Their religion prescribes a number of forms and ceremonies, which they never neglect. They contract marriages with women of their own sect, and would not dare to marry from any other, as other Sunis often do. Every Usbeg would regard such a step as a heinous sin, and they keep themselves aloof from other races who are not strict in this respect, refusing to intermarry with them, or to pray in their company.

Soothsaying.—The Khivans practise divination, the learned among them by observation of the stars, and the vulgar by two methods which I shall describe. According to the first method the soothsayer repeats a prayer, then fetches a book (carrying it on his head), opens it and notes the first letter on the first line of the page; from that he counts down to the seventh line, notes the letter there, and then turns over 7 pages and commences " da capo," and so on. Every letter having its peculiar significance, the soothsayer is enabled to weave a prophecy out of the combination of letters he turns up. The other method is as follows :—As many sticks as there are letters in the alphabet are laid together as radii from a common centre, each stick representing a particular letter. The soothsayer then closes his eyes and throws a number of other little sticks over those arranged on the ground, and the letters represented by the sticks covered in this manner are combined and form the basis of the divination.

Ideas of good and evil.—The Khivans consider every crime committed in the heat of passion to be directly prompted by the devil, and say that when a man feels this prompting in his heart he should refrain from speech until the fit has passed over.

The term " evil " they apply to that act which injures a neighbour, and " good " to that which rejoices the heart and does no one harm.

Language.—The Khivans speak the so-called Jagata dialect of the Turkish language, which much resembles that of the Tartars in Cazan, and widely differs from the common language of Persia. They have several words quite peculiar to themselves.

They also change the letters b into m, m into b, p into ph, ph into p, u into v, v into u, d into t, and often prefix the letter b to words beginning with o. Their writing is the same as the Turkish. The Usbegs talk very fast and continually change their key; any one hearing them converse, and not understanding their language, would imagine that they were abusing each other.

Intellectual culture.—They stand very low in the scale of enlightenment and education. Very few are able to read or write, but some of those few have acquired a knowledge of Arabic and Persian, and write verses in those languages, an acquaintance with astrology and a smattering of medicine. They are nearly in total ignorance of astronomy, only knowing a few of the principal stars. The north star they call "Demur Kasik," *i.e.*, " iron point," because they believe it to be the end of the earth's axis. In Khiva there is a man who can calculate eclipses, but only mechanically; his fame as a learned man is great, and he lives at the Khan's Court. He also practises soothsaying, and is very proud of his attainments, although he does not even know the cause of an eclipse, but believes with the rest of the people that it is brought about by the devil fastening his claws on to the sun or moon, and thinks a loud noise and the firing off of guns necessary to get rid of this dreadful enemy.

The earth they believe to be round and compare it to a water-melon.

Medicine.—They have cultivated medicine more than all the other sciences, and yet it is quite in its infancy with them. Their treatment consists usually in employing remedies the most antagonistic to the disease, for example, they treat inflammation with ice, debility by applying heat, &c.

The profession of physician is hereditary, for they know a number of every-day cures and medicinal herbs, which they keep secret.

They are very skilful in the treatment of wounds. Like all Asiatics, the Khivans are fond of taking physic, and have the greatest confidence in European Doctors. One has only to hold out a glass and say it contains medicine to be overwhelmed with the rush of sick people. In illnesses they often have recourse to witchcraft. An ancient Persian physician, by name Lokman, has a great celebrity in Asia, but, like other Oriental sages, his fame has descended in sayings and *bons mots* rather than in any true medical lore. I do not know if this Lokman really was an expert physician or not, but this is certain that the fame of his skill is universally spread throughout Asia, although no mention is made of any cures performed by him. The following is an anecdote related of him :—

He once sent his slave to the market, commanding him to purchase there "a life," or if he could not find a whole life to bring him half of one, if this also were not procurable, then he was to bring him some poison. The slave returned and said he could purchase none of the articles required, when Lokman proceeded to interpret his commissions, and explained that by "a life," he meant meat, because nothing gives so much nourishment and strength as that food, by "half a life" he meant eggs, as the latter are in a smaller degree conducive to vigour, whilst by "poison" he meant cheese, because he regarded that as hurtful to the system. This and such like foolery have been the means of gaining for him the reputation of a sage in the East.

Khivan physicians lay down four things as the elements of life, the most important of which are the blood and the bile, which accordingly must be taken the greatest care of.

They believe that the blood vanishes from the veins on death, because it does not flow from a corpse. Bleeding is one of their favourite and most efficacious remedies. They often let blood from the head, and have many different ways of bleeding, sometimes making numerous incisions in the afflicted part of the body.

Historical knowledge.—Learned Khivans devote themselves greatly to the study of the ancient history of the East, and have no ordinary acquaintance with it, but they unfortunately mix it up so with wild fables, as to obscure what it really contains of truth.

Mathematics.—They have no knowledge whatsoever of mathematics. Instead of figures they use letters of the alphabet, just as at one time Slavonic letters were used in Russian prayer books. Some, however, have a knowledge of the decimal system of counting and of Arabic notation. They know nothing beyond this, and one of the hardest tasks for them is to express in figures a number containing several hundreds of thousands. They are ignorant of the four simple rules of arithmetic.

Geography.—Being surrounded by desert on every side, the Khivans have only very crude ideas of other countries.

They know all about those in their own immediate neighbourhood such as Persia and Bokhara, which latter, by the way, they hold to be the most powerful monarchy in the world, saying that Greece (which they call " Urum " and by which they understand Turkey) was and is still a great power, but cannot approach Bokhara.

Their knowledge of Russia is derived from their merchants, the Sarts. They therefore know of its division into 52 departments, and compare every department to Astraccan, with which they are best acquainted. They have also acquired from the Sarts some idea of the power of Russia, but they cannot grasp the fact of any one nation being so vast in extent as to contain several seas within its boundaries; they therefore hold that the Russian frontier districts are provinces each under its own hereditary Prince, but that the latter, although in possession of full power over their subjects, are the vassals of the Czar. The Khivans call Astraccan " Khaji Terkhan " which means the free or untaxed Khaji, Orenburg they call " Angi kila," or the new fortress, and Guryev, " Sarajik " or the little fort.

They are much better acquainted with Afghanistan. India is also well known to them, and goes by the name of " Multan." * They have even some vague ideas about Cochin. China they call " Chin " or " Chinimachin." They generally call Europe Frankistan, or the land of the Franks, and call all Europeans by the latter name, with the exception of the English, whom they know as the " Lords of the sea."

The chief instruction imparted in Khiva is religious, their books being the Koran and the works of some Arabic writers, particularly those which treat on philosophy. For some time back their attention has been turned to this study, and they have therefore begun to have their children instructed in reading and writing.

---

* The word Multan is in Khiva a term of abuse.
It is a great insult to call a man " Multan " or Multan Oglu (son of a Hindoo).

Supplement
The Trade Route from Astraccan
to Mangushlak and Khiva and Bokhara

THE Russian ships engaged in the Astraccan and Khiva trade generally repair to the Bay of Kutsh or, as the Russians term it, Mangushlak Harbour, passing between Cape Karagan and the islands of Kulaya and Svatoi. The country about Mangushlak is bleak and bare, but directly the masts of the Russian ships are descried by the nomad Turcomans on the coast, swift horsemen are despatched with the news to Khiva, and Arabs, Khivans, Turcomans, and Bokharans hasten to the rendezvous with the goods they have to barter.

The return caravans go from Mangushlak over the mountains lying to the east of the Caspian to Urganj; Turcoman camels were formerly employed for this, but the Kirgis are now entrusted with the transport of the goods.

The caravans have to march for rather more than 20 days over the mountains before they descend into a valley where the range bifurcates and trends off in opposite directions to two mountain chains in the vicinity.

The mountain road is stony and almost entirely devoid of trees, but wells are sunk in suitable places. Midway there stands a square enclosure consisting of a wall 12 feet high and 1,200 feet in circumference, with a gateway in it. In the interior there are neither buildings nor ruins. The Turcomans call this Olank, and say it was built in ancient days by a race whose name they do not know, who quarried the material from the bed of stone lying at the foot of the enclosure. This is very likely, as the shores of the lake* contain the same kind of stone as that which the walls are composed of.

The banks are steep and high, and only a narrow foot-path leads down to the water.

The lake is very deep and never still, but it contains no fish, and a remarkable circumstance is that since 1804 the

---

* The German translator has made some omission here evidently as no former mention has been made of this lake.—W. S. A. L.

water which before was always salt has been fresh, and that the same sudden change occurred in the same year to many springs in the mountain.

Further in the interior by about a day's journey (or a little more) there is another lake on the left hand side of the road which is exactly 1,800 feet in circumference. Its bottom is muddy, and from the high rocky banks numerous springs noisily discharge salt water into it. In the distance there is a mountain, on which one can descry a square stone castle on a clear day. No one knows what is to be seen there, but a tradition says that the place was built before the Mahomedan era by a conqueror of many nations called Iskander (Alexander the Great) or "Zulkarnain;" that after him another conqueror, called Jamshid, buried untold treasures in this castle; and lastly, that Timerlane once intended to occupy it, but was deterred by some cause or other, which may explain the peculiar name it goes by, *viz.*, Bir-Sa-Kilmos, *i.e.*, "he has gone and is lost," or "he goes away and returns not."

In the mountains there are wild horses, buffaloes, foxes, (here called Karachanki) and hares. The wild horses sometimes gambol up to the caravans; they are smaller than the domestic horses of the country.

There are coral reefs on the Mangushlak coast.*

On the descent to the valley there is a lake which formed itself in the year 1800 in an angle made by the two mountain chains before mentioned.

The name of this lake is Oi-Bogur, it is about 2,400 feet in circumference, is deep, and full of the same kind of fish that are caught in the Caspian. The Turcomans therefore believe that it is connected with that sea by subterraneous channels; but one may more reasonably conclude that the fish came from the sea of Aral, which is connected with the Oi-Bogur Lake, during the spring floods by means of a branch of the Amu Dariya, whilst another arm of the same stream runs away to the south-west at that season, and every year lessens the distance between the point it reaches and the Caspian.

With regard to the sudden appearance of the Oi-Bogur Lake, that must be attributed to the effects of an earthquake. In the interior of the mountain range there are many places where the ground gives out a hollow sound when struck by anything heavy, and there are many chasms, one of which,

---

* These remarks appear to have been set down very much at random.— W. S. A. L.

a very deep and dark one, is said to have been formed by a caravan falling through the thin upper crust.

On the Mangushlak coast there is a volcanic mountain called Abishtsha, from whose open crater sulphurous smoke continually rises ; black stones lie around.

The mountains in this neighbourhood are generally covered with mist ; torrents of rain are frequent ; and the sun, although it often shines, never does so for any very long period together.

From the mountains to Urganj the road lies through level ground. Trees of different kinds grow on either side, and one species called the Sak-Saul is very plentiful.

This tree is about 18 feet high, is very leafy, with long branches, and is so hard that it is difficult to fell it with an axe. Its wood is brittle and sinks in water. In this wooded district there are different kinds of wild beasts, even lions among the rest. Caravans from Bokhara have abandoned this route for some time in order to avoid being attacked by the Turcomans.

They now take either the road to Orenburg or to the Sarotshikovski Custom House.

The caravans take five days to go from the Oi-Bogur Lake to Urganj. From Urganj to Khiva is a distance of 58 miles.

Caravans for Bokhara only go as far as the first town in that country, El-jik, whence the light articles are sent into the interior by land in three days, whilst the heavy goods are despatched up the Amu Dariya on badly built rafts, towed by men, for there the use of neither oar nor sail is known.

Table of the principal Usbeg tribes

USBEG.

Mahomed Ragim Khan.

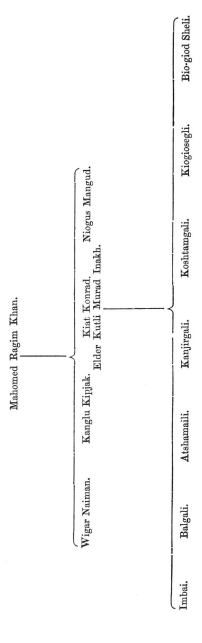

Wigar Naiman. Kanglu Kipjak. Kiat Konrad. Niogus Mangud.
Elder Kutli Murad Inakh.

Imbai. Balgali. Atshamaili. Kanjirgali. Koshtamgali. Kiogiosegli. Bio-giod Sheli.

Notes

by M. Klaproth
Translated from the French edition of 1823 by Kate Thurlow

THE TURKOMAN

The Turkoman are a people of Turkish race who, during the 11th and 12th centuries, swarmed into Bukhara, Northern Persia and, to the west of the Caspian Sea, into Armenia, Southern Georgia, Shirvan and Daghestan. They were a nomadic people and formed the greater part of the population of the countries named above, where they were called TAREKAME, TURKOMAN, and KIZYL-BACHI. According to Persian tradition the Turkomans are so called because at the time of the Turkish invasion of Khorassan the invading tribes married into the conquered race and their descendants were given the name Turkoman, meaning 'resembling the Turks'. This seemingly plausible explanation cannot however be altogether relied upon since other Turkish speaking tribes of people who settled far away from that area also called themselves by the same name, Turkoman. My opinion is that the name Turkoman was derived from 'Turk' and 'Roman' and that it referred to those people who settled to the East of the Caspian sea under the domination of the Altai Turks, and to those who settled in the vast plains to the West of the Caspian and to the North of Palus-Meolidir, spreading later as far as Hungary.

THE UZBEK

The etymological explanation for the name of these people, given by Nikolay Mourav'yov, does not, in my opinion, ring true. The Orientals are great inventors of stories and especially of explanations to fit a word, as can be seen by the wealth of explanations for names found in the Old Testament. Even today, if a town somewhere in Syria, Arabia or Egypt, has a name which would seem to have a meaning, their inhabitants invent a history which provides an explanation for the name. It seems more reasonable to assume that Uzbek is derived from 'Uz', called Guz by Arab historians. These 'Guz' are the same people as the Uigur — a tribe which used to inhabit the countries to the south of the 'Celestial Mountain', namely Bukhara. The old name in China for the Uigur people was Ku-szu, pronounced Guz. The Hoei-hu people were from the same ethnic origin as the Uigurs.

At the beginning of the 16th century the Uzbek spread out from Sihhun (or Jaxartes) towards the West, causing terror and destruction on their way. Today they are the masters of the Balkan countries, of Kharism (or Khiva), as well as of Bukhara, Fergana and the other countries bordering Mount Belout-Tagh. The Uzbek tribes which are found in Khiva are called:—

UIGUR-NAIMAN, KANGLI-KIPTCHAK, KIAT-KONKRAD and NOEKIUS MANGUD. The KIAT-KONKRAD can be divided into the IMBCI, BALGALI, ATCHATAILI, KANDJIRGATI, KOCHTAM-GALI, KOEGOESEGLI, and the BOEGOEDJELI.

THE SARTY OR BUKHARS

The Bukhars are spread throughout Central Asia from the Caspian sea to the north of China. By race they are a Persian people and, apart from the towns of Bukhara, Kharizm and Fergana, they live in Kashgar, in Khotan, Iarkiang, Aksu, Uchi, Turfan and Khamil (known sometimes as Hami). Their mother tongue is pure Persian, and they were given the name Sarty by the Turkish nomadic tribes living in those areas. It has been thought that the name Sarty meant 'merchant' but this is not so; the name became associated with 'merchant' because the Sarty or Bukhars were the only people engaged in commerce in these countries. It would seem that the name is quite old because in the time of Ginghis-Khan, the land given to Chagatai (the conqueror's son), was called by the Mongols 'Sartohl' and comprised Greater Bukhara and the western part of little Bukhara. The inhabitants of the towns in these two countries called themselves 'Tadjik'. This is the old name for Persia and the Persian people, being the name of the Parthes who passed it on to the Persians when they conquered them. The Chinese have certainly used the name Tadjik since the time of the birth of Christ, and they knew Persia by the name Tiao-dji. It was not until later that they changed the name to Po-szu, a corruption of 'Parsi'. It is therefore wrong that until now the Bukhars have been numbered as one of the Turkish races, since their name and their language clearly show that they are Persian.

KALMUK TEA (p. 161)

This tea is known as 'brick tea' or in Russian *kirpichnoy chai*, and Chinese *Ch'uan-ch'a*. It is the staple diet of the Mongols and the Buriates. In northern China it is made from the leaves of a wild bush which resembles a wild cherry tree. The leaves are heated, moistened with sheep's blood, and then formed into large bricks or slabs which are dried in a very low temperature oven. To prepare the tea a few ounces are cut off from the brick. This is then crushed and boiled in water to which has been added half an ounce of kujir (a naturally occurring salt found in the Steppes containing natron and sodium sulphate) in a kettle or tall copper tea-pot. After the tea has boiled it is mixed with butter, fat and a little flour. This beverage, which looks somewhat like milk chocolate in colour, has a detestable taste, bitter and disgusting to the European palate; but for all the nomads of Central Asia it is a great delicacy.

Those poor people who cannot afford 'brick-tea', and there are many, substitute leaves from the following plants:—

	Mongol word
Saxifraga crassifolia	Badan
Tamarix germanica	Balgou
Potentilla rupestris et fruticosa	Khaltalsa
Gticyrrihza hirsuta	Nakhalsa
Polypodium fragrans (this smells like raspberries)	Serlik

They also add roots from a kind of Sanguisorba which in Mongolian is known as chudu.